D1291562

TWO STUDIES IN VIRTUE

CHRISTOPHER SYKES

TWO STUDIES IN VIRTUE

COLLINS
ST JAMES'S PLACE, LONDON
1953

PRINTED IN GREAT BRITAIN
COLLINS CLEAR-TYPE PRESS, LONDON AND GLASGOW

To the Memory of
WILFRED ROOKE LEY
Best of friends and critics

Contents

Acknowledgment

The author and publishers are grateful to the following for permission to reproduce the illustrations that appear in the book: The British Museum (*Richard Sibthorp*), the Proprietors of *Punch* (*Charles Sibthorp*), Mr. Alexander Gordon (*Theodore Herzl*), the Zionist Archives and Library of the Palestine Foundation Fund (*Chaim Weizmann*), Sir Richard Sykes (*Sir Mark Sykes*), and Picture Post Library (*A. J. Balfour*), and to Messrs. Hamish Hamilton for permission to reproduce the map in Appendix B.

Illustrations

Preface

In this book the same sequence is followed as in its predecessor, *Four Studies in Loyalty*: the material is grouped in chronological order, beginning outside experience and ending amid events which, if they were not at all understood at the time by their present chronicler, remain vivid in his mind because of childhood memories of numerous details. A claim is lodged that some neglected points of view have been manned, rather than that a great quantity of new material has been produced.

The story of Richard Sibthorp was told in a biography written by his Anglican successor in Lincoln, J. F. Fowler, and the main facts were condensed by Mr. R. D. Middleton in his admirable *Magdalen Studies* together with all the most interesting material on the subject which is to be found in Magdalen College Library. It would not have been worth adding to these, were it not that both books are one-sided in the same way. Neither of Sibthorp's biographers, in tracing the career of this man who sought the truth in different places, devote any care to considering the Church to which he was more than once irresistibly attracted, and an attempt is made here to make good the deficiency by retelling, with reference to the amazing Catholic story of the nineteenth century, the life of this man from its Georgian beginnings to its late Victorian end.

He passed through revolutions of the soul with a frequency which alone makes him an untypical man of his century. No guess is attempted as to why such " inner crisis," why a moment of abandon and disillusion followed by new faith or stoically born infidelity, such as is commonly reserved to genius at all times, became, in the nineteenth century, an essential, even a normal part of a great multitude of careers of which we have record. It would be claiming too much to insist that the Balfour Declaration was another result of this response to the world, but it can, and (it is believed here) must be insisted that in great part the declaration belonged to the spiritual disposition of its time. This is the connection between "The Damascus Road" and the second essay. They grew together from considering the end of the preceding age and the beginning of our own.

So much has been written on Zionism within the last thirty years that, when producing a new essay, some apology may be thought necessary. Well then, first: a very high proportion of the best Zionist books in Great Britain and America are addressed to a Jewish audience and assume a knowledge of Jewish history rare among Gentiles who have not made detailed studies. This book is primarily addressed to Gentile readers, and some Jewish history has been introduced despite the danger that this may make for some pages of wearisome repetition to Jewish eyes. The more learned reader is asked to remember that ignorance of the historical causes of Zionism was one reason for the grievous misunderstandings which afflicted the British experiment in the Promised Land, and that this is an attempt to undo part of that wrong.

Secondly, we move to more awkward ground. From its beginning the Zionist movement has been helped and damaged by an extraordinary quantity of propaganda. It requires much labour in consequence to discover what were the personal roles because these have been so distorted by friendly but biased versions proclaiming that all depended on such-and-such pioneer, or State official, or politician, or man of influence, and as though to deny a lasting impression, which must surely not be escaped, of something greater than any personal enterprise: of many influences and men brought together in a unique conjunction to produce a unique result. Worse confusion has been wrought on the great deed itself. All kinds of anti-Semitic rubbish have been used to explain it in terms of recondite villainy, and equal absurdities can be found on the other side, of which the most unworthy is the suggestion that the Balfour Declaration was a punishment meted out to the Arabs for their failure to rebel more thoroughly against Ottoman misrule. The purpose of this essay is to bring together in one place authentic historical material free of such stuff, material which in this instance is otherwise scattered over an immense literary field, large areas of which have been regularly sown with the tares of prejudice.

Lastly, let it be said in defence that the opportunity has been taken to publish some new material. Sir Mark Sykes's papers were examined by Sir Shane Leslie in 1922, when the part Sykes played in Zionism was too near and too unresolved to allow a judgment to be formed; and they were re-examined in 1932 by the late George Antonius, who seems, however, to have done his work hurriedly. (They are fragmentary and require much concurrent reading of outside matter to be understood.) By the kindness of Sir Richard Sykes the Zionist material in these papers is used here for the first time. It serves to answer the difficult question of how the Declaration and the Entente were maintained together in our foreign policy. The papers also tell us a good deal about the day-to-day adventures of 1916 and 1917, and correct a view sometimes taken that Sir Mark Sykes was a dreamy individual, full of vague and amiable intentions, who was betrayed by his craftier French colleague. It is plain now that this is nonsense, and that the truth lies rather in the transitional character of his time. In an age when Imperialism was still a lusty growth Sykes and Picot both belonged to the new League of Nations school and were both opposed by Imperialist interests over which they triumphed temporarily and by which they were both finally defeated. The shipwreck of French rule and influence in Syria was chiefly the result of the malign strength in French affairs of Picot's enemies; the ruin of Sir Mark Sykes was occasioned less by the impracticable geography of the Sykes-Picot Agreement, or his responsibility for confused pledges, than by his offending anti-French Imperialist ideas. Yet it may be said that the most interesting thing in these papers, called " The Sledmere Papers " after the name of Sykes's house, is the evidence for the idealist character of British Zionism in the midst of these squalidly dishonest rivalries. That Zionism was sometimes gleefully regarded in London as a novel stick with which to smite Frenchmen in Syria cannot be denied, but it is remarkable that this view belongs to early and inactive stages.

The evidence that there was a French party friendly to Zionism may surprise many people, although this has been mentioned in several places before, notably in Sokolov's history, the memoirs of Dr. Weizmann, and in Mr. James Malcolm's brief and fascinating paper. The last two writers lay particular stress on Georges Picot's Zionist disposition, a point which has been less seriously taken than it deserved. Among contemporary documents, however, the strongest evidence for this is to be found not in the Sledmere Papers but in those left by the distinguished Sephardic Rabbi, Dr. Gaster. Thanks are due to his son, Mr. Vivian Gaster, for generously allowing these as yet unpublished papers to be examined for the purpose of this essay. The part played by Dr. Gaster was extremely important, even essential, and has been strangely neglected.

" The Prosperity of His Servant " cannot unfortunately be taken as definitive. There is Declaration material in the Foreign Office which has never been placed at the disposal of a historian, and under the present hardening rules of security this cannot be available for some years. This modern official secrecy has, somewhat extravagantly, been extended to the private papers of Arthur Balfour which were left by his nephew, the present Lord Balfour, to the British Museum. It is likely that among these forbidden documents there are to be found many further details of what happened to Zionist fortunes in 1916 and 1917; but even when security regulations become less fearful, and the historian is smilingly beckoned aloft, it is unlikely that a theory of the origins of the Balfour Declaration radically different from that recorded by Dr. Weizmann, Israel Cohen, and Nahun Sokolov will ever prevail. This is somewhat curious when we consider how certain elements of it, one in particular, will probably always be conjectural.

Lloyd George was without the writer's itch; he was as averse as Talleyrand to the labour of despatches, and the desire to pin down the moment in literary shape was foreign to him. He wrote almost nothing about Zionism. What is said about Lloyd George in this book is largely the result, therefore, of discussing him with people who knew him, pre-eminent among whom Lady Megan Lloyd George, Mr. Leopold Amery, Sir Harold Nicolson and Lord Altrincham are remembered with gratitude. There is some Lloyd Georgian documentation to be followed, a record of his meeting with Sykes on April 7th, 1917, the minutes of the Royal Commission of 1936, and his own War Memoirs, but these amount to little and it is doubtful whether more exists. He must be guessed at, and it is possible that the man who once said to Mr. A. J. Sylvester his private secretary, " I am always consistent. I want you to take heed of what I *say* rather than of what I *do*," often had to guess at himself. (To Mr. Sylvester thanks also must be given.) Care has been taken not to lay down laws concerning this elusive subject, but in spite of his own traces being covered up or invisible, the view is taken that Lloyd George's role in the Jewish revival is easily drawn because it was straightforward.

A general acknowledgment is due to Mr. Isaiah Berlin for having read the original manuscript of the essay and for making numerous and valuable suggestions notably in regard to the introductory passages.

In dealing with enormous subjects, no matter how deliberate the intention to escape bias, a tendency persists that way if only because it is tempting to make faces at people who get in the way of the neatest theory. When considering Richard Sibthorp it is hard to do justice to the Neo-Ultramontanes: we meet them in their worst aspect in the career of this bothered clergyman, and it is easy to forget that for all their eccentricities these were the people who prevented the sundering of the Catholic

Church by making a relapse into Gallicanism impossible except
on the periphery.

In the same way, when recording Zionism in British politics,
it is difficult at moments not to become exasperated with the
progressives of the early twentieth century whose optimism cost
their successors much woe, but here, as with the Neo-Ultramontanes, we must remember that their ill deeds were positive
and arresting, their good ones negative and thus easily not
noticed, though of greater consequence. This is what we must
recognise: that had the forward-looking enthusiasts been
thoroughly corrected by the massive common sense of such men
as Asquith, European influence in the Moslem East (principally
represented by Great Britain) must have become closely associated
with an order whose weary antiquity prompted revolt not only
against itself (as happened), but against all Western civilisation.
The second of these disasters has nearly happened on several
occasions, but until now, in spite of great and lasting hostility,
the overtaken and embittered world which speaks Arabic and
Persian still looks to the West as the source of the modernity
which it passionately craves. Among many causes this is partly
due to the " men of the Declaration," because they left progressive ideas associated with the memory of generous minds.

CHRISTOPHER SYKES

THE DAMASCUS ROAD

A Study of the Religious Movements
of the nineteenth century

The Damascus Road

IN THE middle years of the nineteenth century, the name of the Reverend Richard Waldo Sibthorp was famous in England. During some years he had been known in Oxford as a prominent Fellow of Magdalen College, and beyond the University, as a preacher of commanding eloquence. Then, in those days of violently running tides in the religion of England, he suddenly became something more, he became a national spectacle. Over the waves of the tempest agitating the Church, there loomed for a short time, as though drawn up to the surface by immense convulsions, the figure of our hero. On him a shocked attention was fixed. For this friend of Dr. Newman did a bold thing by which he seemed to remove all doubts as to the dreaded direction of the Tractarians. On a day in 1841, this supposed Oxford leader "went over," as the saying was, "to Rome." That was the origin of his fame. His fame was brief; it was soon outshone by the similar but greater fame of Newman, and the brilliant notoriety of Sibthorp never flared up anew. Thus only a little of his brightness, which once flashed so amazingly for our ancestors, has traversed the space which separates his time from our own. For all that he is not quite forgotten. He is usually mentioned by scholars of his epoch as a comic character in the background. Lytton Strachey makes a highly diverting reference to him in *Eminent Victorians*, which well indicates the place allotted to him in history, and we must allow that though the judgment of time has been harsh, it has not been unjust. There was piety and courage in his character, but there was beyond question something absurd about poor

Sibthorp too; and yet, for all that, he had the undeniable importance which attaches to absolute sincerity, and sincerity, moreover, which burned in the last years of the age of faith. If we pursue this minor figure through the long stretch of years in which he lived, we must sometimes lose sight of him in the ancient forests of thoughts and belief through which he takes us, and where our quarry sought the shelter of an earth; but at the end of the hunt we may see the landscape in a new light because we have been made to cross it by an unfamiliar way.

Richard Sibthorp was born in the year 1792, the youngest of five brothers, of a rich and ancient Lincolnshire family noted for rigid Protestantism. The father of the family was called Colonel Humphrey Sibthorp, and one day in the seventeen nineties, while travelling in Germany, he met a certain learned French priest called the Abbé Beaumont, former Rector of the University of Caen, and now an exile from Revolutionary France. Colonel Humphrey took so great a liking to this man, that after a brief acquaintance he invited him to return with him to England. Abbé Beaumont accepted and accompanied the Colonel to his family home, Canwick Park, which lies by the city of Lincoln. His benefactor obtained his appointment as chaplain to the small Catholic community of the town, and for fifteen years Abbé Beaumont lived with the Sibthorps. When not engaged in parochial duties, he taught the boys French and Latin.

It may seem odd that a strictly Protestant gentleman should have invited this minister of a faith he disapproved to join his household, unless we remember the times when this happened. The anti-clerical excesses of the French Revolution made Englishmen look with a more kindly eye than usual on the old faith, and on its hardly perceptible remnant in England. In the Pope and his followers they discovered in the sudden chance of war whole-hearted allies against the new and terrible tendencies of Europe. There were French priests living as refugees in this island then, and they were esteemed as martyrs by many people who were not of their mind.

We know almost nothing about Abbé Beaumont; nothing about his French University career, very little about his subsequent life in England; we do not even know what his face looked like; but we do have a record of his great skill in argument, and this is contained in the memoirs of another Lincoln man, and another Fellow of Magdalen, Henry Digby Best, who was about to enter the ministry of the Church of England in 1799 when he was unexpectedly converted by this man. His account is important to Sibthorp's history, for it is the only one we have of his first mentor.

Best relates that he himself was brought up in ignorance of any but the Anglican church. " Of Popes," he says, " I had conceived an idea that they were a succession of ferocious, insolent and ambitious despots, always foaming with rage, and bellowing forth anathemas." When he was a Fellow of Magdalen, and had already been ordained Deacon, he was invited to deliver the yearly Bampton Lectures and he chose as his theme the conversion of the Jews. While studying for this performance in Lincoln, he received a visit from Abbé Beaumont (whom he had met previously) which coincided with another from an Anglican clergyman. He relates how he was impressed by the Abbé's " esprit de son état," and he describes his appearance, typical of a Catholic priest of those times in England, dressed in a snuff-coloured suit, a brown wig, and cornered hat. The three of them began to argue doctrinal matter, and soon came to the question of Transubstantiation, and here we can appreciate from the record the delicate skill of this wily ecclesiastic.

" The Frenchman," says Henry Best, " who talked English well but not currently, was soon overpowered by two opponents; and the Anglican, his retreat thus covered by me, carried off with him the honours of the day. . . .

" . . . At length [the Abbé] renewed the former conversation, with an air as if he had recollected something, though I rather suspect he had prepared himself.

" ' Pray, at what time did the change take place from your doctrine respecting the Eucharist, to that professed by all Christians three hundred years ago? '

" I begged of him to put his question more clearly.

" ' If your doctrine on this point be the true one, it was taught by the apostles, and received by the first Christians; then *our* interpretation must have been introduced at some subsequent period: I ask you to fix that period.' . . .

" ' It was introduced gradually during the dark ages.'

" ' In the first place—*gradually*—that is impossible: the question is, whether the Body of Christ is really or figuratively present: the people must have known in which sense they believed it to be present, and would have resisted innovation. Do you think it would be easy at this day to make the people of England believe in the real presence ?'

" ' No; because they have already rejected it.'

" ' I admit the difference; but at any time it must have been impossible to change the faith of the people without their perceiving it; and the controversy, which the attempt must have excited, would have come down to our days in works written on both sides; the memory of the Arian controversy is not lost.'

" I was struck by the argument and the parallel. He pressed me.

" 'What do you call the dark ages? '

" ' The tenth century is called by Cave, a learned English divine, *saeculum tenebrosum.*'

" ' Berenger of Angers, in the eleventh century, who first taught the figurative sense, found all the world in the belief of the real presence.'

" ' First? You forget the apostles.'

" ' It is for you to prove that they taught the figurative sense. St. John Chrysostom, who lived in the fourth age, preached on this subject like a Catholic doctor of the present day.'

" ' Really? I have his works; I will refer to the passages.'

" ' Will you give me leave to send you a treatise on this subject, entitled *La Perpetuité de la Foi de l'Eglise touchant l'Euchariste?* '

" . . . I assented, and he wished me a good evening." [1]

To the end of his days Richard Sibthorp asserted that by an agreement made between him and Colonel Humphrey the Abbé Beaumont never attempted the conversion of his young charges, but we can imagine how conversations, such as that recorded by Best, may have deeply impressed the listening children of Canwick. The second brother, Charles, grew up with a lasting fear of foreigners and of the religions they followed. The youngest one, Richard, gave precocious signs of an un-English style of devotion. One day, to the distress of his parents, he was found praying before a crucifix. It is related that William Wilberforce was present on this occasion and that he said to Colonel Humphrey, " That boy will become a Roman Catholic."

As often happens in large families, the youngest was the favourite of the mother. She was a forcible lady who ruled Canwick and the Sibthorp estates equally with her husband, the Colonel. She was reputed to have much sense of humour, and was noted in Lincoln for wit. We may picture her to ourselves as a highly characteristic County lady of her time: a managing person, certain of herself, and of her authority. It seems from what we know of her that the bond between her and her youngest son was somewhat stronger than the usual maternal hold, and that this circumstance had some influence on Richard's career.

He went to school at the age of seven to the establishment of the Reverend John Smith of Eltham in Kent, and we learn, perhaps with surprise, that here he was exceedingly happy. In an age of ferocious pedagogy Smith was evidently an exception. From Eltham Richard Sibthorp went to Westminster School, and at the age of seventeen, in 1809, he matriculated to Oxford University. He spent a year as a member of University College,

[1] It should be noted that Best's family on the maternal side had only recently become Protestant. They changed their religion in 1745 from motives of anti-Jacobite patriotism.

and then became a scholar of Magdalen. In Oxford usage these scholars are called the " demys," because, in the past, they used to receive allowances half (demi) the size of those paid to Fellows.

There was a long family connection between the Sibthorps and Magdalen, which was then in the care of its most famous president, the great Dr. Martin Routh. Anyone who studies Oxonian history of the early nineteenth century begins after a while to weary of the word " venerable," for it was applied to Dr. Routh with great regularity by those who knew him, echoed by those who knew them, and further echoed by following generations. At the time of young Sibthorp's demyship he had been President since 1792, and although he was as yet only fifty-four years old, he was beginning to be regarded as a marvellous survivor from an olden time. He wore the clothes of his youth without any alteration of style, and many memorialists, in recalling him from their undergraduate days, draw attention first to what his Vice-President, J. B. Mozley, called his " awful wig." A powdered bob-wig was an unusual sight in the Oxford of 1810. He still wore it as part of his everyday dress, in his last and hundredth year in 1854. He was famed for learning, for breadth of outlook, for a strong aversion to Popery and democracy, for deep piety. His Churchmanship was described as " that of the best Caroline Divines," his politics those of a Whig belonging to the later school which leaned more to the throne than Parliament; he was generous, witty, and possessed of unwearied mental vitality to the last. He has been the subject of so much panegyric that it is difficult to discover what human flaws if any were to be found in this noble character. Thomas Mozley, in memoirs written twenty-eight years after the President's death, accused him of morbid vanity concerning his longevity, and his early taste for antique dress gives some point to the charge, but Cardinal Newman, who had known him well, and far better than Mozley, replied to this with a heated denial. It must be admitted that in his final years Dr. Routh certainly grew extravagantly conservative and opposed some needed reforms of discipline, but under the same impulse he opposed plans to rebuild much of the loveliest of all Oxford Colleges, so we of a later time should be grateful for this weakness. To Henry Best, whose conversion angered him, he behaved on one occasion with cruel and subtle discourtesy, less excusably because he was his host; but that is a single event in a century, and there exists one great positive proof of his venerability. At the age of ninety he wrote a perfect model of the most difficult of all imaginable letters: an exhortation to a criminal whom he had once known as a parishioner, and who was about to be hanged. For the sake of Colonel Humphrey this truly good man took young Sibthorp under his especial care.

The impressionable youth from Lincoln was, however, under another and stronger influence, unknown to his family, or to his college, or to any but one friend of his own age. He used to correspond with a man called Francis Martyn.[1] We know something about this man Martyn from contemporary records. We are told that he was a fine horseman, was to be seen riding at speed over the Lincoln country on a smart cob, dressed in buckskin breeches and top boots, very much in the style of the English squire-parson. He holds a place in our history. He was the first Catholic priest since the Reformation to have been educated and trained entirely in England. He had been ordained by his close friend Bishop Milner, and (through Martyn no doubt) Milner also corresponded with the young demy of Magdalen. We should glance at that Bishop for a moment.

At this time John Milner was fifty-eight years old, and held the positions of Catholic Vicar-Apostolic of the Midland District and Parliamentary agent for the Irish Bishops. He was said to understand the complexities of Parliamentary procedure better than most members. He was much disliked by his fellow Roman Catholics because he spent a great part of his career in preventing various Emancipation measures from passing into law, on the grounds that they contained excessive reservations. For this he was accused of secret protestantism, of a love of mischief-making,

[1]We do not know how they met, but this probably occurred in Lincolnshire.

and even worse things. His personality was impressive. In speech and dress he was wholly eighteenth century, calling everyone "Sir" in Johnson's style, and always wearing knee breeches, bands and his hair powdered. We learn that he was abnormally devoid of a sense of humour. He never made jokes and was perplexed when they were made to him. His character contained other oddities. Unlike most pontifical functionaries of the Roman Catholic Church, he had no taste for ceremony, finding great tedium for himself in the elaborate poetry of Catholic ritual. His crozier was of the meanest, being merely a metal hook which for ceremonial purposes he rammed on to his walking stick, and his conduct at the altar was slovenly. He rejoiced in the smell of smoke from wax candles, and when saying the Last Gospel at Mass, he had a way, disconcerting to many pious people, of leaning over and puffing out the left-hand candle so that he might enjoy the goodly smell as he recited the words of Saint John. But above all things, this Bishop was a man of gigantic strength of mind. His brief and interesting book, *The End of Controversy*, contains one of the best summaries and defences of Catholic doctrine ever written. In wrestling for the soul of the young demy Dr. Routh had no mean opponent.

Trouble began soon. According to University gossip, Richard Sibthorp was once more indulging his taste for crucifixes, and had one hung in his room, but the truth about his religious behaviour outran this surmise. He used, secretly, to attend Mass in the little Catholic chapel of St. Clement's. During his second year at Magdalen, in October of 1811, he suddenly disappeared.

There followed frantic scenes. Colonel Humphrey was told, whereat, in the highest agitation, and insisting on the strongest possible measures, he despatched his eldest son, Coningsby, to Magdalen with a detective. Arrived there, Coningsby discovered from Richard's friend and confidant, an undergraduate called Zachary Biddulph, first about the Roman devotions of his younger brother, and then about St. Clement's. He went to Richard's rooms with his retinue, and in the excitement of ransacking, a little model of the Venus de Medici was hurled into the fireplace and shattered, under the supposal that it was a statuette of the Virgin Mary. And then in the midst of the din Biddulph broke down and confessed what had been most secretly confided to him. Richard Sibthorp had gone to Martyn's house at Bloxwich in Staffordshire. His purpose was dreadfully clear.

Coningsby acted with vigour. He obtained a chancery order, and accompanied by an officer, and presumably by the detective, dashed off to Bloxwich. There at Martyn's house they told him that his brother had gone with Martyn to Wolverhampton. They dashed on to Wolverhampton, where they found him, just where they thought they would, in the house of Bishop Milner.

What happened then is not recorded in any detail. All we know is that there was an irruption into the Bishop's house, after which the pale young man was taken back to Oxford under enormous protection. Sibthorp himself did not refer to the matter in his later years, but he gave two contradictory accounts shortly after. "If ever Popery gains the upper hand," he said when he was an ordained clergyman of the Church of England, "I do not expect that her friends will forget how nearly they had me within their clutches. An interval of two or three hours had (humanly speaking) seen the deed done, and myself a member of the Church of Rome. But in that interval God stretched forth His arm and plucked me out of the net."

This was said a few years after. Nearer the time he said: "I fled to Bishop Milner . . . and was brought back a prisoner, sighing for St. Clement's."

Which of these utterances expressed his deepest feelings? Without question, both.

He was taken back to Lincolnshire, and there in his family home subjected for three months to the ministrations of a certain Mr. Swann, who enjoyed a reputation for piety of a strictly English sort. For a few weeks he was sent southwards to Kent to receive further exhortations from the Reverend John Smith, his old master, and then back to Mr. Swann. He was obliged to read a great mass of holy treatises. All this may suggest a rather lowering regime against which a youth of spirit might have rebelled, but Swann and Smith were evidently men of tact. They succeeded in their undertaking with the result that young Richard Sibthorp became convinced of having done a deed of horrible iniquity. He turned away from Rome with disgust.

In the meantime a correspondence was held between Colonel Humphrey and Dr. Routh. The former did not minimise the enormity of what his son had tried to do, but he put the blame for it on " the well-known Milner, who," he said, " has been in the habit . . . of fixing the fluctuations of his mind," and he thought he perceived a sinister agent nearer home: Abbé Beaumont, who was still on the scenes, no longer at Canwick, but living as Catholic chaplain in the town of Lincoln. The Colonel suspected him of having " had a deep and busy hand in the plot." This was not the case. The Abbé remained far away in the background, taking no part in what he had undoubtedly begun, and it is somewhat strange that no one appears to have taken the trouble to go down from Canwick to discuss Richard's upheavals with that mysterious figure. He now leaves the story.

In January the affair was concluded. Dr. Routh forgave this favourite pupil. Young Sibthorp wrote to him a letter of abject contrition, and at the same time broke off relations with his Catholic correspondents. He returned to Magdalen in the spring, and in the following year, having obtained a creditable degree in Divinity, commenced studies for Holy Orders. He had committed a foolish indiscretion, such as young men are prone to do, and now he had settled down, so it seemed. But if there was one thing poor Sibthorp was never to succeed in, it was in this act of settling down. . . .

At the end of two years' study he was ordained deacon, in

1815, shortly after the death of his father, and he preached the maiden sermon of his long pulpit career the same year, in Magdalen Chapel. We would expect him to have seized this opportunity for a display of orthodoxy, but he did the opposite. He disturbed many members of this, his first congregation, by extolling the founder of the College, Bishop Waynflete, as a " burning and shining light," without at the same time passing any strictures on the corruptions of Rome under which that great man had laboured.

Soon after delivering his sermon Sibthorp left Oxford for a curacy in Lincolnshire. He owed the appointment to his mother because, wishing to have her youngest and favourite child near her in her widowhood, she had brought some pressure on the Bishop of Lincoln. Under Mrs. Sibthorp's influence our hero joined the Evangelicals then at the plenitude of their great influence.

There is a portrait of Sibthorp made about now when he was still a young man at the beginning of his public career. He appears before us in gown and broad white bands, his high collar exaggerating the effect of great length in a pale worried face, and his dark hair brushed forwards over a high forehead. He wears modest whiskers in accordance with gentlemanly custom. There is a melancholy expression in the large curious eyes, and in the small down-pointing mouth, but, though this melancholy is tense, it is not such as to make the personality of the man clear; on the contrary, the portrait fairly announces the presence of a secret. It shows a face perfectly adapted to an emotional nature which at the same time was devoid of ordinary passions. The delights of the world and the flesh seem to have had no meaning for him at all. There is no evidence that he ever loved a woman apart from his mother, and even here he was unusually restrained. He was not one of those men who are dominated by that emotion throughout life: as we shall see later, the supreme cult of motherhood in Christian observance had no sensuous attraction for him. He belonged to a type more common among Oriental nations than our own: the instinctively pious, the naturally mystical. He could not conceivably have followed any profession not ecclesiastical.

From the date of his first curacy he was an Anglican Minister for twenty-six years. Most of this period was the least eventful of his life and we need only to record it very briefly.

In 1817 he was ordained priest. His rector, when signing the recommendation for him to receive sacerdotal orders, added the words: "good but queer." The young man had a curious knack of getting into trouble and to this the Rector was probably referring. Shortly before one Lincolnshire clergyman had felt obliged not only to preach but to print a sermon against his doctrines, and there had been much uproar over a sermon Sibthorp preached in a barn, when he was carried away into addressing the local inhabitants while staying with some friends.

Soon after ordination he removed to Hull, again under the influence of Mrs. Sibthorp, for Hull was an Evangelical stronghold. We have a glimpse of him stalking through the streets of that harsh city. We are told that he became known there for "the solemnity of his manner." After a year he returned to Lincolnshire as Vicar of Tattershall. We find him writing a letter to Dr. Routh because further allegations had been made against his orthodoxy, and so against his becoming a Fellow of his college. But once more the venerable Dr. Routh extended his generosity to him, and he was elected a Fellow in July of 1819. He remained Vicar of Tattershall till the year 1825.

By that time he had made a considerable reputation for himself as a preacher. We may measure his early fame by the fact that there is a lengthy description of his style of delivery to be found in an unlikely place: namely in an edifying and unreadable novel of the period, called *The Bishop's Daughter*.[1] We learn of his "singularly musical voice," and "a power, a solemnity, a pathos in his sermons which left among his hearers nothing to wish." There is extant another memorial of him written by a parishioner. It seems that he usually commenced in a low hesitant whispering voice, which then rose during a

[1] *The Bishop's Daughter*, by the Rev. E. Neale 1842.

crescendo sustained by him through the longest of his performances and culminating in notes of massive musical power. In 1825 he left Lincolnshire for London.

The city of " Corinthian Tom and his friend Jerry," the fabulous London of George IV, can never be understood unless we remember the element which determined its character. We should forget the drinking and the horseplay, and think first of the Evangelicals, of whom it has been wisely said that their discipline, " secularised as respectability, was the strongest binding force in a nation which without it might have broken up, as it had already broken loose."[1] We must picture to ourselves the most distinctive feature of late Georgian life: demure little white meeting houses, called " proprietary chapels," in which well-connected persons of Evangelical views worshipped with their dependants, and in which, during four years, the young clergyman from Lincoln ministered.

The centre of Evangelical piety was the sermon, and so very soon Sibthorp, since he was remarkably gifted in this line, became well known among the London following. Several of his sermons were published, and even to-day, more than a hundred and thirty years after, something of their power can still be discerned from the yellowing printed pages of these works. There is one called " The Character of the Papacy," which is the most polished, both in construction and style, of all these performances. It is interesting among other things because along with much violent abuse of the Bishop of Rome it contains expressions of reverence for the Catholic Church such as were rare at that time, most of all among members of his party.

As often happened in that age, his sermons led to his being " lionised " by people in fashionable society. We hear of one evening when he was asked to dinner by a pious nobleman, and how during the meal he heard a frequent noise of the front-door bell, and of numerous people arriving and going up the stairs,

---

[1] G. M. Young, " Portrait of an Age," the terminal essay of *Early Victorian England*. Oxford University Press 1934.

and how on reaching the drawing-room with his host and hostess, for this was no port-loitering place, he found a sizeable assembly awaiting him, and at one end a chair and table with a Bible ready. His host invited him to preach. " I remembered nothing of it afterwards," he said, " I was told I had done admirably; but I was resolved I should never do so again."

During this period he experienced what seems to have been a telepathic experience. He was staying at Canwick in the May of 1827. One day at about twelve o'clock he left his mother lying on a sofa and went for a walk in the grounds. Suddenly he was aware of " something—it was no voice but a kind of impression as if from the air "—urging him to go back. He could almost make out the words " Go home directly! " As soon as he arrived he found his mother's maid in a state of distress. " I think my mistress is dying," she said, and a few minutes later Mrs. Sibthorp expired in her son's arms. It was the belief of her son that the mysterious utterance which sent him back proceeded from an angelic being. This moving occurrence probably strengthened his Evangelical confidence in his intuitions. During the rest of his life he was liable to be moved by lights and instincts and inner promptings.

After the death of his mother he returned to London, where he took the familiar course of smothering his grief in an excess of industry until signs began to show of dangerous mental strain. His restlessness became uncontrollable, he was plagued by insomnia, and his doctor warned him that his mind might give way. He used, after preaching a sermon on the subject of the Devil, to suffer fits of gloom which brought him near to delusion. " That sermon makes me miserable," he said, " I have preached it three times. Each time I believe it has been distinctly useful; and each time I have suffered from deep depression. I believe Satan dislikes that sermon."

In 1829 Sibthorp left this London life of little plain chapels, pious gentlefolk, drawing-room sermons, and visitations of the poor, and returned to Magdalen College. He did this because it had been made clear to him that he was favoured for election

RICHARD WALDO SIBTHORP

to the Vice-Presidency by Dr. Routh, who was now entering the fabulous period of his life when the "awful wig" was becoming a thing wonderfully removed from the prose of ordinary experience. An undergraduate asked him one day if it was true that he had once seen Charles II. He replied to the undergraduate that this was not true. He explained that he had known a lady whose mother had seen Charles II, and this was doubtless the foundation of the rumour. He had known Dr. Johnson.

Not far from Oxford there was a small rustic church under Bagley Wood. Here Sibthorp began a new career of preaching with the same success as he had enjoyed for the last fifteen years, and "the church," we are told, "was always full to the doors." We have a singular record of this part of his life because among his congregation was an undergraduate called William Ewart Gladstone. In after years, the latter told how he "used frequently in summer to walk out from Oxford . . . to hear Sibthorp preach in the evenings to a purely peasant congregation." At the distance of much time he recorded "a soothing, general recollection, a venerable visual image in the mind's eye, and a moral certainty that the preaching was, at the least, of singular grace and charm, which drew me again and again out of Oxford, where preaching was abundant, and *good* preaching was to be had. I may illustrate this," he adds, "by saying that I never went out of Oxford to hear a preacher, except in this case, and on one other occasion."

We learn from Mr. Gladstone that in University society Sibthorp was the most prominent of the few Evangelical Fellows of Colleges. The movement, he tells us, was only a small force in the Oxford of 1829 and Sibthorp's representation of it was personal. There was a Mr. Bulteel in whose church our hero occasionally preached, but though these two were of the same party they did not always make common cause. The old trouble began again, so much so that on one occasion Bulteel felt obliged to rebuke in an afternoon sermon "the error that Christ died for all men," as, "his brother Sibthorp had mistakenly taught them" in the morning. Sibthorp may easily have picked up this notion from Monsieur Beaumont, or from Francis Martyn.

He was not made Vice-President of Magdalen to his great disappointment. But this was not all. He suffered another humiliation at the same time. He used occasionally to preach at Lincoln, congregating about him such enthusiastic hearers, that he decided in 1830 to settle as a curate in that city of his ancestors. He bought a house in the Minster Close. Then, once again, difficulties arose. There were complaints that he was not the sort of person wanted by his prospective parishioners, and the Bishop decided against him. Sibthorp sold his house in the Close and went to the Isle of Wight, where he spent eleven years.

It was his intention to lead a life of mystical retreat henceforward. He bought a small privately-owned church at Ryde from a certain Mr. Hughes Hughes, and built himself a house with a garden, at a place called Holmewood, an hour's drive away, and here he consecrated all his energies to the loftiest uses of the soul. From his letters we know a little of his style of living. In those days, when not only politics but religious leadership too, was the business of the gentry, it seemed perfectly in order that this mystical hermit of the Isle of Wight should keep at least six gardeners in his employ, and sometimes more.

People who witnessed Sibthorp's holy retirement were impressed. He preached every Sunday, and once in the week, running to great length. "He could not stop," said one of his hearers, "he saw no way for stopping." A retired military man said that he felt translated into celestial regions when he heard Sibthorp preach on the text " Holy, Holy, Holy," as also on more ordinary occasions did a servant who waited on him in his lodgings. She felt, so she said, as though she was in a supernatural presence when she entered his room. He busied himself in pious works. He organised a " Provident Society," and collected a choir of twenty-four boys, who were educated and lodged at his own expense. Every Friday, at six in the evening, he held a debate on religious matters with ten or fifteen gentlemen. He cultivated edifying and harmonious relations with his brother-clergymen, but not long after the beginning of this regimen he gradually began to find the most interesting part of his life outside the Isle of Wight. His attention soon began to wander from his hermitage back to where he came from.

Stirring events were taking shape on the mainland within the Church of England. The story is too well known to need re-telling here, of how, having originated in Cambridge a little while before, the Oxford Movement was launched by John Keble in the July of 1833, whereafter the leadership was taken by Newman from whose writings the party were called "The Tractarians." For our purpose we need to remember the dates. The first of the famous " Tracts for the Times " appeared in the year 1833, and the last, Tract 90, in 1841, that is, throughout the period when our hero dwelt in the Isle of Wight. In this famous movement, in which the foremost of the young teachers of Oxford endeavoured to revive the splendours of pre-Reformation belief and practice in England, without, at the same time, diminishing the national character of the English Church, Sibthorp played a very peculiar role.

He often left his island retreat for visits to his revered mentor at Magdalen, and during these times of refreshment he came to know Newman and the Oxford generation which followed him, and among these men, all much younger than himself, he formed the lasting friendships of his life. Of these friendships the most conspicuous was with Newman's friend, John Rouse Bloxam. It was this man who led the ritualistic part of the Tractarians because he knew more about Catholic customs than the others, indeed the others only knew what they were told with reluctance by an apostate priest called Blanco White. Bloxam was considered as the most Romishly inclined of his party. These new affections and alliances of our hero led to a simple and curious misunderstanding.

The ordinary Protestant Englishman of the time, watching

the events of Oxford from outside, did not take to the novel teachings of Keble, Pusey, Newman, and the rest of them. Although the Tractarian leaders stressed repeatedly and in strong language the unshakable firmness of their loyalty to the national Church, the onlooker was of a different mind. He smelt Popery in this thing, and furthermore he seemed to detect a particularly pungent Popish odour about the tall dark solemn man who walked in the midst: Dr. Newman's and Dr. Bloxam's constant companion, the gentleman-hermit of Ryde. He took it that this man, older than the others, and of far wider priestly experience, was one of their leaders along the hated Roman way.

Strangely enough Sibthorp, against all appearances, had next to nothing to do with the movement. He shared much with the Tractarians but all of it on the surface; beneath was a profound difference. They were attracted from their Protestant surroundings towards the old faith, he struggled against memories of the compelling power of Rome. They were in danger of having to renounce success for the sake of their consciences. That was never his problem, and never could have been. Wherever he had followed his profession in the Church of England, he had met puzzling failure. With the considerable advantage of family influence, of wealth, eloquence, the patronage of Routh, and an amiable disposition, he had yet contrived to miss all chances of promotion.

In one respect only was he with the Tractarians. He came to share Bloxam's delight in sacred ceremony, and it was soon noticed at Ryde that his behaviour was beginning to undergo alteration. Hitherto he had, in common with all the Evangelical party, conducted his services in that austere manner inherited from the Puritans of the seventeenth century, but now, towards the end of the eighteen thirties, luxurious forms began to be introduced into St. James's Church. He dressed up his choir in cassocks and surplices. A choral service was held daily. He erected a cross on the altar, until ordered by the Bishop of Winchester to take it down. We do not know that he wore vestments or used incense, or lighted candles, but his decoration of the church was such as to excite the disapprobation even of a distinguished Roman Catholic friend and family connection of his, the architect Pugin.[1] " I think," the latter wrote to Doctor Bloxam, " his intentions *truly admirable*, but to speak the blunt truth the Sanctuary looks amazingly like one of the modern Catholic chapels, there is too much finery to produce the solemn effect . . . I feel truly anxious that we should avoid anything trifling or too gay about the altar . . . a modern altar always produces a mingled feeling of sorrow and disgust in my mind." The Catholic priest in Cowes became a frequent visitor to Holmewood, and conversation with him caused Sibthorp to question the validity of his orders.[2] A visit paid to him in 1840 by a Hull friend, Mr. Dikes, depressed the latter deeply. " In proportion," he wrote on his return, " in proportion as we hear of rich ceremonial at St. James's, there is less said of Missionary breakfast parties, at which Churchmen and Dissenters were ' as one heart and one mind.' " In 1835 Sibthorp had described the Vatican as " Satan's Masterpiece," but in 1840 he was impressed by an undeniable connection which he believed he had discerned between the Old Jewish Dispensation, and the Roman Catholic Communion. News of all this reached Oxford.

In spite of these constant warning tremors, the final act astounded his friends. It happened about the middle of October in 1841. Sibthorp sought out his friend Dr. Bloxam in Magdalen. He told him that a member of his congregation on the island wanted to become a Roman Catholic, for which reason he would like to have an audience with Bishop Wiseman, then Principal of St. Mary's College, Oscott, near Birmingham, to discuss the matter with him. He asked Dr. Bloxam, who had made the acquaintance of the newly arrived Bishop, to arrange a meeting. Bloxam agreed and wrote to Wiseman. An answer came back.

[1]They used to address each other as " cousin," Sibthorp, in his letters, usually writing the word between inverted commas. It seems impossible to discover the relationship. It has been suggested that the term was used playfully with reference to the fact that they were both Lincolnshire men.

[2]This appears in a letter preserved in the Oratory, Edgbaston, kindly shown to the writer by the Reverend H. Tristram.

" Reverend and dear Sir,

I shall be most happy to receive Mr. Sibthorp on the day you mention.

I remain, dear Sir, your obedient servant,

NICHOLAS WISEMAN "

Shortly before leaving Oxford for this interview, Sibthorp went to Dr. Bloxam's rooms and was with him some time. As he left he met Dr. Newman in the cloisters. The younger man knew more than anyone else at Oxford, more even than Dr. Bloxam, of our hero's latest leanings towards Rome, for it was to him that he had confided the doubts raised in his mind by the priest of Cowes. Newman sought for some way in which to express his disapproval. As they spoke together he asked about his immediate plans.

" I am going to Oscott," said Sibthorp.

" Mind you don't stop there," said Newman abruptly, and they parted.[1]

But he did stop there.

On the 27th of October of 1841 Richard Waldo Sibthorp was received into the Roman Catholic Church at Oscott.

As though a stone had been cast into water, the agitation of this event spread rapidly. England was moved.

The action came as a sudden and painful, even a brutal humiliation of the Established Church, most easily accounted for in general opinion by the folly of those Oxonian tamperers who had allowed themselves to be fascinated by the " august superstition " of Rome. Rumours were spread that Newman was the real author of this business; Archdeacon Samuel Wilberforce even asserted that Newman had taken Sibthorp personally to Oscott. Angry letters and articles appeared in many papers

[1]This is Dr. Bloxam's account. There is in existence a somewhat different account given by Cardinal Newman in 1881, who describes this interchange as taking place at a dinner party. Bloxam's account is the one followed by Fowler, who had almost certainly heard it from Sibthorp as well.

until a calm judgment was attempted in the most eminent of them.

Leaders appeared in *The Times* on the 10th and 13th of November in which, while the Tractarians were defended from abuse in other journals, heavy charges were brought against the convert. He was accused of revolutionary leanings. " He entered avowedly into politics at Ryde," *The Times* said, " and presented the anomalous picture of a Radical clergyman."[1] He was accused of dishonesty. *The Times* said that before yielding to Bishop Wiseman, he had sold St. James's Church to a Catholic purchaser, while still an Anglican Minister.

In the midst of all this uproar and libel, the most libellous paper then in England, *The Tablet*, showed a decent restraint, making no mention of the matter beyond printing a letter from Mr. Hughes Hughes to *The Times* denying the alleged sale of the Church. It was evidently *The Tablet's* policy to re-enforce the victory with a masterly moderation. In their issue of the 23rd of October, however, two days after the conversion, there had appeared by coincidence a very unfortunate sentence. A recently published book called *Barnaby Rudge* was reviewed in this number, and the writer of the article found much to criticise in the unhistorical picture of Lord George Gordon contained in the fiction. He reproached Mr. Dickens with having exaggerated Gordon's influence. " Parliamentary history," he said, " will show that all through the year of the riots he was the buffoon of the House of Commons, the Colonel S-p of his day." The suppressed name could only be that of Colonel Charles de Laet Waldo Sibthorp, Member for Lincoln, and our hero's brother, to whom he was deeply attached. We shall hear of him later.

At the end of October Sibthorp came back to Oxford, " looking worn and agitated," so recorded Dr. Bloxam, " and no longer a member of the Church of England." Here his friendship with Newman, which had meant much to him, and was to influence him in the future, came to an end. He called on Dr. Newman and urged him to follow his example, and

[1] Sibthorp was, in truth, a Tory, but he did once vote for a Radical on the island.

" he only threw me back," said Newman afterwards, " by the 'methodistical' character, as I felt them to be, of the reasons which he gave for the step which he had taken." They did not meet again for many years. During this same brief visit, Sibthorp wrote a letter to the President explaining that in sincerity he could have done no other than what he did do, adding that he would ever offer the prayer, ". Floreat Magdalena." The old man summoned Dr. Bloxam to him, and as he read out this letter he broke into a passion of tears.

Oxford sank into something of that state of melancholy which was to overcome her in 1845 when Newman left Littlemore for the last time. Pugin alone struck the jarring note. He sent a jubilant letter to Bloxam, beginning: "I cannot express my delight, and I may add, my surprise, at hearing of our mutual friend the Reverend Mr. Sibthorp having made his profession of faith . . ."—which was not well received.

As to the convert himself, after a few days in London, he took a train northwards to St. Mary's College, Oscott, near Birmingham, and there he settled, amid Pugin's new Gothic buildings, to study for the priesthood and to deal with the campaign of pamphleteering which his action had provoked.[1] He was ordained by Bishop Wiseman on May 21st, seven months after his admission. In obedience to his directors, Father Sibthorp, as he was now known, took up residence in Birmingham, and was attached to the Cathedral of St. Chad's.

---

[1]The sequence of these productions was as follows. In reply to a pamphlet by the Rev.W. Dodsworth of Christ Church, St. Pancras (later to become a Roman Catholic himself), Sibthorp wrote his brief and able defence of his action, called " Some Answer to The Enquiry: Why are you become a Roman Catholic? " This led to a further pamphlet by Dodsworth, and a further reply by Sibthorp, called " A Further Answer to the Enquiry: Why have you become a Roman Catholic? " (Note the change of verb.) Dodsworth's second pamphlet was supported by a pamphlet by the Reverend G. E. Bilber, 'Presbyter of the Anglo-Catholic Church,' entitled " Catholicity versus Sibthorp, or Some Help to answer the Question whether the Reverend Richard Waldo Sibthorp, D.D., is now or ever was a Catholic." Next appeared Richard Blakeley, 'a layman of the Irish Branch of the Catholic Church.' In the meantime the Reverend William Palmer of Worcester College, Oxford, who must not be confused with his interesting contemporary and namesake, William Palmer of Magdalen, produced two pamphlets in answer to Sibthorp's original one. The last of all these pieces was a long and massive production: " A Serious Remonstrance," from the clergy of Hull. (Magdalen Studies).

It was thirty years since his first attempt to join the Catholic Church. In 1811 he was young; he was now nearly fifty. He looked around him at the undiscovered country which Abbé Beaumont had, perhaps unintentionally, pointed out to him. Let us try to see the view which met his eyes. . . .

From a distance the Catholic Church, then in the tenth year of Gregory XVI's pontificate, presented a spectacle of majestic unity, but within it was a scene of party strife. Clergy, laity, Bishops, theologians, artists and journalists, were joined in a mêlée in which mud and missiles were being exchanged with such vigour that it might have seemed impossible that the combatants professed a common faith.

The main antagonism was between two parties: the Gallicans, who wanted a high State influence in Church affairs, and the Ultramontanes, who considered that in any matter touching religious life, even remotely, the Pope should be allowed authority superior to any sovereign or Government. This ancient contest had been revived and had taken on a strange shape in these mid-nineteenth century years. Before the French Revolution, when the debate centred round the claims of the French throne, the Gallican party had been the progressive one: the party of change, advance, and new orders; but after the Napoleonic wars, at the time of the French Restoration, Gallicanism became part of conservatism. In England the devout, small, and very conservative Catholic minority was for the most part Gallican in spirit and practice.[1] This was not because the English Catholics were untypical or rebellious, but was due rather to the central paradox of Rome itself in the reign of Gregory XVI, the last of the Popes who remembered the old regime, the last great extravagant patron of art to rule in the

[1]Ullathorne relates that he was brought up on Gallican principles at Downside, where Maistre's work *Du Pape* was frowned on. Milner's opposition to the Gallican Blanchardist movement in the early nineteenth century was strangely feeble for so vigorous a man. He only required priests to acknowledge that Pius VII was not a heretic or schismatic!

Vatican, a man who was haunted by the ever-present threat of revolutionary carnage and barbarism.

It was under his rule that the Ultramontane movement revived, chiefly in France, with the object of making the Papacy what it had been in its greatest days. Gregory XVI did not like this movement. Although privately convinced that Papal Infallibility was an essential doctrine, his own conservatism agreed far better with the Royalism of the Gallican party than with the Liberal tendencies of his new champions.[1] It followed very naturally that since he could not support his enemies, and would not encourage his friends, his rule became hesitant, and in spite of the growing strength of the new centralising party, Catholic life within different countries was conducted with an unusual amount of freedom from central control.

The English Catholics, having spent a long period of decline, lasting over a hundred and fifty years, at the end of which they were the least noticed and least influential body in the country, had suddenly, and for unexplained reasons, become one of the great minorities. Twelve years after the Emancipation Act of 1829 they numbered around 900,000 and were increasing by two to three thousand yearly.[2] The challenge of unexpected power confronted them, and required intelligent government. This they did not receive from the perplexed Vatican, nor from within their own community.

In 1842 " the well-known Milner " had been dead fifteen years, and the future Cardinal, Nicholas Wiseman, was not yet in a position of importance outside his college. The senior Catholic bishop, Thomas Griffiths, was a worthy nonentity, and for practical purposes the strongest influence in ecclesiastical matters was exerted by a highly puzzling figure, Peter Augustine Baines, titular Bishop of Siga, and at this time Vicar-Apostolic of the Western District. His story throws a strange light on

[1]The interested reader should consult the recently published essay by Lord Acton, " Ultramontanism," in *Essays on Church and State* (Hollis and Carter) for an account of how the conservative Ultramontanism of Maistre became "avant-garde Left" under the influence of Lammenais.

[2]Statistics prepared for Bishop Griffiths in 1842. Their accuracy is open to some question, but they may be taken as an adequate indication of the dimensions of the case.

English Catholic life in those days. He was fifty-six years old and had behind him a career of success, disappointment, intrigue, and cruelty. He had been educated by the monks of Ampleforth and joined their monastery as a young man. In 1823, when he he was only thirty-seven, he was made a Bishop. It may have been that he harboured resentment against his educators, or he may sincerely have disapproved of monasticism, but however that was his first act after consecration was to indulge in a lengthy and sordid quarrel with his own order, the Benedictines, which continued almost to his death. In 1826, he went to Rome, where he was invited to preach for a season at the Gesù, and his sermons, delivered, we are told by Wiseman, in "a tremulous voice," brought him so much fame that he was noticed by Leo XII. A deep friendship immediately grew up between that most unpleasant of Popes and the English Bishop, and it was reliably reported that Leo XII had decided that as soon as it was possible to establish a hierarchy in England, Baines should be the first of its Cardinal Archbishops. Suddenly this glittering prospect vanished with the death of Leo. His successor, Pius VIII, ruled only for a year, and when Gregory XVI was elected in 1831, Baines, though known to Gregory, was somewhat forgotten at the Papal Court. It seems likely that for the rest of his life Baines was struggling, unscrupulously and in vain, to recapture the commanding position he had enjoyed once and for so little time.

He became Vicar-Apostolic of the West in the year of Leo's death, 1829. In the same year he left the Benedictine order with Papal permission, after having done everything in his power to subject the English monks to his will. The great orders enjoy some degree of independence of episcopal authority, and Baines wanted the Benedictines of England to renounce their privilege. After failing to achieve this by intrigue in the first part of his career he decided to renew his attack with direct violence. He turned first to the monastery and school of Downside in Somerset. He was armed with instructions from Rome based on his own misrepresentations, and when these were questioned, and an appeal lodged against them, he placed the monks under a species of interdict (without any reference to Rome), forbidding them to exercise priestly functions outside their house. He went further and reported to the Vatican that the Benedictine order in England had been established in an irregular manner, and that in consequence the English monks were not valid Benedictines at all. He then turned to the North and attempted once more to break up the monastery and school at Ampleforth. He almost succeeded. He persuaded the three senior members, including the Prior, of the invalidity of their monastic vows, and he got them, and all the novices, and half the school, to leave Ampleforth for his own seminary and college at Bath. They left, taking more of the furniture, pictures, and livestock away with them than was considered their rightful portion by those who stayed behind, and the streets of York were packed with a long procession of cattle, tumbrils, carriages, and monks all going southwards. In the meantime Baines had bought the magnificent property of Prior Park on the outskirts of Bath, it being his intention to establish here a great centre of learning, a sort of Catholic Eton and Oxford of arresting magnificence.[1] He had hardly settled down at Prior Park when he engaged in two other quarrels, one with the Benedictine nuns in his diocese, another with the Jesuits. At length in 1833, and very late in the day, Rome intervened, and having suspended this violent Bishop for a short while, restored order of a kind, allowing the validity of the English Benedictines in the following year. But the quarrels went on.

Like most Catholic ecclesiastics of that time, Baines was more Gallican-minded than the men who followed in later years, though here he was somewhat undecided. He championed both schools at different times and so provoked a double measure of conflict. It was he who introduced the intensely Ultramontane preacher, Father Gentili, into England, making him one of the chief directors of Prior Park, and it was Father Gentili who first

[1] In his excellent history of Ampleforth, the late Dom. Cuthbert Almond doubts whether he intended founding a University. The assertion is made by numerous other authorities, including Bernard Ward.

introduced many Italian devotions into English custom which were then hardly known, and much resented. Then Baines quarrelled with Father Gentili, and with those converts who, in the manner of many converts, enjoyed luxuries and extremes. At this moment, 1842, he was in serious trouble, having been again rebuked by the Pope, this time for a Pastoral letter, delivered in 1840, in which he publicly dissociated himself from, and even ridiculed the new practices. He made references to the credulity of those who gave " heed to foolish old wives' tales," and discouraged prayers for the conversion of England and the cult of " The Sacred Heart,"[1] as absurd extravagances. He made pointed allusions to the arrogance of the newly converted to their former Anglican co-religionists. This utterance caused furious disgust which led finally to official disapproval of what he had done. The quarrel between the followers and opponents of Baines had burst out anew over this, and was perhaps fiercer than at any time in his pathologically quarrelsome career.

The most prominent Catholic layman in England was Frederick Lucas, a recent convert. He was the first Editor of *The Tablet*, founded in 1840. He was of Quaker origin, a brother-in-law of John Bright, but he seems to have carried over none of the gentle piety of The Friends into his newly adopted religion, and it is difficult to believe that he was ever sweet-natured. He championed the Ultramontane cause, though this did not prevent him delivering sharp attacks on the Pope when the latter and he were not in accord. He was a man to whom polemics were as needful as food, and he spent the last sixteen years of his life, from his conversion to his death, in organising strife between his co-religionists and Anglicans, between the traditional Catholics and the Converts, and fanning the flames of the ancient quarrel between England and Ireland. Hardly a number of *The Tablet* appeared without an article directed against one or other of Lucas's numerous opponents and written in offensive language. In the dispute over the " Queen's Colleges "

[1]This cult, which may be described as that of the Divinely and humanly emotional character of Jesus Christ, is founded on the spiritual experiences of Saint Margaret Mary Alacoque in the late seventeenth century.

in Ireland, *The Tablet* threatened a religious civil war in England, in the course of which, Lucas prophesied, all the major industrial cities would be laid in ruins. When a Diplomatic Relations Bill was before Parliament with the object of exchanging embassies with the Vatican, he summoned a public meeting in London to protest against this move whose object, he said, was to use the Papacy as an instrument of oppression in Ireland. The demonstration concluded with jeers and catcalls against the old Catholics for having failed to oppose the Bill in the House of Lords. He called Sir Thomas Redington (a pious and able Catholic politician not of his party) " the slave of Pontius Pilate." When he fell into disagreement with another convert, Thomas Chisholm-Anstey (a man almost as intemperate as himself), he put an announcement in the papers that they were not on speaking terms. He called Catholic Bishops crypto-Protestants when they disapproved of his conduct, and described the Anglican divines of Oxford as pagans. The hysteria over " Papal Aggression " in 1850 is partly explained when we remember that people in England only knew Catholicism by Lucas and *The Tablet*.

Towards the end of his life, ten years from this date, Lucas became involved in a famous quarrel with Archbishop Cullen, the chief of the Irish hierarchy, who disapproved of Irish priests joining political movements, while Lucas took the opposite view. The quarrel was carried to Rome, and when the Pope, with much kindliness, it seems, but with much firmness too, reproved Lucas in a private audience for his journalistic excesses, the Editor of *The Tablet* could hardly understand what was being said to him, and bitterly resented the Pope's words. He was ordered by the Pope to write a personal statement to him on his opinion in the Irish question. He did so in a very able document (uncompleted because his health failed while writing it), but, being who he was, he could not resist putting in some threatening hints as to what might happen to the Pope if he did not agree with his conclusions. He never understood why this caused offence to the Vatican authorities.

But that part of his violent career lay ahead of these years in the early 'forties. What we must note now is that while the most influential English Catholic ecclesiastic had raised party storms by his tempestuous character, this influential layman increased those storms.[1]

Between the " old Catholics," as the traditional followers of the old faith were generally called, and the converts, the dispute was in early and not very clear stages, but a division was already evident, the old Catholics following time-honoured English practices of austere moderation which had become vaguely associated with Gallicanism, and the converts preferring Italianate luxuries which they decidedly associated with Ultramontanism. The old Catholics were accused by the converts of timidity, because they kept their religion hidden away, avoided using traditional Catholic terms, such as " Mass " (which they still called " Prayers "), and maintained their churches free of much ornament. The converts were irritated to find that the old Catholics had insensibly come to adopt many Anglican ways and were in danger of losing some of the greatest things in their heritage; for example, monastic life was so little understood in England that, under old Catholic influence in the houses of Downside and Ampleforth, the rule of the order was hardly followed, and attempts to impose the Benedictine silences or to adopt the Benedictine habit were resented as " un-English " and unpractical. The old Catholics were also accused of hanging back in the Parliamentary struggle. In modern language, their rough-tongued opponents might have described them as " wet." The converts, on the other hand, were accused of saucy ostentation, and of play-acting, and if there was much truth in the charge that the old Catholics were unworthily shy of such finely tested systems as the Benedictine Rule, or that people such as Shrewsbury and the aristocratic politicians were weakly good-

[1]To understand Lucas some things must be remembered in his favour. In the last years of his life he became a Member of Parliament, and as the political champion in the House of his co-religionists he behaved with wisdom, and astuteness. The other is his highest claim to be forgiven his many faults. Before the Emancipation of 1829 the English and Irish Catholics had a sense of unity, which was somewhat lost afterwards. Lucas could have made his self-appointed task of lay Catholic champion much easier and more pleasant if he had ignored Irish questions. But he did the very opposite and thus made his co-religionists free of English guilt in the Irish disasters of the time.

mannered in their defence of Catholicism in Parliament, it was equally true that the other party did many things likely to exasperate opinion needlessly. We hear of convert clergy imitating Italian manners with extraordinary theatricality: appearing in the street wearing knee breeches and buckles, at that time the usual dress of a priest in Italy when not gowned, but outlandish in England. " Some even went to such lengths," relates Bernard Ward, " as to spit in church, a practice which they said denoted the feeling of being at home. . . . One well-known convert allowed a small dog to run about his church, declaring that the collar bells had a devotional effect." Both sides confused doctrine and devotion and suspected each other of heresy.

There was one very curious and intensely bitter controversy raging in the Catholic Church then, particularly in France and England, which has since entirely disappeared. This was concerned with the Gothic Revival, and what made this struggle so particularly fierce in England was that it centred round the fanatical character of Augustus Welby Pugin, that wonderful and enormously eccentric genius who has appeared in this story already, as Sibthorp's friend and supposed relative. It is surprising that Dickens never portrayed this man, who reminds one so vividly of the Pickwick Papers that it is easy to fancy in a vague moment that one has met him as the companion of Jingle and Snodgrass, rather than in the history of England. Pugin was a man who thought, lived, and felt in terms of architecture, and in terms of Gothic architecture only—no other sort at all—and whose deep piety was powerfully influenced by this taste.

It was quite wrong of Ruskin to say that his conversion to the Catholic Church was sentimental, and merely undertaken for æsthetic reasons. On the contrary, the man was tormented throughout his Catholic life by what seemed to him the hideous art with which its mysteries were surrounded. Few odder documents exist than the journal which he kept during his visit to Rome. " The churches here are frightful," he cries out in his agony; " St. Peter's is far more ugly than I expected,

"UNDERTAKERS CAROUSING AFTER THE BURIAL
OF PROTECTION"

*From a Cartoon of 1852 by John Leech. The central
figure is Disraeli. That on the extreme left
is Charles Sibthorp*

and vilely constructed. . . . The Sistine Chapel is a melancholy room, the Last Judgment . . . a painfully muscular delineation . . . The Scala Regia a humbug, the Vatican a hideous mass, and St. Peter's is the greatest failure of all. *It is quite painful to walk about.*"

Not only his appreciations of art, but his friendships and his estimates of men were influenced by Gothic architecture and sometimes expressed in its technical terms. When he met William Ward, whom he admired, it seemed to him strange that so fine a man should live in a house without any mullioned windows. He was narrow, even in his love of Gothic. He wrote in a letter: "If any man says he loves Pointed Architecture and hates screens, I do not hesitate to denounce him as a liar!" Towards the end of his life his entirely exclusive preoccupation with Gothic style even affected his taste in food, and he evolved means of making Gothic puddings. Surely that last detail could only have been invented by Dickens—but no, it is a record of fact; the thing really happened.

The influence of this amazing man on Catholic custom was held in disfavour at Rome, and by some of the English Bishops, being associated with extreme Gallicanism. This was a mistaken idea which probably arose from the fact that Pugin took his enthusiasm to heretical lengths. He regarded Gothic architecture as an almost essential part of the Christian faith, the high leaping arches as a tremendous and unique symbol of the Resurrection, and Rood Screens as utterly indispensable to a Christian's communication with God. He felt equally strongly about medieval style in ritual, chanting, and vestments. "What is the *use*," he once said to a priest who was about to enter a church to conduct an evening service, "what is the *use*, my dear Sir, of praying for the conversion of England in a cope like *that*." We must remember that though he was supreme in the art of angry jesting, he had little of what is commonly meant by a sense of humour. When the Gothic Revivalists began to be looked upon as very dangerous men at the Papal Court, Bishop Baines began the offensive in England, refusing to attend the opening of the church of Uttoxeter because Gothic vestments were to be used, and thereon battle was joined. At this time, in 1842, the controversy was at its height, cutting across the division between the old Catholics and the converts, and creating desperate enmities in both camps. It was not to be calmed till the end of the nineteenth century.

Apart from these main feuds between Ultramontanes, Gallicans, the great orders, the secular Bishops, the old Catholics, the Converts, the Irish, the English, the Italianisers and the Gothic Revivalists, there were many other lesser quarrels which made almost as much noise. The autobiography of Archbishop Ullathorne presents an almost incredible picture of bickering, spitefulness, intrigue, and scandal-mongering in the English Catholic community. It is true that in many places, probably in most, Catholics were entirely unaware of these alarums and excursions, but it was impossible for a clergyman, in the midst of the pother, with many years' experience of a very different life, not to be shaken to the soul by what was going on around him.

We last saw Sibthorp in Birmingham. He was installed in the clergy house near the recently built Pugin-Gothic Cathedral of St. Chad's. His troubles now began in earnest. Throughout his career he had been used, at those breakfast parties, for example, on the Isle of Wight, to clerical companions drawn from county families and from the upper middle class, gentlefolk whose behaviour was informed by the graceful reserve peculiar to the Church of England. Here in the Birmingham clergy house he was thrown amid coarse people. His companions were Irishmen from rough humble homes. There was no friend for Dr. Routh's lost sheep. There was none who knew or cared about the Universities, none sharing any of his other secular interests. He had known few Catholics before conversion. He was not prepared for the fact, which met him forcibly among these priests, that as a result of many years of penal legislation most Catholics in England were grossly uneducated. They were ignorant and common, and he minded it.

After a short time this delicate fish out of water sought solitude. He took a private dwelling in Edgbaston, that suburb which rises clean and pleasant from Birmingham on a nearby hill. One person who knew him at this period says that he did this as a result of a breakdown in health, but another put the matter more bluntly: " He refused to live with the clergy."

He often preached in St. Chad's, with still undimmed eloquence, drawing great congregations to hear him. But in this, the most successful part of his ministry, the appearance of a difference between his own and regular Catholic practice, was noted. The blunt friend, previously quoted, described his adventures in the pulpit. " He preached a great deal," he said, but added, " and generally without a trace of Romanism." We know what was meant by this from Sibthorp's own testimony given many years later. It is usual for Catholic sermons to be centred on the subjects of the New Dispensation: The Saviour, His Mother and Apostles, The Church Triumphant, and the Communion of Saints; but Sibthorp's sermons still bore a Puritan character from his Evangelical days, and were largely centred on the Old Testament. This was not offensive but novel to Catholic audiences, whose Church has for many centuries been sparing in the use of Old Testament matter. The discovery of this fact shocked him. It was to shock several of the later University converts. It shocks some people still.

We are to imagine him during this Birmingham career as occupied with frequent prayers, and his priestly duties which lay for the most part among the very poor, but pursuing this life in a lonely manner, almost as a personal enterprise. In July, he wrote words which sound strangely from a priest who has been ordained but two months before: " I am still here, but still unsettled. I am not one of the clergy, strictly speaking." The unhappy man had already made plans to leave Birmingham for somewhere more agreeable, somewhere with a friend in it.

The Gothic Revivalists had just carried off a new victory.

Our hero's marvellous friend Pugin, two years after the completion of St. Chad's, was commissioned to build another large church, the Catholic cathedral of St. Barnabas in Nottingham, in spite of strong Ultramontane opposition. Sibthorp, as we have remarked, was a man of means, and he contributed a thousand pounds to this undertaking, informing the authorities at the same time that he wished to remove from Birmingham to this other city. He bought a house in Nottingham. Then for the first time he felt the weight of the severe and autocratical discipline under which the Roman Catholic priesthood is governed. His superiors disregarded his request for change—a request which, after his contribution, he had considered almost as a formality—and no orders came for him to go to Nottingham. It is likely that he had incurred disapproval by siding with the Gothic party. Because of the way his individualism was tolerated people in Birmingham often called him " the spoilt convert." But—poor Father Sibthorp! Perhaps it would have been kinder, and wiser, at his time of life and in this friendless world, to have spoilt him a little more.

In the autumn of 1842 there occurred an event which gave rise to much speculation later on. During a visit to a country gentleman near Birmingham, he went for a drive in the course of which he was thrown out of an open carriage, and flung with great force on the road. He landed on his head. The injury was as severe as it could be, short of death. Some people said that he was not in full command of his reason after, but there is no evidence for this, or that the accident influenced his behaviour. He suffered a great physical shock, it is true, but the person who emerged from the disaster was precisely the same as he who suffered it. There was no break in the queer consistency of his life.

He spent a long convalescence at the end of which he returned to his duties, where he found an urgent task awaiting him. A certain Miss Isabella Young, one of Dr. Pusey's penitents, was in Birmingham. She wished to become a Catholic, and Father

Sibthorp had been appointed her instructor. Upon her he now exerted the eloquence for which he was famous, and in due course she was received into the Catholic Church. It does sometimes happen in human intercourse that when a man conveys a lightly held opinion to someone who accepts it, he himself loses it by that act of giving.

As winter drew on he left Birmingham for a brief holiday, and went to Oxford.

"There is a quondam member of the College, visiting us just now," wrote James Mozley to his sister on the 20th of December, 1842, "namely Sibthorp; he is with Bloxam and dines with the President to-day. I have not seen him and probably shall not, though I believe he is prepared to receive callers. . . . It is rather curious that S.'s fall from his carriage seems likely, from what I hear, to have the effect of withdrawing him from a public and important position among the Roman Catholics. They say that his head has been so much affected by it that preaching will be a great exertion. Bloxam thinks that half from this, and half from not liking his new associates particularly, he will probably retire into private life."

Mozley's gossip was true. Sibthorp seems to have spoken of his inner life somewhat freely as people often do in the midst of sudden happiness. He must have found Oxford, that delectable, half slumbering and noble-souled Oxford of the mid-nineteenth century, very pleasant after the dark modern misery of the nineteenth-century Midlands. He must have found it very pleasant to sit and talk again with Dr. Routh and Dr. Bloxam.

Within a fortnight of his return to Birmingham talk about this Oxford visit led to a new storm in the newspapers; not a great nation-shaking storm as before, but a storm of sorts. It can be followed in a correspondence which appeared in *The Tablet* on the 28th of January, 1843. First was printed a letter from Wiseman which had already appeared in *The Morning Herald*.

Two Studies in Virtue

" St. Mary's College
Birmingham
3rd Sunday after Epiph. 1843

SIR,

My attention has been called to a paragraph in which it is stated that ' The Rev. Mr. Sibthorp is reported to have already serious differences with his brethren of the Romish Priesthood; that he refuses to pray to the Virgin, or to be a party to auricular confession; that an appeal is now pending to Rome . . . and that should the decision be adverse, Mr. Sibthorp, it is said, will secede from the Romish Church. . . .'

A paragraph, much in the same strain, appeared a short time ago in *The Record*, or some other religious paper, and went what is called ' the round of the papers.' . . .

Had there been the slightest ground for any one of the statements put forth in that paragraph, I must, from position, have been acquainted with it, and Mr. Sibthorp, whom I have seen this very evening, is aware of my intention of writing this contradiction. . . .

I am, Sir, your obedient servant,

N. WISEMAN, Bishop of Melipotamus "

This was followed by a curiously self-revealing letter from Father Sibthorp:

" *To the Editor of 'The Tablet'*
DEAR SIR,

My attention having been directed to a paragraph in your paper of last week, extracted from the *Morning Herald*, I beg to assure you that, as far as it relates to myself the statement it contains is as *false* as it is *foolish*. It is *foolish* to charge me with dissenting from the Catholic Church, because I will not worship the Virgin Mary. Assuredly I do not WORSHIP her; but neither does the Catholic Church require me to WORSHIP her, or any but God.[1] But I ask her intercession, and, as you

---

[1] In Catholic as opposed to Anglican parlance the term " worship " is very widely used for almost any act of reverence. In his brief novitiate Sibthorp does not seem to have discovered this.

well know, must do so, many times a day, while saying my Breviary Office. And it is *foolish* to accuse me of disapproving of auricular or private confession as a practice of the Catholic Church, when the Protestant Church of England at least commends it on some and frequent occasions. See her Communion Service, and office for the Visitation of the Sick.

It is *false* that there are differences on these points between my clerical brethren and myself. And it is *false* that a reference or appeal has been made to the Pope etc. At least, if these statements are not false, I am, to this moment, not cognisant of any such facts.

In short, the whole paragraph in the *Morning Herald*, as it relates to me, is a fabrication from the beginning to the end: the invention, probably, of the same ingenious but not over scrupulous person, who lately forged the letter signed ' Bernard Smith,' denying his conversion to the Catholic Faith.[1]

I am sure you will do me the favour to insert these few lines; and regretting that I am obliged to obtrude myself on the notice of your readers, I remain,

Dear Sir, your faithful servant in Christ,

R. WALDO SIBTHORP

Edgbaston, January 24th, 1843 "

No comment seems to have been passed by Wiseman on this defence of the sacrament of confession on the grounds that it was not forbidden by Protestant tradition.

He did not stay much longer in Birmingham. He wrote to the Vicar of Canwick in April: " I now dare speak of nothing as fixed, but live only by a day at a time. . . . I excuse your harsh words against the Catholic Church. I wish we had not given you reason to say anything against us. But do not lay the faults of her members on the Church itself. However I am sick and weary of controversy . . ." and later in the month he wrote, yet more suggestively, to the same friend: " I am pretty

[1]The interested reader should consult Mr. R. D. Middleton's *Magdalen Studies* for an account of these forgeries.

much like him of old, who went forth not knowing whither he went . . . and may say, in the words of the hymn, ' Guide me, O Thou Great Salvation.' "

In June Mozley's prophecy was fulfilled. He retired from Birmingham, and went to live in the Isle of Wight once more. He said many years later that this place had a peculiar effect on him.

Not much is recorded of this second Isle of Wight period where he lived as a recluse. We know of a visit paid to him from Chichester by Archdeacon Manning, but nothing of what passed between them. We know that he had an oratory attached to his cottage and that he said Mass in it, attended by his local fellow-religionists. We know also that in September his acolyte forgot to extinguish the candles after a service with the result that the oratory was gutted by fire. The climax came fittingly very shortly after that.

One day in the first week of October, the venerable Dr. Routh, now in his ninetieth year, received a letter which contained great news for him.

" I am sure," wrote Sibthorp, " I shall find in your kindness and the friendly interest you have always shown respecting me, an excuse, if I needed one, for troubling you with a few lines. Indeed I should think myself wanting in duty and gratitude if I did not write to you, and be myself the first to communicate what I hope will have your approbation. I resolved in Lent last to go into retirement, that I might leisurely reconsider the step I took (certainly hastily) in joining the Church of Rome. I came here in June last, and the result of much consideration and most painful and anxious reflection—not, I hope, without hearty prayer to God to guide me right—has been that yesterday morning (October 1) I received the Holy Communion in the Parish Church of this village, as declaratory of my return to the Church of England." . . .

The die was cast, he thought. He was home once more.

The third Sibthorp storm which now blew up was strictly
of the nature of a local disturbance. It made little noise. It was
considered to the interest of the Anglican side to say little and
The Times made no mention of the matter at all. This final
storm involved few people, but it was most dreadful for those
few.

The shock fell with immense force on Bishop Wiseman, even
affecting him physically so that he was obliged to lie in bed for
twenty-four hours. He admitted with tears that the fault was
chiefly his own, and he reproached himself for having received
Sibthorp into the Church at their first meeting without lengthy
instruction, and then for having ordained him after only half
a year.

The Tablet, which might have been expected to break on this
quarry in full cry, showed at first grave and thoughtful restraint,
dealing with the incident in a leading article entitled " Converts
and Conversion." This was for good reason. In his timing
Sibthorp enjoyed a remarkable stroke of luck, because it so
happened that another priestly scandal of this scandalous era had
afflicted the Church a little before his secession. There had just
occurred the case of Father Oxley, which was alleged to have
been of an exceedingly sordid nature, involving not only apostasy
but some doubtful money transactions, so that in comparison
the sincere fall of Sibthorp seemed almost wholesome. He was
treated with respect and with forbearing grief, at first that is—
only at first.

It was suggested, at first (and almost certainly wrongly) that
the injury to his head had temporarily disordered his mind, and
the familiar mistake was repeated of assuming that he was
representative of the Tractarian Party. He was called " the
brightest light that Puseyism has yet brought us." Then the
correspondence and the comments left the subject of Sibthorp
for a while. The debate ranged over the whole topic of Catholic
England, from time to time coming back to our hero. But the
latter, meanwhile, blundered into Lucas's hands and excited that
fierce man's carnivorous disposition.

Sibthorp had determined to conduct himself with gentlemanly moderation in this crisis of his soul, but suddenly he found this discipline too much for him, and he gave way to a violent fit of indignation. He wrote to an Anglican clergyman, a friend of his, called Mr. Bickersteth: "The conviction I am come to after most painful deliberation, is that the Church of Rome is the Harlot and Babylon in the Apocalypse. I believe her to be an adulterous and idolatrous Church, especially as it respects Mariolatry." This was more than Mr. Bickersteth could keep to himself. A few days later he attended a Church Missionary meeting in Bath, where he read the letter publicly amid applause. A report of this meeting appeared in the local press and so found its way to London, and thus to *The Tablet*. "Those who know their man," wrote Lucas, "and see us snap up a Sibthorp, laugh at us and say: 'How dreadfully these poor Papists must be off for decently educated priests, when they make such a pother about a Sibthorp.'" Such was one of many deep wounds inflicted upon him. More than twenty years after Sibthorp remembered with pain what had been said, and how much he deserved it.

In the autumn the storm gradually died down in the Catholic press. The last reference to him in this year, at the very end of November, was in a letter publishing an odd rumour that Sibthorp had not really left the Roman Catholic Church, but continued a faithful member in secret. This was contradicted by the Editor.

The resentment of his Catholic co-religionists at what he had done was, however, not the greatest he incurred. The Tractarians at Oxford banded together against him for they were not only shocked by what he had done, but exasperated by hurt pride at being seen by the outside world as the followers of this eccentric clergyman, belonging to an Oxford age much earlier than their own, who was not of their party, whose spirit wobbled between faith and faith, and who made religion laughable. Their feelings were well expressed by William Ward in a letter which he wrote to Ambrose Phillips de Lisle: "By this time you have doubtless heard of Mr. Sibthorp's step. How unspeakably dreadful! It makes one sick to think of it. I hear that quite moderate people among ourselves are extremely disgusted. . . . His reception among us will be, I fully expect, of the most repulsive character; I, for one, shall decline any intercourse with him whatever."

James Mozley treated the affair with ridicule. He wrote on November 7th: "He has suffered, Bloxam says, amazingly throughout. But there are some persons who possibly enjoy these spiritual uneasinesses and doubts."

And now let us consider "poor Sibthorp" himself during his ordeal, the ordeal of being ground to pieces by great forces which he had invoked carelessly.

Having shut the gate of Rome behind him, and having incurred at the same time the contempt of his Oxford friends the Tractarians, coming back just as they were about to set forth, and so having made Oxford an uncomfortable place for him to live; having cut himself off from his past, he turned to the Bishop of Winchester in whose diocese he had both lost and recovered his Anglican faith. He returned to him like the prodigal to his home, but he was not so successful as he expected to be. The Bishop was not in the mood of the father in the parable. He had had enough of this man.

Charles Sumner was the Bishop's name. Sibthorp could hardly have chosen one less likely to sympathise with his troubles. Sumner had suffered not a little through the Catholic Revival in his successful but not supremely successful career. He stands in our history as one of the last of those princely rulers of the English Church of whom Bristol, in the eighteenth century, marked the extreme limit of grandeur and extravagance. This later huge, dignified, mellifluous prelate, of no great learning or brilliance, according to his biographer, but "richly cultivated" and renowned for graceful manners, was supposed to have owed his first promotions to a remarkable service which he performed for Lord and Lady Conyngham when he was tutor to their son. The youth, so people said, while travelling abroad for his instruction, fell in love with a Swiss maiden of the middle class, and would have made her his wife, had not the tutor, for the sake of his patron, retrieved this dangerous situation by marrying the girl himself. The story was consistently denied by the Conynghams and by his Swiss family-in-law, and may have been no more than a fable based on an exaggerated estimate of his courtier-like qualities and character. What is certain is that the Conynghams were so delighted by their son's tutor that they presented him to George IV in the first year of his reign. The King took an instant, one might say a furious liking to him, making him a Canon of Windsor (without consulting the Prime Minister, Lord Liverpool, an action which nearly shook the Ministry to pieces) and personal chaplain both at Windsor and Carlton House. The King even went so far in his passion as to forbid Sumner to travel abroad, because he wished this man and no other to be at his side at the hour of death. But before that event the two friends had quarrelled. Charles Sumner was not a courtier in a contemptible sense; he could endanger his success for his principles. In 1829, in opposition to the King, the sacred side of whose character was largely occupied with detestation of Catholicism, Sumner, already Bishop of Winchester, voted for Emancipation. Judging by his letter on the subject to the King, he did so for fantastically ill-informed reasons, it being his belief that when the old faith was no longer threatened by penal laws, and had been deprived of the glamour of martyrdom, the Irish nation would swiftly embrace the Church of England as their own.[1] Yet, absurdly wrong as was this judgment, it was sincere, and he preferred to lose the patronage of George IV, and the prospect of Canterbury, rather than obey the King's wishes in so grave a matter. When he saw the extent of his miscalculation, the rapid and vast expansion of the Catholic Church in England, the revival of some points of Catholic doctrine and ceremonial among the Tractarians, he repented of his support, and at this moment he was passing through the climax of his second mood.

As a natural consequence he received Sibthorp's overtures

[1]Some English Catholics embraced the Church of England after the Catholic Relief Act of 1792, on the grounds that hitherto their adhesion to the old faith had been a point of honour, but was no longer so. Sumner doubtless had this in mind.

coldly. He did not want him any more. But the man persisted, and the Bishop, obliged to arrange some sort of welcome, contrived such a one as assured that this time Sibthorp's repentance must be final. He made a hard condition for him, namely that he should live in retirement at Winchester, as a faithful Anglican, for three years. Sibthorp consented. It thus came about that he was living as a private person in Winchester during the year 1845, which saw the greatest upheavals of a century in the Church of England, saw the " parting of friends," the secession and conversion of Newman, that blow, to use the famous words of Disraeli, " under which the Establishment still reels "; and so, because the attention of historically minded persons was bent on greater events, the figure which had once seemed the most prominent one among all English Churchmen, the gentle perplexed figure of our hero, passed into an obscurity from which it never came back. But he had many more years to live, and many strange things were still to happen to him.

When the three years were over he applied for Church employment once more but at this the Bishop made a further demand. He now required Sibthorp to sign a declaration of adherence to the Church of England, " especially in regard to the principal points of difference between the English and Roman Churches." Sibthorp took offence at this request, which he described as " vague." This term roused the Bishop not a little, and he sent back a letter to which Sibthorp did not reply; indeed the letter had the effect of making him withdraw his application. What the Bishop wrote was this: it was necessary, he said, to have a signed assurance from Sibthorp as to his convictions because he, the Bishop, had been informed by a Roman Catholic priest that he, Sibthorp, was in the habit of attending Roman Catholic services. . . .

The acccusation was true, though " habit " was a strong word. According to Dr. Bloxam (who may have accompanied him on these excursions), he had, in the course of his three years' retirement, attended Mass once in the Catholic chapel in Lincoln's Inn, and once in Warwick Street; he had also been to Vespers once in a chapel in Chelsea. By his own account these experiences repelled him. He sincerely preferred the Anglican to the Roman Catholic Church, but from the latter, for reasons perhaps not clear to him, he could not entirely keep away.

After this there was no more to be said as far as Winchester was concerned. He turned to his family home and petitioned the Bishop of Lincoln. But he met the same difficulties.

Bishop Kaye, though a man of deeper mind, resembled Sumner in his ideas. Like the Bishop of Winchester, he was a supporter of the Evangelical Party, like him he was an opponent of Tractarian ritualism, and he had always been what Sumner became: an opponent of Catholic Emancipation. It was natural that he should follow Sumner in exacting assurances from Sibthorp, because our hero had wandered into those very sloughs and thickets which both Bishops regarded as the dreadfulest dangers threatening the progress of the soul. He wrote to the elder brother Charles showing the logic of his wishes. But against this discipline Sibthorp plunged and kicked. He wrote to Bloxam: " In withdrawing from Rome, I never dreamt to become her hostile opponent. The quietest course possible, I am clear without a doubt, is the properest under my circumstances; I will take no other, God helping me, be the result what it may. I shall not wonder if this prove the decisive hitch. The Bishops want more from one man than the law of the land and the rules of the Church warrant them to ask; and *I will not give it.*" Later in the year 1847, he wrote: " My own health and peace of mind demand a settlement some way. The Church of England has no bowels of compassion, no feeling, no forgiveness."

In December a compromise was reached. Sibthorp was required to sign a recantation which was not to be published, but entered in the Registry of the Diocese, in exchange for which he would be received into the ministry once more. Sibthorp agreed, and gave his recantation. He sent copies of it to Dr.

Bloxam, and to the ancient President, who shortly after, for the third time, re-admitted him to Magdalen College. On the 23rd of December of 1847 Sibthorp was once more appointed an active clergyman in the Church of England. He was fifty-five years old. He settled in Lincoln.

For a space we will consider a different world from that of a cathedral city. We will not digress from our theme; we will examine very briefly an influence upon its main personage.

There is an element of resemblance in this story, full of false parallels, though also of illuminations. Henry Digby Best shared Magdalen and Abbé Beaumont with Sibthorp, and though so different in character he can remind us also of Newman because he startled the University first with sermons and then with a conversion, and much later with an apologia. Newman in his turn shared something with Sibthorp. People living at the time were very impressed by their resemblance. They saw Newman as Sibthorp's shadow, as plunged by the projector of that darkness into frightful places, while Sibthorp himself, in the years after his return to the Church of England, was sometimes disturbed by guilt at the thought that his conversion in 1841, and the " Anglican landslide " to Rome in 1845, were closely connected. But apart from unworldliness of temperament, Newman and Sibthorp were in fact joined by not much more than coincidence and caricature. Viewed from certain angles, Sibthorp is a comic Newman. In his turn our hero was reflected in another. A grotesque of himself was ever present in the person of his elder brother, Colonel Charles de Laet Waldo Sibthorp, who, since the early death of Coningsby Sibthorp in 1822, had been the head of this ancient family. He had followed the military bent of his father. In youth he had served in the Fourth Dragoon Guards during the Peninsular War, and was now Colonel of Militia. Soon after inheriting the family estate he had turned to politics.

From 1827 to 1855 Colonel Sibthorp sat in the House of

Commons as Member for Lincoln, with a brief interval after his failure at the election for the first reformed parliament. If much strangeness can make a man great, then this Sibthorp was great indeed. His character was a dark and highly emotional confusion of loyalties and principles. He had fierce attachments, most markedly to the well-being of the gentry, to an unchangeable constitution, to a throne safe-guarded from the designs of foreign princes, to a sacredly English England, and these attachments were bound up with a passion to protect their objects so strong as to keep him in a state of perpetual alarm. At any hint of changes in the eighteenth century England of his first youth, even of very small changes such as a reduction in the numbers of drum-majors in the Army, he saw total disaster falling on this island in the way of an avalanche. It is a grave condemnation of our own age that the maddest visions of this maddest of politicians have been so abundantly fulfilled within a century, though it must be added that they have never been fulfilled for the reasons he put forward.

For years his appearance was one of the curiosities of the House. It is preserved in numerous caricatures of him by John Leech, and Richard Doyle, and in a few by Thackeray. He had the dark complexion of his family and contrary to the fashion of that time he wore a beard, a somewhat wispy one. His most usual dress included short and wide white trousers showing eight inches or so of his Wellington top-boots, a short bottle-green frock-coat, a very high stick-up collar, rather like Gladstone's collar but more open at the throat, on his head a lofty white hat. He wore a great deal of jewellery and rings, and carried a large rectangular quizzing glass at the end of a silk ribbon in the forgotten style of fifty or even a hundred years before. He is described in 1847 as looking " like the débris of what must once have been a magnifico. A majestic air of tawdry grandeur reminds you of how King Joachim [Murat] might have looked when he found that the game was up at Naples."[1]

He has one serious claim to a place in Parliamentary History,

[1]Frazer's Magazine, 1847. Vol. XXXVI.

and that is as the originator of the " Chandos clause " in the first Reform Bill. Lord Chandos unfairly appropriated the credit of introducing this amendment, and the clause should in justice have been called after Sibthorp. He has also one spectacular claim. It was he who in January of 1841 moved for a reduction of Prince Albert's annuity from fifty to thirty thousand pounds. Sir Robert Peel, the Leader of the Opposition, had not been consulted about the annuity by Lord Melbourne, and irritated at this neglect of courtesy, but doubtless seeing party advantage therein, he rose up in high wrath, and to the astonishment of Sibthorp and of the whole House, seconded the Colonel's motion and defeated the Government. This reverse led to a change of Ministry; it was the beginning of Lord Melbourne's political decline; and because of what Sibthorp had contrived against her husband, the Queen would never visit Lincoln while he was its Member. In party Sibthorp was a wavering supporter of Sir Robert Peel until the latter embraced Free Trade. He was a passionate believer in the Corn Laws, and when they were repealed he was left without a leader. But he continued to represent Lincoln as an independent until his death.

The House of Commons has always had a jovial side. Provided he is of high quality, a comic man finds the best of audiences there. It thus came about that this passionate voluble fanatic was, throughout his career, one of the darlings of Parliament. He spoke very often, and though he introduced an extraordinary quantity of irrelevant matter, particularly irrelevant personal abuse into every speech he made, he never seems to have been called to order, nor to have been requested to withdraw his wildest utterances. He would rise to speak, say, on the Corrupt Practices Bill (which he opposed for many years) or on Army reform, and into his observations he would introduce lengthy digressions on the desirability of pulling down the National Gallery, the dangers of the new cheap postage, of barrel organs, of Commissioners and Commissions, nearly always using certain favourite expressions: " humbug," " one scabbed sheep spoils the whole flock "—this frequently applied to Lord

John Russell—" scratch me and I'll scratch you "—this for
Commissioners; commencing every peroration with the words
" For myself," and often ending with a declaration that even if
he was killed for his honesty he would do his duty to the last.
He used to refer to " The Infernal Reform Bill—that vile engine
of robbery and oppression "; he described the Maynooth grant
as " a system for the encouragement and protection of beings
who are little better than devils incarnate." The House never
took the smallest offence[1] at these outbursts: members of all
parties leaned back on the benches and roared with laughter
while he was delivering these hobby-horse-ridden orations. In
his long career he was only once interrupted. They loved
" Sibby " at Westminster.

In spite of the disorderly nature of his hate-infested mind,
his political career has an easily discernible shape. He moved
from hatred to hatred by precise stages, beginning with Catholic
Emancipation and moving through his Reform Bill phase to a
personal detestation of Lord John Russell. He started on a fresh
scent with his campaign against the railways, and in this phase it
is possible that he moved by accident into an august position in
history. He foretold every sort of calamity from this invention,
and frequently confided to the House his personal dismay at
being compelled to use such transport. He often said that he
looked to a day when the steam-engine would vanish as an evil
dream. Somewhat similar views, expressed with a similar touch
of crazy moral enthusiasm, can be found expressed by Lebedev
in *The Idiot* by Fedor Dostoyevski. The great Russian used to
read Parliamentary reports and the Colonel's speeches may
have served him as raw material.

His feelings on Catholicism, Reform, Railways, and the
rest were mild compared to those which he brought to the last
great rage of his life, the Exhibition of 1851. He delivered his
first speech on this subject on the 18th of June of 1850, and he
kept up a series of loud and sullen bellows against " this great

[1] But he sometimes took offence at the House's reception. See Hansard, July 5th, 1831, and June 17th, 1836, for the best specimens of his injured manner.

humbug," as he called it, " this unwholesome castle of glass,"
" the palace of tomfoolery," and " this big bauble," until the
end of 1853.

The Crystal Palace touched the very essence of this man's
mind. The objections of our English Cato to Prince Albert's
venture were numerous, but they were without exception connected with a deep-set fear, the deepest, the most essential of all
his fears, and which excited all his numerous anxieties, namely an
uncontrollable dread and loathing of people and things not
English. He warned the House that the Exhibition would
tempt foreigners to visit these shores. He described their object
in so doing as four-fold: to under-sell, to burgle, to rape, but
chiefly to spy. He had always mistrusted Prince Albert on
account of his foreign birth and he saw now the climax of a
treacherous career: the enticement of other foreigners to London
in order to disturb our English peace. He always spoke as
though the hatefulness of foreigners was an agreed fact, not
worth argument or illustration because so self-evident. He
called them " hypocritical foreigners."

Charles Sibthorp is a curious example of a commonplace
phenomenon: namely that historical significance may be independent of grave character. In the early Victorian years, at the
time of these utterances, his conservatism obscured the fact that
he was the herald of a new age. Violent nationalism had often
been expressed in modern times before, but not often in the
extreme terms he used, with much pretence of seriousness. He
declared himself the champion of the English rural gentry, but
he spoke the language of the mob. He would have been much
surprised, no doubt, to learn that he was a progressive, a prophet
of what was to be,[1] yet this was his role. Like the gallant and
idiotic Nicholas Chauvin, he symbolised more than his con-

[1]Even sometimes (by coincidence) in matters of detail. He proposed more than
once, for example, that the Government should set financial impediments in the way of
foreign travel from England, and this, fantastic then, seems no tyranny to the present
age. Doyle, who drew the best caricatures of Colonel Sibthorp, seems to have made a
curious error in representing him as holidaying in Athens in 1850. The allusion was
perhaps to his collection of works of art. He was a considerable amateur of Greek and
Roman objects. Although he wished to pull down the National Gallery, he was not
a Philistine.

temporaries deemed possible, or he himself in all likelihood.
The brothers, Charles and Richard, were separated by their
religious differences, but they never lost affection. When Richard
Sibthorp joined the Catholic Church, the Colonel besought him
with tears to undo the deed, and he rejoiced over his brother's
return to the Church of his ancestors. Much later we see the
extent of that elder brother's influence. What we should note
now is that they shared certain characteristics: originality,
patriotism, and deep seriousness. Amid the laughter of the
House of Commons, which he endured for twenty-six years,
Colonel Sibthorp retained an unmovable seriousness.

The city of Lincoln lies in the narrow east-west valley of
Withan. The southern upland is covered by Canwick Park, the
home of the Sibthorps; the northern by the medieval town of
Lincoln, from whose centre the Minster rises forth in unsur-
passed majesty. Here on the northern hill, Richard Sibthorp
settled down, as comfortably as his odd nature allowed him to.
The Bishop of Lincoln very sensibly agreed to his ministering
in an individual fashion suited to his singular and intractable
character. It so happened that he had arranged a fitting outlet
for his energies.

He and Pugin had drawn plans for a venture which was to
occupy our hero the rest of his life. In medieval England there
were places called " Bede-Houses," meaning " Prayer-Houses,"
asylums for the poor attached to monasteries and other religious
foundations. The inhabitants paid rent in spiritual kind, being
obliged to attend certain offices of the Church. Sibthorp, disgusted by the vulgarities of Rome, but yet desirous, as the pupil
of Routh and the friend of Bloxam, to mitigate if possible the
Protestant character of the Church of England, set himself to
revive these forgotten foundations. He used up a large part of
his fortune in the establishment of Bede-Houses in Lincoln for
the reception, according to their charter, of " poor, honest,

Lincolnshire folk, thirteen women and one man,[1] communicants of the Church of England, and natives, or twenty-year residents in Lincoln town, in the parishes of St. Peter in Eastgate, Canwick, Washingborough, Waddington, and Harmston." The houses were called after St. Anne in memory of his mother. They are still there, used for their original purpose.

Two connected lines of one-storied brick dwellings, built in a medieval style, the eaves of the high roofs jutting out far so as to shelter the way between the front doors, the whole compound approached through a gate in the College fashion; mullioned windows; in many places the initials of the founder, RWS; a well in medieval style; high chimneys of antique shape; such were some of the chief characteristics of the Bede-Houses as completed by Pugin in 1848. The site was a half mile or so from the Minster, on the outskirts of the old town. There was some difference between Sibthorp and Pugin over the construction of the chapel, so this was entrusted (three years later) to the architect William Butterfield. From these dissensions between Pugin and Sibthorp no quarrel arose, and this was somewhat remarkable and should be noticed. We have seen, already, how Pugin was apt to read dark purposes into architectural opinions differing from his own. In these last years of his short life, his narrowness was getting ever narrower, both in architecture and religion. He had almost severed relations with William Ward on the subject of Rood screens. Yet here he was amicably disagreeing with, and building for, an apostate priest. The fact is an illustration of the unmistakable character of Sibthorp's sincerity. He was a man whom people forgave. Dr. Routh was for ever forgiving him. Wiseman had done so, and now the fanatic Pugin forgave him too.

In a small house next door to the Bede-Houses, and also built by Pugin, our hero dwelt in Lincoln for seventeen years, right into his old age. It seemed that at length the high-minded prodigal had found a lasting and honourable place at the hearth of his ancestors. Praying and consumed in pious works, the

[1]To act as porter and watchman.

good man seemed contented, as he had reason to be. In Bishop Kaye he had an affectionate superior who was one of the greatest of Victorian Churchmen; he was allowed to practise as a clergyman in a manner suited to the strong vein of originality in his character; he lived in constant sight of one of the noblest edifices raised by Christian hands to the glory of God.

He was profoundly unhappy nevertheless. No sooner was he safely back in the Anglican priesthood, than he was shaken by doubts as to whether he had done right. The disturbance in his soul took a painful form. He complained of intolerable boredom.

To his friend Dr. Bloxam he made an intimate confession shortly after the commencement of this Lincoln life.

" We have," he wrote, " of God different vocations. ' And so,' you will say, ' do you feel called to be a saint? ' I do . . . True indeed, I at present scarce do touch with my toes the threshold of this sanctuary; but I do touch it, and resolve, God helping me, to go further in. Pardon me for saying what seems so full of pride and empty vain conceit, that the ordinary clerical life in the Church of England would be the death of my soul. I do not mean by ' ordinary ' the low, worldly standard, but the better, and respectable, and useful and actively busy."

Soon, very soon indeed, after his reinstatement as an Anglican clergyman, he began to cast anxious backward glances towards Rome. It seems probable that an incident marked the beginning of this fresh season of doubt. A year after the opening of St. Anne's one of his Bedeswomen died, and he realised, with a considerable shock, that he could not administer Last Sacraments to her, as he would have done in the same circumstances in Birmingham. In a letter to Bloxam from Lincoln, written shortly after he described himself as a proud heart struggling, and referred to his vexed thoughts as he re-officiated amid what he called " the desolations of the sanctuary."

This soon became one of his most frequent moods. On many occasions, particularly when corresponding with his great friend, he spoke of his late religion in terms of warmth and regret, such as strike the reader as astonishing in a practising Anglican minister. But there was another side. On certain occasions he spoke in a directly opposite sense, with sincere and passionate disgust. For this he found a strong incentive. It was well for what little contentment he could enjoy in Lincoln that when he looked with longing to the glories of Rome, he caught sight of something which filled him with sufficient distaste to stop him going nearer. For instead of the Communion of Saints, he saw more and more often, as he peered across, the fantastical figure of Frederick William Faber. He remembered then, in all their repulsiveness, the things which had offended him within the fold.

He must have known of this strange man long before. He may have met him at Oxford in the 'thirties when Faber, a Tractarian undergraduate, knew Sibthorp's friends, Dr. Bloxam and Dr. Newman, and had been noticed by the venerable Routh. However that may be, it is not till 1848 that Faber is mentioned in Sibthorp's correspondence. After that he becomes a frequent theme. He becomes the first of a series of obsessions whose violence reminds us, for the first time in the story, that our hero was the brother of Colonel Charles.

Faber had things in common with Sibthorp. He was an Evangelical by upbringing, of a very extreme Calvinist and Protestant kind, until Tractarian life made him more receptive. While still a young man, in the eighteen thirties, he became attracted, and then repelled, by the Catholic Church, just as Sibthorp had been twenty years before him. After some hesitations a visit to Belgium in 1839 finally, as it seemed, strengthened him in the disgust he felt for what went on under the Roman obedience. With a sense of lasting accord with the Church of England he became Rector of Elton, in Northamptonshire, in the same year. It is difficult to see why, but Wordsworth said to him shortly after his ordination and appointment: " I do not say you are wrong, but England loses a poet." Faber wrote a great deal of verse during the remainder of his life, and most of it, in spite of its evident sincerity, is of a low order. It is hard to believe that even if he had devoted all his immense energy to writing he would ever have been of great literary account; nevertheless there is this impressive different judgment.

Within a few years the influence of Rome, which had seemed ineffective on him, worked vigorously, just as in Sibthorp's case, and his church of Elton became a scene of Romish ritualism, more Romish indeed, than that of any other ritualist in those days of exciting revival. He conducted services not only in honour of the Rosary, but of the much questioned Sacred Heart as well. At last, in November of 1845, he left the Church of England. He went away from Elton with the good wishes of his unhappy parishioners.

After that November day he ceased to resemble Sibthorp.

As soon as he had been reordained as a Catholic priest, he took to Roman practice with frenzied zeal. The man who kept a devotional dog in Church was soon left far behind by this convert. When he was put in charge of the first London Oratorian Church, Faber turned King William Street, where it was situated, into a little Italy—he and his clergy rustling to and fro in the streets at all times in their habits, an astonishing sight in those days—while within the Church the manners and customs of Catholic lands were carefully imitated, regardless of what was likely to please or repel: his painted plaster statues, clusters of little metal emblems, and votive candles causing especial offence. Faber saw himself as rebuilding a ruined city, but the old Catholics sighed for the days of Bishop Challoner's stoical devotions. Pugin suffered more than most, for under Faber's vigorous leadership the tide began to turn against the Goths. Sibthorp watched Faber's career with nausea and fascination. It became almost his main preoccupation. He read his *Lives of the Saints*, the first of which was published in 1848.

" The Life of St. Phillip Neri is a disgusting volume," he wrote to Dr. Bloxam, " I cannot get through with it. Mr. Faber is an extravagant of the first water. What a different sort of Catholic was Cardinal Bona, or Fénelon, Bossuet, and many more! The former sort are excrescences which want *reducing*."

Again a little later, he wrote: " Faber has produced another

volume. I feel less and less disposed towards these specimens of
' the saintly,' not denying that there was true sanctity in them,
but sadly mingled with enormous superstitions, puerilities, and
extravagances. Faber seems to have a taste for these; to delight
in promenading them before you, as if the maintenance of these
things was an exhibition of strong Catholic faith. A wiser man
would keep them out of sight." He wrote very frequently to
Bloxam in that strain.

Faber's *Lives of the Saints* are not wholly contemptible as
studies in the psychology of sanctity, but as historical records
they are almost unbelievably absurd. Miracles are piled on
without the least critical examination and with an undisguised
emotional delight. The result was peculiarly unfitted to his
audience. A reader, who had been brought up to believe that
a gentlemanly self-control was among the highest virtues, was
puzzled what to think when he read of Saint Phillip Neri that
" one day, speaking of the Passion, he was surprised by such an
extraordinary fervour, that he began weeping and sobbing; he
could hardly get his breath, he trembled all over, the seat shook,
and not the seat only, but the platform on which it stood, as if
someone had shaken it with his hands."

At moments the extremes of Father Faber threw Sibthorp
out of his determination to speak no ill of the Church he had
quitted. " Might not a person," he wrote to Bloxam, " show
up the weak points of the Roman Catholic Church, as Newman,[1]
you say, does those of our own? What a volume might be
written on that Church, as at present developed in England, by
one conversant with her! . . . I dare to pronounce Rome a falling
Church . . . She will never again triumph. Her struggles are
those of death." But in the event he stuck to his earlier decision
to say nothing, and possessed his soul in patience.

It is not impossible that his preoccupation with Faber arose
from psychological causes. It may have been a way in which he
becalmed a frequent sense of guilt. There is a curious document
among the letters to Dr. Bloxam, dated the 16th of October of

[1]At this time Newman and Faber were producing the *Lives of the Saints* in collaboration.

1849, in which he describes how he found himself at Birmingham in the course of a journey. "I steal through that town as one, that is ashamed, flees from battle. I always feel a *very peculiar attachment* to Birmingham; and an oppressive recollection of my days of interesting ministry there. I have not known a happy day since. . . . Yet do not suppose my eyes are less open to the evils of that Church of which I am yet a priest, or that I think more tolerable those corruptions which seem the delight of some who have gone into her. Indeed, it is by strange peculiarity that I cannot shut my eyes to her beauties or her defects. . . . I called at St. Chad's where as usual I was most kindly received, and I went away *sad at heart.*" The wording makes it clear that this visit to St. Chad's was one of several.

By the year 1854 when the Bishop of Lincoln consecrated the completed chapel of St. Anne's Bede-Houses, Sibthorp was beginning to grow old. His health was delicate, and the final period of his life began early, soon after he was sixty. "The fire of his youthful eloquence," we are told by his biographer, "may be said . . . to have died out. His sun, in this respect, had gone down, or was kept permanently under cloud; but there remained the soft, tender, lovely afterglow—the pensive, pleading, persuasive style so well adapted for those among whom he ministered. Who can ever forget his hand partly raised—rather stiffly—as he spoke; and his upturned eyes?"

In December of the same year, Martin Joseph Routh did at last die, three months after his ninety-ninth birthday, and Oxford could hardly believe that so catastrophic and postponed a loss had really befallen her. He was followed to his grave by a huge concourse of divines, fellows, dons, and undergraduates. Sibthorp was among them, the beloved and wayward child. He had corresponded with the President up to two years before his death. Cousin Pugin had died three years before this, quite early in life and mad; and in the next year his frantic brother

Charles was to die. But Bloxam was to outlive both his friends Sibthorp and Newman.

As must happen to ageing men, he was surviving into a new age, not thus only, physically, by these deaths, but as regards certain spiritual circumstances as well. The religion of his youth was now a distant and imperfect memory. The great days of Evangelicalism had come to an end with strange abruptness. Between the 'forties and the 'fifties, according to Gladstone, it ceased to be a great spiritual power in the life of England, and something of the truth of his statement is testified by our hero. " The major part of the Evangelicals," wrote Sibthorp to Bloxam, as early as 1850, " appear full of bigotry in their way, and idolatrous of their own right of judgement."

The loss to him of Evangelicalism increased the anguish of his predicament. He had now no alternative to Rome if he were ever to become convinced that the middle way of compromise where he now travelled was not the right one. And thanks to what he had learned from Evangelicals, or from Abbé Beaumont, from Martin, Milner, or from Wiseman, he found it increasingly difficult to believe that this road was the right one.

In 1857 he felt the need of an assistant and obtained the help of the Reverend John Fowler, who was to be his memorialist, and from whom we can learn much. He recorded early in his Lincoln days that Sibthorp's melancholy became a more regular feature of his life at this time. " When his past troubles," Fowler said, " and his present distractions had told their tale, his weakness showed itself—naturally enough—on Sundays. It was then that his morbid mind drew contrasts."

So he might have ended his days as a melancholy, perplexed, bored, and ailing Oxford Fellow who was dissatisfied with his position, when a new influence suddenly entered his life and forced him into action. The year was 1863. One day Sibthorp was at his usual occupation, watching from out of his Lincoln boredom the glitter and diversity of Rome, when he caught sight of something which he had not seen before. He found that unnoticed by him a tremendous figure had been standing there, throughout his lifetime. The name of this phenomenon was Jean Baptiste Vianney, better known as the Curé d'Ars.

To understand the rest of the story we need to have some rough notion of the modern saint who transformed this elderly gentleman's mind.

Vianney was born of French peasant stock near Lyons in 1786, a few years before Sibthorp. Between the ages of three and seventy-three, when he died, this man used every moment of his time not occupied by business in prayer. Only one discreditable action is recorded of him. In 1809 he deserted from the Imperial French Army. It seems that he fell into a trance while praying, and that while he was in this helpless state his regiment marched off, and he was unable to find it again. As a deserter he became liable to the death penalty, so he went into hiding. He was a man who criticised himself unsparingly, yet he never referred to this incident except in jocular terms, so it may be assumed that he did nothing worthy of blame.

In 1812 (having been pardoned by decree) he went to a seminary at Verrière near Paris, where he studied philosophy and theology, but without academic success. In consequence of his failure in the schools there was some question as to whether he was eligible for priesthood, but his director, a man called Balley, intervened, and in 1815 obtained his ordination. As a mark of confidence Balley appointed Vianney his confessor. In later years the Curé d'Ars defended his lack of book-learning with audacity and wit. When a fellow-priest once told him that many people considered him ignorant, he answered: " They are right. But it does not matter. I can teach you more than you will practise." To one who asked him who was his master in theology he gave the reply: " The same as St. Peter's."

In 1818 he was appointed to the curacy of Ars, situated near his birthplace, in Les Dombes. The village was said to be without spiritual life of any kind, and the scene of repulsive debauchery. We have several accounts of the Curé's life, written by witnesses, but unfortunately these are all marred by prudishness, for from them we learn of nothing worse going on at Ars than occasional dances on the village green, and some jollity in the public houses. It may be supposed that this dancing and tavern-life is an euphemism for a degraded amorality.

We are told by his companion, Abbé Monnin, that he was, at this time, without social graces. " His face was pale and angular," he records, " his stature low, his gait awkward, his manner shy and timid, his whole air ordinary and unattractive. There was nothing in his appearance except the singular brightness of his eyes." These handicaps proved unimportant. He entirely changed the life of his parish in a few weeks. At the beginning he spent his whole day on his knees in the little village church praying; he could always be found there when wanted. This life of solitary prayer, interrupted only by urgent matters and sleep, lasted a short time, because soon the village people took part in his life and found they had need of him at all hours. They joined him at prayer at two or three in the morning and again in the evening after their work. They contributed to rebuild the church. On solemn festivals they would go with him for long processions in the countryside, carrying gorgeous banners and shrieking hymns at the tops of their voices. He heard confessions, for two or three hours a day, until, as his fame spread and people came to him from far off, he was obliged to stay in his confessional for a great part of every day, sometimes all day, sometimes for days together.

He built a chapel to St. John the Baptist, and his parishioners believed that he did so in answer to a vision. Of this he would only say: " If you knew what has happened in this chapel, you would not dare set foot in it." This supposed vision was the first of a great mass of such happenings alleged to have taken place at Ars. They cannot be judged together. Some of them are very weakly attested, some are open to ordinary explanation, some which are well attested defy unbelief, but chiefly they are difficult to judge because Vianney, like many saints, attached little importance to such things.

He founded an orphanage in 1825 which he named " La Providence." Because Jesus Christ said that we should take no thought for the morrow, Vianney, in the administration of this place, took no thought of any kind for the morrow, with frequently resulting chaos. On such occasions he would pray for Divine assistance, a proceeding which, according to every extant record, never failed of result, sometimes in extraordinary ways. Whatever time he could spare from parochial duties (which included the support by him personally of the destitute of Ars), he spent in his confessional. His short hours of sleep, rarely more than three, and often two, were disturbed by violent manifestations of unseen hostility, sometimes audible throughout the village, and never, so far as was discovered, attributable to a human or other terrestrial agency.

The neighbouring clergy became exasperated. They asserted that Vianney showed a clear case of delusion, and that he was communicating his hysteria to his unfortunate parishioners. But after a single meeting with him at St. Trivier-sur-Moignans, they withdrew their charges.

During the eighteen thirties and forties his fame spread throughout France. Some twenty thousand people came to consult him every year. He received them in his confessional. He radiated a force to which none who met him was indifferent. We have the testimony of Lacordaire, Leon Bloy, and Bernard Ullathorne, among many others. He was credited with the inexplicable faculty of healing by touch. He had telepathic powers of a high order: he sometimes told people what they were about to confess, or should confess, before they had uttered a word. Often he told penitents to go back to their parish priests as they had come to him through trivial curiosity. Certain of his pronouncements have something of the ring of his Master's. "It is a strange thing," he said to a cynic, "I have met with many people who repented of not having loved God; never with one who sorrowed for having loved Him." A penitent asked him whether it were not rash to give indiscriminately to the poor, because they might abuse such kindness. He replied: "That is a responsibility of the poor. You must answer as to whether or not you gave." Some of his less intelligent penitents gave grotesque accounts of him which led to a renewal of angry criticism by the clergy. He rejoiced at this, and never denied the absurdest allegations. He said that all experience comes from God and is therefore capable of being sanctified. He usually slept on the floor with a log for a pillow. When he needed more bodily comfort he slept on boards on straw. He scourged himself, wore hair shirts, and so on.

Three times he decided to leave Ars for some more peaceful retreat: once in 1840, once in 1843, and the third time in 1853, He returned from his first two flights in obedience to compunctions, the third was an unsuccessful attempt which was forcibly prevented by the villagers who had warning of his design. It was not because he sought any relaxation of his intolerably arduous career that he left, or attempted to leave, on these occasions. He went because he regarded the life of a curate as a wretchedly low one compared to the ideal life of withdrawal and contemplation. He maintained that the highest activity of man was to be found nowhere outside a life of prayer, and that his looking after the poor of Ars, his conduct of " La Providence," his almost ceaseless ministrations in the confessional, gave him no time for the following of a loftier vocation. He regarded himself throughout as a very ordinary person. However, to the end he was compelled to attend to the poor, the orphans, and the penitents, converting many hundreds and even thousands of the latter, never, according to the Abbé Monnin, in a superficial manner.

Only once did his judgment of human beings falter, and that was over the affair of La Salette. In that place, in the Savoy mountains, two peasant children, a boy and a girl, professed to have seen an apparition of the Virgin Mary in 1847. When news of this reached the Curé d'Ars he encouraged the making of pilgrimages to the scene of this wonder. Later, in 1848, the boy was brought to see him. When the child was alone in the presence of this overpowering man, he confessed that the vision was a fraud. After this the Curé refused to have anything to do with La Salette. But in the meanwhile the Bishop of Grenoble, excited by a party in favour of these visions, had given much encouragement to acceptance, and even to pilgrimages. The Pope was persuaded to take a favourable view. For several years Vianney refused all part in this enthusiasm, until, suddenly, he declared that since the Bishop of Grenoble and the Pope accepted these miracles he must perforce be wrong, and he withdrew his objections. It may be that for once in his life, as the devotees of La Salette still insist, the Curé d'Ars behaved in a stupid and careless way when interviewing the boy, but on examination of the statements that Vianney made to Monnin, and of the boy's later excuses, particularly those concerning Vianney's supposed deafness, of the improbable nature of the messages said to have been confided to these children by the Mother of God, and of the subsequent histories of those same children, most enquirers will feel that Vianney was right in his first conviction, and that he would have done a finer service to his Bishops and his Church had he stood by it and not allowed himself to be impressed by his superiors.[1] In the manner of saints he sometimes took virtues to shocking limits, and one of his virtues was humility. Not long after his change of opinion over La Salette he died, in 1859.

Such in outline was the story.

Four years after the death of Vianney, Sibthorp read of this man who had fled from his parish in the same year, in the same month, as he had fled from Catholic priesthood in the Isle of Wight. He read it sitting in his Pugin-built dwelling next to the Bede-Houses; next door to *his* " Providence." His life was changed from then on. He suffered an immense upheaval.

There is nothing strange in the fact of the heroic virtues of the Curé d'Ars overwhelming Sibthorp. But to understand the dimensions of the case we must remember that there was another side to the great Frenchman's career which could not have been more perfectly calculated to repel an English person of refined, moderate, gentlemanly outlook, such as this Lincoln divine.

[1]The interested reader should consult the article on La Salette in the Catholic Encyclopædia, though this account needs to be supplemented by Monnin's account in his Life of Vianney.

We mistake Vianney if we consider him a model removed beyond all criticism; he was a saint with undeniable short-comings. He was a peasant, living among peasants, practising religion according to their ways, and in consequence some of his sermons, expressed in the fierce or maudlin language of simple people, may easily disgust learned or more sophisticated ones. Strangely enough this particular stumbling block, the largest to most educated readers of his life, is unlikely to have worried our hero. Evangelical sermons were not dissimilar in style, and the question is one of style. More likely to distress him was Vianney's devotional behaviour. He delighted in relics and kept about five hundred of them; he maintained also an excessive collection of devotional objects: rosaries, crucifixes, little blessed pictures, statuettes, scapulars, and other toys and trinkets of the kind. He spent much time in violently sentimental devotion to the child-saint Philomena, who almost certainly never existed.[1]

Whatever was superstitious, fantastic, or absurd in Faber's missionary endeavours could be found much more plentifully and much more grotesquely in the life of the Curé d'Ars. Did all this matter very much—that was the question. If the reality and need of sanctity is admitted, an answer suggests itself: that the significance of Vianney's life lay so deep that these sports and extravagances on the surface had of themselves little if any importance. The argument can be carried farther. It can be maintained that Vianney achieved sainthood, and exerted the power belonging to that because, among other things, his spirit was given freedom; it was not stunted or turned in upon itself by the deprivations of Puritanism. We may suppose some such thoughts to have occupied Sibthorp's mind from what happened. From the testimony of people who knew him, we know that after reading about the Curé d'Ars, his days as an Anglican were numbered, and that this Frenchman remained his model to the end.

---

[1]Philomena's supposed tomb was identified by an error of archæology which was later corrected. The whole story is well summarised in the article ' St. Philomena ' in the Catholic Encyclopædia.

Sibthorp wrote a letter about his great discovery to Dr. Bloxam. After describing the Abbé Monnin's book, he asked how it was that the English Church in the nineteenth century seemed unable to produce such men. The extremes in the story, the Philomena business, the trinkets, and so on, had not failed of their effect: "I should add," Sibthorp wrote, "that there is a considerable sprinkling of real superstition in the saintly Curé's life." He went on to say: "May God keep me and everyone He loves from a purely respectable religion!" Then there was a postscript: "I have all Faber's works, but they are really unreadable."

The letter was singular in more than one way. Although Vianney was to be one of his preoccupations during the rest of his life, this was the only letter he wrote on the subject. It was also among the last in which he mentioned Faber. The latter had died the year before, but what he stood for ceased to obsess our hero after November of 1863: this was the last of his Lincoln letters in which he passed strictures on Roman superstition.

The effect of Abbé Monnin's book on Sibthorp was unexpectedly strengthened soon after. In the May of 1864, Dr. Newman whom he had not seen since their conversation in October of 1841,[1] published the first instalment of his *Apolgia pro Vita Sua*, and Sibthorp followed it fortnight by fortnight to the end. It decided him. It was now, not earlier, and only now for a short time, that he came under Tractarian influence.

He said nothing of his intentions, but he began to make new plans for the conduct of the Bede-Houses. He said he wanted to see his foundation in the state it would be in at his death, which could not be long delayed, so he persuaded Mr. Fowler to take over the direction, both temporal and spiritual, of his thirteen dependents. In the course of making these arrangements he disclosed that more than ten years before he had been offered

---

[1] Mr. R. D. Middleton takes the view that Sibthorp and Newman had met with Bloxam in London.

a Lincoln Parish, and that he had declined this on grounds of conscience. He explained: " I am actually an ordained priest of the Roman Church, with all her obligations on me."

In November he left Lincoln. From London he wrote a significant letter to his successor shortly after.

" I went last week," he said, " to Clapham, to see a friend[1] who is in what is called ' retreat,' previous to ordination. I found him in the house formerly occupied by the Thorntons, and where used to meet Macaulay, old Mr. Grant, Mr. Wilberforce, and the leading Evangelicals, lay and clerical, of fifty or sixty years ago; the identical house where the Bible Society was set on foot, by men all great in their goodness, and some good in their greatness; the house celebrated in a remarkable article in the Edinburgh some twenty years since, entitled ' The Clapham Sect.' Now it is occupied by another kind of Saints—the Redemptorist Fathers; men, I believe, not less holy, and certainly more self-denied as to matters of daily life. It was very singular, and called up many thoughts, to find myself walking with these monks (for though not monks, they are somewhat of a monastic body) in the very gardens, and among the very shrubs, where old Mr. Wilberforce used to play at tilt and tournament with his sons, the present Bishop of Oxford, and the three who joined the Church of Rome. These Redemptorists are the parochial clergy of the Roman Catholic parish of Clapham. They have a flock of above sixteen hundred souls. It is impossible not to be struck by their appearance and whole demeanour, and not to admire their laboriousness." He entered into a description of their duties, comparing them favourably with those of the Church of England. He ended: "With all that I have said of the English Church, I esteem and venerate her from my very heart."

In January of 1865 Sibthorp left the Anglican Communion for the second time, and was reconciled to the Catholic Church.

[1]He almost certainly referred to his nephew George Yard, who was converted and ordained in this year.

His friend Wiseman, now a Cardinal and an Archbishop, and the Catholic Primate of Great Britain, was still alive. He was bedridden, hardly able to move, but he was able to receive his favourite convert, for whose earlier calamities he had taken the blame, and he insisted that Sibthorp's first Mass after reconciliation should be said in his private oratory. This was done. Less than three weeks later the Cardinal died. He had for some time ceased to play any part in the Catholic rule of England. Unknown to most of his flock, his age had already come to an end. That of Manning had already begun.

Sibthorp was seventy-one years old.

The act of rejoining had been done slowly, in contrast to his first tempestuous act of conversion. It was no shock to those who knew him. Dean Jeremie of Lincoln wrote to Mr. Fowler: " The information you have had the goodness to give me causes much pain, but no surprise." The Bishop wrote of " my sorrow, not my surprise, at your tidings," and paid some tribute to the saintliness of Sibthorp's character. No public notice was taken of him this time. *The Tablet*, which was still an extremist paper, though no longer, since the death of Lucas, the exultant or foul-mouthed partisan it had once been, let the matter pass in silence. So did the national papers. There was no storm.

Sibthorp entered the one brief golden period of happiness in his life. During February he went on a sort of modest triumphal tour of the Catholic shrines and personalities of England. He celebrated Mass in the chief Catholic churches existing in London then: York Place, Baker Street, Portman Square. A little later we find him at Great Marlow saying Mass in the private chapel of an unnamed noble household recently converted, and at the end of February visiting Birmingham, where he was presented to the Bishop, Bernard Ullathorne, and where, at Edgbaston, he met Dr. Newman for the first time in twenty-five years. The latter had changed little in externals since his Oxonian Anglican days. Samuel Wilberforce, who never spoke to Newman after 1845, once found himself in the same house about this time. " I heard the unmistakable voice," he recorded in a letter, " like a volcano's roar tamed into the softness of a flute-stop, and I got a glimpse (may I say it to you?) of the serpentine form through an open door—' The Father Superior.' "

While Sibthorp was taking some refreshment with the Oratorians of Edgbaston, Newman came in and welcomed him. In the course of conversation he gave the convert-apostate-reconvert some advice. He urged him to go back to Lincoln and say Mass there in the little chapel, that in which Abbé Beaumont had officiated, and to do this privately though not in secrecy; not to seem ashamed of his change of faith, but yet not to invite attention and so hurt the feelings of his successor at St. Anne's, or of his former Bishop. Sibthorp did all this. He and Newman never seem to have conversed again.

He began to make arrangements for his permanent residence. It was remembered that he had not been treated with generosity to his age and station in the eighteen forties, and this time there was a wish to make amends. It was proposed that he should be of the clergy attending St. Barnabas's Cathedral, to whose building he had contributed. He agreed. He preached the first sermon of his new career in Nottingham, some time in the spring of 1865, though he had not yet, as early as this, settled in that ancient and hideous town. He records his deep delight in the discharge of his priestly functions. Before the November of 1863, he had never written a happy letter in his life. Now, all his letters were happy. He received a personal message from Pius IX conveying his blessing.

He was invited to attend the consecration of Wiseman's successor, Henry Edward Manning, and he described it to Bloxam: ". . . a very splendid and solemn ceremony; only too crowded round the altar by the multitude of attendant clergy. He looked like Lazarus come out of the tomb in cope and mitre—a richly vested corpse, but very dignified and placid. It is a very wonderful promotion. It is sixteen or seventeen years or rather more since he called on me in the Isle of Wight . . . as Archdeacon of Chichester. I was in retirement then. . . . Dr.

Newman was there, and I just saw him to shake hands with him. As his manner is, he kept retired."

Shortly after the ceremony of consecration we hear of him taking three hundred and fifty poor children for an outing in Richmond Park, and then in October of the same year, he went to Nottingham, where he was to live till his death. After some changes of address he at length lighted on a house near the Cathedral in Wellington Circus. This was the last of the many houses he bought during the course of his life.

His position was unusual. He was now an old man, relying for social intercourse on a circle of Anglican clergymen, or former Protestant parishioners. Rome found it judicious to unstiffen her habitual attitude of uncompromise before his strange predicament, and so it came about that with the relaxations of discipline normally extended to people of his age, such as his being excused all fasts, there went some novel ones. He remained a Trustee of St. Anne's Bede-Houses so that this Anglican foundation was administered, during fourteen years, by a Roman Catholic priest. We may notice a symbolic scene. When his old friend the Vicar of Canwick died, it seemed proper to everyone under the circumstances, that Father Sibthorp, wearing his surplice with Anglican ministers, should lead the long procession of Lincoln clergy who took part in the burial. He had made his bed with much elaboration and many changes of plan. At first he found it comfortable to lie on. For three years he lived in pious and uneventful bliss.

In 1868 death drew near at last. He suffered what he described as "an organic seizure," a total breakdown in health which, after passing through a phase of extreme danger, left him permanently weakened. Occurring in his seventy-sixth year, and to a man whose health was frail, this physical crisis clearly signalled the end, and Father Sibthorp met it with this understanding. When he had recovered sufficiently to take note of his surroundings he wrote edifying letters to his closest friends declaring his faith and resignation, and composed himself for death. But he was mistaken, as men not often are in such a pass, when he supposed his life to have reached its final stage. It was to be prolonged. Simple story-telling pictures with a moral are not often found among the wares of experience: the spectacle of Sibthorp's storm-racked soul at length making harbour at the sunset hour of life was too lacking in complexity and esoteric meaning to please the taste of nature. To his utter confusion this man was destined to live into extreme old age and suffer great consequences from so doing.

He recovered almost completely.... Between his re-conversion and his illness he had been too wrapt up in spiritual delights to show much curiosity about Church politics. Now he began again to look around him. It was one—it was perhaps the supreme misfortune of Sibthorp that he had a way of turning up at the worst possible moment, like a man whose visits invariably coincide with a death or an outbreak of fire. If we try again to recapture the view which met his eyes in the years around 1870 we shall see that much was going on likely to disturb this delicate-minded old gentleman.

Since the year 1843, when he had left her, the Catholic Church had changed in many ways. In the place of the hesitant unhappy Gregory a formidable personage now occupied the Papal throne, the famous Pio Nono, on whom history has not yet made up her mind.

Even at a calm period a man such as he must have made a mark on the world, but Pius ruled during years in which the Papal States were destroyed, and in which the pathos and drama of his position was so heightened as to thrill the imagination of men and to bring out the best and the worst of his great but imperfect gift of leadership. His nature was passionate. Unlike his predecessor Gregory, he urged the pace. It was in keeping with his character that the break between Catholicism and the world of advanced thought occasioned by the *Syllabus Errorum* of 1864, should have been caused less by what the Syllabus said than by what it appeared to say. He took no pains to charm his opponents, and seemed indifferent to the fact that his polemical style of address could serve as a fatal encouragement to the more foolish of the sheep in his care. Towards those of the latter who professed devotion to him he showed, in the later part of his reign, a very tender partiality in contrast to the disapproval he maintained against people who contested any fraction of his policy. As befitted a time of violence, this leader prized unconditional loyalty before all things, and consequently he was apt to mistake criticism for treachery, and fanaticism for strength, as men do in war.

It is wrong to think of Pius as a simple man: his virtues and his faults are all open to much qualification, but he made a very simple impression on the Catholic Church of his time. It was that of a second Hildebrand who was determined to establish the form of Papal authority for all time in terms of rigid centralism and unprecedented power.

The rule of the Catholic minority in England was changing as drastically in character as that of the Papal Court had already done in Rome. The appointment of Manning to the Archbishopric in 1865 was made on the Pope's intervention and established the new age. It was the culmination of an important tendency. Wiseman had said long ago that if ever Anglican divines came into the Catholic Church, then the traditional holders of the old faith, with their defective learning, must be prepared to withdraw and give first place to the newcomers. This had happened. With few exceptions the luminaries of Catholic England in 1870 were men who had been distinguished Anglican clergymen in the first part of their lives.

These converts had already changed many things. Gone now were the knock-about days of Frederick Lucas and Bishop Baines. These able new men had composed most of the quarrels which had agitated the former time, and, since they never shook off the manners of the Church of England, they instituted conventions in the Catholic English flock which agreed well with " the respectable tone," as it was called, of the Victorian age. This new decorum was all very well so far as it went, but that was not far. Whereas the disorderly community of the Baines time seemed united from a distance, nothing could disguise the essential division of these later Catholics. Their party cleavage was formed by a single issue, part of a world-wide debate, at which we should look briefly in order to understand the meaning of our story.

Since the fall of the French throne in 1830, and the consequent decline of conservatism, the Gallican party, which had shaken Europe and braved Rome since the seventeenth century, had been gradually weakening. By 1850 it was extinct. An entirely new danger swiftly rose over its corpse and imperilled the Church. This danger did not come from challengers of Papal rule, as had the old one, but from the triumphant Ultramontanes.[1]

The new episode, like the Gallican one, opened in France, and then involved the whole Catholic world. A familiar thing had happened. When, after the defeat of their enemy, the victorious party began to become intoxicated with success, it split into two: a moderate wing, and an extreme one. The moderates were at first led by Lacordaire and Montalembert, and then by a group of Bishops; the extremists were led by two ardent churchmen, a journalist of gluttonous devotionalism called Louis Veuillot, and a fanatical priest, the Abbé Gaume.

During the sixties these extremists (or as they were later called), the " New Ultramontanes[2] " grew important: the party of Veuillot and Gaume, from being looked on with grave suspicion in the early days of Pius IX began to be accepted as the real Catholic party: the moderates as lukewarm and unwilling subjects of the Pope, living on the verge of schism. This change

[1]See Chapter V. " The Catholic Revival and the New Ultramontanism " in Wilfred Ward's *W. G. Ward and the Catholic Revival.* Also Lord Acton's essay " Ultramontanism " mentioned on page 42 f. above.

[2]This appellation was invented by Wilfred Ward and has led to considerable confusion, as later historians have been encouraged thereby to refer to the struggle between the New Ultramontanes and the Moderates as one between Ultramontanes and Gallicans. In fact the main infallibility struggle was exclusively between Ultramontanes. The Extremists sometimes called the Moderates " Gallicans," but this was abuse and intended as such. Gallicanism was a weak small hidden force which later became apparent and strong in the Modernist Movement.

was due chiefly to the appearance of the Syllabus. The extremists proclaimed this as their justification. In contrast, the moderates appeared always to be toning it down if not explaining it away. In this controversy the Pope, by not intervening, appeared to favour the extreme side, and this was probably his intention. But the extremists did not finally come into their own until they began to organise publicity for a definition of Papal Infallibility. It appeared, again by contrast, that the moderate leaders opposed this doctrine. Some of them did, but the majority accepted it with a reservation: alarmed at the shapes it received from Ultramontane handling, they strove for a postponement of any definition till a calmer moment. The men who were to save the Church, notably Felix Antoine Dupanloup, Bishop of Orleans, were thereon represented by extremist propaganda as cowards slinking away with sheathed weapons, and the Pope found himself in agreement with this view. Nevertheless, though the weight of propaganda throughout the Catholic world was with the New Ultramontanes, the weight of learning was more evenly distributed, and there were moments in the late sixties when it seemed as though " The Minority " or " The Inopportunists," as they were called, were about to win the day. But they reckoned without the Party Manager on the other side. In Rome on June the 29th of 1867, three days after the Pope had made the first public announcement of the forthcoming Vatican Council, Archbishop Manning made a solemn vow that he would bring about a definition of Infallibility within his lifetime. He accomplished his vow and grew to believe that he had accomplished the victory of his party as well.

In England the division was as absolute as in France. Newman was the leader of the moderates. Opposed to him on the other side was this much more able leader of men, Archbishop Manning, yet though he now led the New Ultramontanes, he was not at first extreme in that extreme party. For what he took to be the best interests of the Church he acted the part of the inflexible man, but he was not really as narrow or unaccommodating as his dreadful appearance strongly and artfully suggested. Left to himself he might even have become a councillor of restraint. The desperate, passionate, reckless element of the extremist party in England was headed by another convert, William George Ward, a man of abundant personality who exerted an extraordinary influence on his friends. In the critical year of 1870 he seems to have obtained an absolute ascendancy over the mind of Manning. We have already noted Ward as Sibthorp's critic and the subject of Pugin's disapproval. He had been converted largely by Newman, and one of the strangest things in the struggle was the curious relationship which existed at this time between Ward, Newman and Manning. It was Ward who kept alive the antagonism of the other two, and yet this man who almost controlled Manning's opinions had no affection for him, while for Newman, whom he injured through-out thirty years, he retained all his youthful feelings of deep love and admiration. By that contradiction the ferocity of the struggle can be measured. As he watched the gorgeous ceremonial of Manning's consecration, Father Sibthorp would have been very shocked to learn that even at that moment the new Archbishop received a note sent from Ward, then in Ireland, urging him to guard against Newman, and not to forget his " disloyalty " to the Holy See, and his " worldliness."

This odd, lovable, deplorable man Ward filled a role as the Editor of the *Dublin Review* closely similar to that of Louis Veuillot in French journalism. In exquisitely constructed articles he attacked in number after number the school of the moderates, whom he described as " minimisers " on the grounds that they wished to reduce to insignificant proportions the imposing authority vested by Christ in the Supreme Pontiffs. He, like Veuillot, took up the cry for more, wider, and frequent powers of infallibility, to be manifest in almost every Papal utterance, for, he said, by the terms of a definition on such lines there would be laid up an immense store of infallible doctrine for the guidance of man. Between them Ward and Manning promulgated a great deal of stuff of this kind and frequently admonished Newman for the dangerous trend of his thoughts.

Meantime, in France, unknown to Ward, enthusiasm, such as he encouraged in the *Dublin Review*, was being carried to astounding lengths by Veuillot and Gaume, whose newspaper the *Univers* was said to exert a greater influence on the French clergy than the pronouncements of the French hierarchy. The journalist and the priest demanded, by implication, and sometimes even by statement, that the Popes should be looked on not as sovereigns but as a succession of inspired seers.[1] Some of the poems addressed to Pius IX and published in the *Univers* came near to idolatry. The Pope never protested.

The Council assembled in 1869 and the outcome of the struggle was never in doubt after Manning had rallied the extremists. They were led by a Frenchman, Archbishop Dechamps of Malines, and the position of Manning has been well described as that of the " Chief Whip[2]" of the New Ultramontanes. Few prelates carried greater weight in Rome, and the fear with which he was regarded by the moderate school was in no way unjustified. He was determined to bring about such a definition as would have satisfied all the daydreams of the Catholic journalists. His English enemy was not there. Dupanloup had invited Newman to come to Rome as his theological adviser, but he had refused. By now Newman had apparently given up all hope that a frightful disaster could be avoided. He wrote to a friend: " Can anything I say move a single Bishop? . . . What could such as I do, but cry out, bawl, make violent gestures, as you would do, if you saw a railway engine running over some unhappy workmen on the line?[3] "

---

[1] " We all know certainly only one thing, that is that no man knows anything except the Man with whom God is for ever, the Man who carries the thought of God. We must . . . unswervingly follow his *inspired* direction."—Louis Veuillot, *L'illusion Liberale*. cf. " The Pope is a ruler, not a philosopher."—Newman.

[2] Sir Shane Leslie.

[3] We may recall another more famous expression of his views. In one of his letters to Dr. Bloxam Sibthorp mentioned Dr. Newman's letter to Bishop Ullathorne, on reading which he had been " startled at one or two strong expressions." He was referring to a private letter written by Newman which was later published in the *Evening Standard*. How it got there has never been discovered, and Manning's defenders have been at pains to accuse other prelates of treachery. In Manning's own memoirs there is, however, an intriguing passage. " Odo Russell gave me all information. . . . From him I received J. H. N.'s letter to the Bishop Birmingham."

As regards trying to impress Manning there was not much else to be done now beyond bawling and screaming. His mind was shut and he moved forward with the relentless cunning of fanaticism. Strangely enough, it was this very fact which rescued the Council from extremism. He overplayed his hand in a way which provoked a revival of the moderate school. It had been settled, not without protest, that the questions to be voted by the Council on the Papacy should be formulated before submission to the grand sessions by a Committee known as the " Deputatio de Fide." It was the wish of the Pope and many of his advisers that this Committee should be formed of members of both parties, but Manning ignored the Pope's wish, and by means of skilful lobbying saw to it that only extremists were elected. As a result the moderates were forced into the role of " His Holiness's Opposition," and this not only intensified the vigour of their debate but alarmed many of the committee, extremists as they were, into moderate ways, as the possibility of schism became remotely apparent. Then a remarkable chain of events served to strengthen the still seemingly hopeless position of the minority. The President of the " Deputatio de Fide " was Cardinal Bilio. He was described by Lord Acton as " a Barnabite monk, innocent of Court intrigues, a friend of the most enlightened scholars in Rome, and a favourite of the Pope." He was not an extremist, being, let us remember, the only member of the committee not elected under the conditions organised by Manning. His position was strengthened by the death of the presiding Cardinal, Reisach, and his succession by a weaker man, Cardinal de Angelis, for this had the effect of throwing much of the management of the whole Council into the hands of Bilio. In the end the moderates prevailed in this sense: that, though the definition finally adopted under Bilio's guidance reserved infallibility to the Pope alone speaking as the successor of St. Peter, and not as the delegated chairman of the Bishops, it confined this to doctrinal pronouncements by the Pope " concerning faith and morals," uttered " ex cathedra," and binding on the whole Church. It is sometimes said that the term " ex cathedra" was chosen because it was vague, and that in employing it the unscrupulous advisers of Pius IX did not commit him to narrow or wide terms. This is not so. There was included in the Canons of the Council,[1] so as to afford a detailed interpretation to a contemporary enquirer of the dogma's applicability. This introduction rigorously confines Infallibility to expressions of the Church's perennial teaching, and under the severest conditions. It shows the influence of Fénelon's writings (though it claims less for Papal Authority than he did), and may have had a further origin in Dupanloup. Its immediate origin was in Bilio, though he was the author of a small part of it only. But for reasons which become apparent in the last stages of our story, these two facts, the partial triumph of the moderates in 1870, and the sober precision of the dogma, were not so easy to see then and have not been recognised since in popular ideas. What the world saw as the dogma was solemnly ratified by Pius IX on the 18th of July was not the event, was not the Pope " on his knees in the dust, confessing his ignorance before the throne of God,"[2] but the capture of the Papacy by voluptuaries of religion. For that reason the act which its promoters believed would immediately open a second Hildebrandine age, marked the beginning of a weakening of Christian influence before powerful new religions, which was to have multitudinous results both outside and within the Church in the succeeding years when the West entered its final heritage of power.

We return to Nottingham and our elderly Catholic priest who in 1872 reached the age of eighty. He lived a life of pious routine, following his great model in sanctity, the Curé d'Ars. His main inner concern in his last years was the study of St.

[1] The Article on the Vatican Council in the *Encyclopædia Britannica* (eleventh edition) by Karl Theodore Mirbt, which Lytton Strachey seems to have followed closely in *Eminent Victorians*, contains no mention of the Historical Introduction.

[2] Bernard Shaw. In the Preface to *St. Joan* he gives an accurate account of Catholic claims regarding canonisations.

Francis de Sales, while in the world he spent what was left of his considerable wealth in caring for the vast numbers of Catholic destitutes in Nottingham, reserving a small sufficiency for his comforts and tastes. He lived simply, but as a gentleman: he kept two servants, and, according to Bloxam, who visited him in his last period, two acolytes as well. This probably means that two boys were under contract to serve his Masses and that he paid them some sort of stipend. We learn, somewhat to our surprise, that this holy man continued a collection of rare china which he had been forming over many years.

About the time of his eightieth birthday he began to lose his hearing, but we must not think of him as decrepit until the very last. He recorded the amusements of his leisure. He was a little unsteady on his legs so he rarely walked more than he needed, but he still took bodily exercise in bowls. He had indoor fun too. He used to play bagatelle and cribbage with his young nephews and nieces.

He enjoyed the reward of extreme age: that of becoming fabulous. He was one of the last people alive who had known the eighteenth century, who had been a grown-up man while the French wars were raging sixty years before, and he would describe Shelley as he remembered him from his days at University College. He suffered one of the calamities of great age too, that of becoming an exaggeration of himself through the distortions worked on things by time. Little ecclesiastical jokes continued to ring in his correspondence, but they became offset by grumblings. Exaggerated in him grew the Sibthorp harping, and like the Colonel aforetime he sometimes apprehended enormous dangers where an ordinary eye sees none. His affection for Oxford never grew less, was always tender and solicitous, but now began to include a queer alarm at the risk the University might incur from the increasing fashionability of boating. "I hope," he wrote to a friend in 1873, "I hope your second son will come out of Oxford unscathed . . . Discipline is nearly extinct; cricket, athletic sports, and boating are uppermost. And that vile annual boat-race in London injures very many very

95

seriously." Four years later, in 1877, we find him still on this theme: "I like not the annual boating contest, in London observation, and, like Epsom Races, collecting the London world, high and low, gentles and rough, to look on and bet on it. Nor do I like the Balliol Broad Church—the muscular Christianity."

But he had deeper worries, at first occasional, then insistent, finally so overpowering that they needed expression. "Not the infallibility!" we find him writing in one letter, "For on that my lips are closed " ... "I am no Ultramontane," he exclaimed on another occasion, "but an old Catholic, though not in the Alt-Catholic meaning."[1] Gradually the strain of silence became beyond his bearing. At last he took the course of unbosoming himself to Dr. Bloxam. "I don't like Newman's last letter about the Infallibility," he wrote in October of 1872. "I think it shows a want of temper." Two years later we find him writing that Newman's "Letter to the Duke of Norfolk " " does not so far satisfy me; nor as I see meet my first and continued view of the dogma of personal infallibility of Popes." In a letter of April, 1874, we can find what this " continued view " was. "It is not required," he asserted, " that the Pope should issue a Bull or a decree. An Allocution, to any assemblage in his principal apartments, getting abroad as it will do, will suffice to make otherwise willing combatants lay aside their swords and rifles."

In the later years of the nineteenth century it could seem to this admirable disciple of St. Francis de Sales a self-evident infamy that any authority, even one which he believed came directly from Jesus Christ, should interfere in any way with national initiative, even in the abominable case of war. But rather than condemn him for such a preference, we should recognise that it was ordinary, and recognise, with a shock, that in following his long life we are confronted at the end of it with our own age.

[1] The Alt-Katholische Party was the new name of a Dutch Jansenist sect which had renounced obedience to Rome in the early eighteenth century. It was reconstituted in 1870 when numerous German Catholics joined it after the Vatican Council.

But, it may be asked, how could it come about that he, a Catholic priest, was so ill-informed; that he could believe that almost any utterance by the Pope, " to any assemblage in his principal apartments " was open to the great claim ?

The answer to that question is that at the end of his life we meet not only the age of nationalism, but the age of " press propaganda " too.

The world of the present has learned to suspect arguments produced at the top of the voice, but the mental habits of eighty years ago were in this regard not so heavily conditioned by experience; they were in some respects more trusting, and so those who trafficked in false mental currency sometimes enjoyed easier success. The emotional religious journalism of the late nineteenth century was such stuff as modern propaganda is made of, and it had the power to take in its contrivers. The New Ultramontanes could not believe that they had missed total victory in 1870. After the storm was over even so acute an observer as Manning could write of the Council with, it seems, entirely sincere boastfulness: " Some (the moderates) who ought to have led the right side went wrong. . . . But the Church decided against them . . . we . . . were right after all. An Oecumenical Council justified us, and the Catholic Church believes and teaches what we said." The very opposite of this statement would have been more true, but Manning spoke with a semblance of great authority, and he was only one of many doing the same thing. Veuillot, more deceived by his own enthusiasm than any other, was still writing at the top of his form, and receiving a very full and public measure of approval. It was by no means unnatural for Sibthorp to believe that the most grotesque versions of the Papal claims were authentic. He never seems to have read the text of the dogma. It is probable that, like many others, he simply did not dare.

One man, Dr. Newman, could have changed his mind, but never did so. Birmingham and Nottingham are not many miles apart but the journey was not made by either. They never met after 1865. It is not possible to say why. Newman rarely gave up an Oxford friendship, but he did allow this one to lapse. He may have resented that element of caricature of himself in Sibthorp which was usually mistaken for close resemblance. On the other side, though Sibthorp owed his reconversion in part to Newman, this did not mean that he understood him. This man who appeared to an early admirer as the living image of Julius Cæsar, to Lord Acton as an old woman with a toothache, to Lytton Strachey, seeing him from afar, as a dove, and to Manning, seeing him close, as the embodiment of bad temper, this complex human being was made for misunderstanding, and was without question misunderstood by Sibthorp. One man could have brought the two men together, and that was Bloxam, the intimate friend of both.

He never did so. He was never likely to. Newman entertained a constant dream that Bloxam would one day be a member of his Edgbaston Community, but he perhaps never understood the antipathy of this man to certain essentials of his friend's religion. Bloxam was a broad-minded ritualist; but side by side with his admiration of Catholicism he had, in a surprisingly strong degree, the old, seventeenth-century, nationalist, English, Miltonic, Bunyanine antipathy to the very notion of Roman dominion, and the authority of " Giant Pope." He accepted none of the claims of the See of Peter. Newman would probably have been much appalled to know that to the last his letters to this most beloved of friends were ruthlessly edited. In their correspondence, the word " Catholic " in Newman's handwriting is invariably prefaced by the bracketed initial " R " for " Roman " in Bloxam's. It is idle to accuse such a man of mischief-making. He never led his two friends back into their old affection because it was to the interest of everything he held sacred, using that term in its literal sense, to keep them apart. Apart they remained.

When he was eighty-two years old Sibthorp asked the Bishop of Nottingham for permission to retire from active work.

His request was granted. He occupied his leisure with a final venture.

"I want," he wrote to Dr. Bloxam, about this time, "to lead our Catholic people into some knowledge of, and reflection on, Scripture truth; . . . I remember Mr. Yard saying to me, in a tone of sorrow and vexation, 'It is of no use to speak to our people about Jeremiah's birthplace; they don't know there was such a person as Jeremiah." So, in his retirement, he began the compilation of a devotional book, modelled on the "nosegays" of St. Francis de Sales, in which for every day in the year there was a different set of prayers for private use, and a lengthy quotation from Scripture, the whole called "Daily Bread." The task occupied him from 1874 till the beginning of 1876, when it appeared. To-day it is occasionally found in High Church Anglican establishments, and, very rarely indeed, in Roman Catholic ones. It was adversely reviewed in *The Tablet*. It was the last of Sibthorp's many many failures.

The letters to clergymen and former parishioners continued as before, most of them expressions of his resignation to the death which was so long, and, for his happiness, so disastrously delayed. He dwells much on dangers besetting the Church of England, and is opposed to an Anglican union with Rome, as he maintains that such a step must weaken the throne, yet in spite of this incongruously strong Anglican loyalty, not unknown to other University converts, he still contrives to feel fairly securely established as a Roman Catholic in this protracted penultimate phase. But though the sense of security is still asserted, it is evidently smitten with a deadly malady. Every time he mentions infallibility we seem to see it becoming weaker, and the conflict of his nationalism and his faith growing stronger. Over and over again he notes the danger of Papal authority cutting across national allegiance; of an Italian being enabled, in certain circumstances, to order an Englishman to desist from war in spite of his sovereign's command, and in this reiterated insistence on the classic beliefs of a new age we hear again, and now quite unmistakably, the voice of Colonel Charles. The influences which formed him begin to show like the outlines of bones in an ancient countenance.

In the summer of 1876 the Catholic Primate announced that he would make a visitation to Nottingham, and the old man trembled. " I dread the coming here of Cardinal Manning," he wrote, " I would get out of the way, if I could: for the excitement does not suit me, nor the Ultramontane and teetotal[1] impetus—from both of which I turn away, and Cardinal Manning encourages."

Cardinal Manning was remarkably well-informed, and there could be little doubt that he knew Sibthorp's story well, and in detail, and everything about his " Inopportunist " leanings. Sibthorp had good reason to dread him. But when he arrived in Nottingham the Cardinal took much pains to be agreeable to this venerable being whose name recalled undergraduate days, when his friend Gladstone used to go to hear him in the little church under Bagley Wood, even though in that far-off Oxford " preaching was abundant, and good preaching to be had." He asked for Sibthorp to come to sit with him for a whole evening, and he did his visitor the signal honour, which the latter recorded with pride, of accompanying him to the stairs when it was time for him to go home. Before he left the town, he returned this visit, calling on Sibthorp in his own house.

The Cardinal made a public appearance, and Sibthorp heard him preach in St. Barnabas's. He was disappointed at the thinness of his matter. For all the unexpected goodness of his nature, this Prince of the Church could never make up for the loss of Newman.

Two years later the last phase of Sibthorp's life opened.

In the spring of 1878 Pius IX died in Rome. After a brief conclave Cardinal Pecci was elected to the throne in his stead. For many years, till very shortly before his election, Pecci had lived as a Bishop in Perugia, and in consequence he was not much known outside his diocese, hardly at all outside Italy.

---

[1] In his later years Cardinal Manning leaned more and more towards prohibitionism. This led to some breaches, notably a temporary one with his successor Herbert Vaughan.

When he assumed the name of Leo and people remembered the harsh rule of the last holder of that Papal name (Bishop Baines's friend), it seemed to many that a policy of scorpions for whips was signalled. It is important to this story to remember that the character of Leo XIII, unlike that of his predecessor, was not immediately manifest. In December of this same year Sibthorp was struck down by what he called "an attack of an inflammatory kind." From this he never recovered, and though he lingered for several months, it was never in doubt now that he was dying. Attended by a nurse he spent most of his remaining days stretched on a sofa in his sitting-room, surrounded by his china, praying incessantly when not correcting proofs for the second edition of *Daily Bread*, or receiving callers, most of them Anglican clergymen.

As befitted the life of Sibthorp, the last climax of his life came suddenly and unexpectedly. As he lingered and grew weaker, he received one day in March, a little before the day of his death, news which shook him to the very soul. Leo XIII, in order to make amends to Newman for the ill-treatment which he had suffered under Pius, made him a Cardinal.

The day after this news was made public Mr. Fowler travelled from Lincoln to Nottingham to pay his last visit to the founder of St. Anne's Bede-Houses. To his surprise he found Sibthorp in a state of distraction. "What a mistake——" the old man gasped. "What a mistake Dr. Newman has just made!" Mr. Fowler ascertained his meaning. He tried to divert the conversation to milder topics; but the unhappy gasping creature on the sofa would take no comfort. Weakened by anxiety, and in a voice hardly audible he endeavoured to say over and over again that Dr. Newman had made a terrible mistake, and after some minutes' silence, when Mr. Fowler was trying to tell him about St. Anne's Bede-Houses, Sibthorp burst out again: "Tell the Bishop of Lincoln that I think Dr. Newman has made a great mistake. I am too ill to do anything. But tell Bishop Wordsworth what I say."

After this visit he summoned the strength to write a letter

to Bloxam. "I wish to express to you my entire and decided disapproval of Dr. Newman's last step. The Cardinal's hat! Oh! It is a very sad step. I don't mince the matter. You may let him know it.

"Whatever you do, 'do not be tempted to leave your present position' is the closing advice of your old friend.

"I see how the wind blows, but do not blow with it."

This was the last of his hundreds of letters to the man whom he had loved for so many years.

On the 24th of March he wrote to Fowler: "I cannot write. It pleases God to deny me all strength. I beg you to stop people talking of me as if I was good, or anything but the vilest of sinners. I have no righteousness, no hope, except in Him; if He has not mercy upon me, I perish.

"Tell the Bishop that I have not a doubt that Dr. Newman is quite wrong in taking the Cardinal's hat; but I am so ill, and suffer so heavily and frequently, that I can do nothing. The Bishop may make known my judgment, such as it is." On his death-bed he harped. It was the most persistent habit of his family.

But what was he harping about? Why did he mind Newman being a Cardinal? Why did he not mind Manning being one? We can only guess. At the end of his life he seems to have looked on Newman as a kind of dissenter tolerated within the Church, a kind of leader of hesitant Anglican-minded Catholicism, and perhaps he saw the Cardinalate as a badge of the extremest New Ultramontane fanaticism, and as a betrayal of people such as himself. We cannot know because he was beyond explaining himself. We can only feel quite certain that his brother would have warmly seconded his disapproval.

He wrote one more letter to Fowler, the last letter of his life, asking for prayers that his pain might be lessened. In April he was still alive, holding on to life with the marvellous tenacity of delicate people. He found a special solace in reciting to himself the words of the English burial service, and he spent most of his conscious hours in that exercise. He received the Last Sacraments from the Bishop of Nottingham. He died on the 10th of April of 1879, in his eighty-seventh year, reading the Book of Common Prayer till it fell from his grasp and lay open on the floor.

His coffin was placed in St. Barnabas's, and on Tuesday of Easter Week a solemn Requiem Mass was sung for the repose of his soul *coram episcopo*: that is to say in the ceremonial presence of the Bishop, by another minister. According to the terms of his will, he was to be buried at Canwick, so on the Wednesday morning his body was conveyed to Lincoln. He had asked that the English Burial Service, which had soothed his agony, should be read over his grave. Such a proceeding is not outside the discipline of Rome, provided the reading is private and not solemnised, but Catholic opinion was not consulted, and (very fittingly indeed) the rule was inadvertently broken. This Catholic priest was buried in Lincoln with the full ceremonial of the Church of England, *coram autem episcopo Anglicano*.

When Mr. Gladstone heard the details of his end, he recalled his lifelong interest in the career of this unusual man whom he described as a "truly elect soul." He wrote to Mr. Fowler: "The circumstances you have mentioned respecting his interment is most soothing, most touching."

Obituaries appeared in the Catholic, Anglican, lay and local press, and the storms of the eighteen forties were recalled, but only very faintly. The appearance of the memorial compiled by Mr. Fowler[1] a year later was little noticed outside Catholic society, and the Catholic press was uneasy at its Anglican tone. Sibthorp fell back into the obscurity from which he had been only a little raised by death. He was never to take the prominent place in history into which he seemed to be thrust in his middle years, and which he never sought. Thus to-day this once famous man is only known to the erudite. As we remarked at the beginning, that is not altogether an injustice. He was a queer

[1]Dr. Bloxham to General Rigaud: "Fowler's Memoir is *my notice* very much enlarged." (Magdalen Studies.)

fellow and a queer place suits him well. Yet in so far as he is remembered outside his Bede-Houses he does not, like his better-known brother Charles, merely enjoy the fame of a ridiculous person. He is more satisfyingly and more deeply enigmatical.

The little band who remember him to-day are not quite sure whether to consider him as an Anglican who was gravely burnt by the fires of Rome, or as a Catholic whose inborn Englishry thwarted him in the prosecution of his way. It would be tempting to suppose that his real harbour, which he missed in storm and fog, was the Anglo-Catholic communion where he would have been spared anxieties concerning Papacy, but against this we have his own testimony written within two years of his death. " I consider the Ritual Party in the Anglican Church " he wrote, " to be infatuated men, wrenching . . . the Anglican Church to pieces." We must also remember the presence in his life of Dr. Bloxam. That man was one of the founders of the Anglo-Catholic movement, and it seems incredible that if this movement had been our hero's true destiny the fact would not have become plain in the course of a friendship which lasted over forty years. Sibthorp, who throughout his life was exceedingly garrulous about his inmost experiences, never declared this preference. Yet the possibility that he had some such unrealised wish cannot be set aside for all that, because, since there are signs, especially in his behaviour over Newman's Cardinalate, that his ultimate aim was not clear to himself, it were absurd to define any close terms for the solution of the riddle. He must always be a mystery. . . .

He received the sacraments for the dying at the hands of his Bishop, and so, whatever the real truth, it is allowable to consider him at the very last a Catholic acknowledging the Roman obedience. If we do this, a strange picture comes before our eyes. He had been treated with forbearance, magnanimity and tolerance during his second Catholic priesthood, and yet his distress of mind as he lay on his death-bed in Nottingham reading the book of Common Prayer was due to intolerance elsewhere in his Church, of a familiar and appalling kind. As we look at them from a distance we can see that the historical crime of the New Ultramontanes was not their enthusiasm but their insistence that they, and they alone, preserved the Apostolic traditions. In the eye of old Sibthorp they made the Church appear monstrous and dangerous, to be entering a period of superstitious power-seeking; but to a subsequent generation they made the Church appear as an emotional experience, of secondary importance.

The long pilgrimage which this doubt-smitten old gentleman made through the length, almost the whole length, of the nineteenth century, ended in characteristic confusion. We may lastly draw attention to one factor of the hesitation which caused that confusion.

Sincerity is a virtue which has been so much tarnished by being invoked as the excuse for bad deeds, that it requires to be adorned sometimes by the lustre of great sacrifices. No one should refuse honour to conversions on the Damascus Road, but it is usual when this is done to consider those who travel that way as obedient to one voice. In the case of very remarkable circumstances or of very remarkable men, two such conversions are sometimes gravely acknowledged, but not more, for if a larger number are allowed the awful drama has a way of turning to comedy.

Our hero took very much more than the agreed ration; he was converted five times, and perhaps nearly six. It would have been very much pleasanter and easier, and in worldly eyes more dignified for him to have kept silence as to the later flashes and promptings which came to him, and to have stayed still in his old age. But such was his innate truthfulness of mind that for the sake of his voices he ran a risk which is almost as painful as that of martyrdom, namely the risk of being funny. And when all is said, he is distinctly funny. To sincerity he made that most painful offering.

But his comedy must not make us forget too much else.

One part of his story is very remarkable, because it illustrates uniquely something often unnoticed in his century. This man, in whose character doubt was essential, was never tempted for one second to doubt the existence of God or the reality of the Christian revelation. We meet the beginning of our own times at the end of his life, but joined so smoothly to traditional faith that we hardly notice the contradiction between old and new. Sibthorp was a modern man in the restlessness of his search, but untypical in his scope. He lived an intellectual life and was wholly unaffected by infidel ideas. This was not easily accomplished by men of his curiosity living at the same time. It became more difficult a little later. This is in some ways the most interesting thing in his story, and we shall consider it again when we discuss the very different world and the very different method of search pursued by subsequent generations amid greater disasters in an enlarged field.

THE PROSPERITY OF HIS SERVANT

A Study of the Origins of the Balfour Declaration of 1917

> Let them shout for joy, and be glad, that favour my righteous cause: yea, let them say continually, Let the Lord be magnified, which hath pleasure in the prosperity of His Servant.
>
> Ps. 35

> Let them not say in their hearts, Ah, so would we have it: let them not say, We have swallowed him up.
>
> Ps. 35

The Prosperity of His Servant

THE AGE, which in England was occupied by late Victorians and the subjects of King Edward, and on the Continent saw the growth of the German Empire, this time of European glitter and success is not open to any brief description. No age, especially one which is fully recorded, can truly be so, but most ages, thanks to our slovenly simplifications, seem to be, with the result that history is intelligible at a great expense of accuracy. The word " Victorian " suggests a uniform notion wherewith to measure the diversity of the English nineteenth century. Something of the kind is true of every age of which there is popular knowledge, so that the exception of this one, in which the nineteenth century closed and the twentieth opened, is somewhat of a freak of chance. Whatever we may say of this tremendous historical epoch we can as easily unsay. This age of material triumphs beyond any recorded hitherto, and in which one civilisation was diffused to so extreme a degree that a time seemed near when a single mode of life would obtain over the whole world, was not only without an appearance of special character, but did not believe itself to possess one. There was no master impulse with which to conform, or against which to react. This age of the realisation of vast dreams was also one of vagueness.

We can learn something from its architecture. Modern techniques made it possible for builders to work on unprecedented scales. But no architectural fashion predominated, so that when the capitals of Europe were rebuilt in this time of wealth and outlay, and almost every Western style was revived and used in colossal edifices, the result was curiously inconclusive. The modest streets of poorer ages conveyed definite ideas regarding forms and preferences. The new splendours could make no such impress on the imagination.

Something of the same excess of variety is to be found in those arts which did not decay: neither in its literature, music, or painting can we make a catalogue of schools, tendencies and groups without recognising that energies were dispersed into numbers of different currents such as we rarely find in all history, and that progress and reaction were no longer complementary but occupied with entirely separate matters. But the most astonishing of all evidences that this was a time of abnormally indefinite mass-momentum is to be found in the field of sociology.

Model states in which destitution and its attendant horrors were virtually unknown were erected in Scandinavia, Denmark and Holland, and the same work was begun on a vaster scale in Germany and Great Britain. It was possible in the years around nineteen hundred to foresee at a great distance a whole Europe and America, then a world, redeemed from the degradations of physical want, a thing such as had never been visible before, in any common or literal sense. Yet this wondrous transition has never excited much emotion of gratitude or admiration towards the men who were there bringing it about at the time. Sociologists find more to delight their minds in contemplating the earlier years when the struggle to relieve penury appeared hopeless to the cruel and merciful alike, and the great moment of change from hope to accomplishment is not held in honour. This later neglect of so abundant a spring in human endeavour may strike us as odd, but even stranger than that was the indifference of the men and women of the time. In England there was not much passionate reform literature such as we find typical of the early nineteenth century; there was no coherent element in English life, no Evangelical movement, to take charge of the excitement of men at the great marvels taking place about them, because there was not enough excitement for such looking after to be needed. It is perhaps to the credit of human nature that when we in North-West Europe saw the earthly paradise from afar we recognised that it was not what we wanted.

The age wanted religion; it hunted for it high and low. Allusion has already been made to the fact that this hunting for divine truth became a very different thing from the enterprises of the good Sibthorp. It was such as suited the termination of the " Age of Faith." We must examine that expression for a moment as it is one that can both elucidate and confuse the episode which we are examining.

Since the days of Chateaubriand historians have often asserted that some time in the early fifteenth century this " Age of Faith " came to an end, gradually giving way thenceforth to an age of scientific logic and self-reliance in which religious exercises took a smaller and smaller part. This cannot be true. If it is true how, for instance, do we explain the enormous output of religious writing which continued undismayed; what are we to make of the life of Dr. Johnson, and how did it come about that as late as the nineteenth century the doings of Lammenais excited the whole of France and those of Newman the whole of England? It was not because his interests were eccentric that the subject of our first essay was briefly famous. We find Gladstone at the end of his life and of four Premierships, declaring that the conversion of Manning was " the severest blow " that ever befell him. How can such an utterance make sense nearly five hundred years after the end of the " Age of Faith "?

The truth of the matter appears to be that not until the nineteenth century did the disposition to look down on organised faith, a behaviour which had received precise philosophic expression from Kant, become not only admissible, but something more than respectable: it became, in many minds, a condition of freedom, and the classic age of atheism opened. As a very rough generalisation one may say that modern atheism, that is acting as a force influencing multitudes, first flourished in Germany and France, beginning largely as a reaction against the clerically-minded Restorations in the eighteen twenties, while in England it came in a purer form, unattached to political loyalty. The abandonment of religious belief by great hosts of people was not a violent occurrence to appearances. It fell in with a vast expansion of wealth, and seemed in some sort to be associated with a benevolent change in destiny. A new picture of the earthly fate grew visible: of man striding into a sunlit expanse, leaving behind him dark mental contortions with the complexities and woes of his once all-besetting poverty. If a man could live without religion, now, if ever, was his chance. But he found that he could not do this, the Age of Faith would not be exorcised, and so the first age of modern mass atheism came to be an age of spiritual search in which Christian orthodoxy still held a prominent place, but gradually became untypical. This was largely because the search for religion took as broad a character as is possible to imagine: we are reminded of the age of Constantine, of the statue of Apollo erected in likeness of the Roman Emperor from whose diadem sprang golden rays fashioned from the nails by which Jesus Christ had been fastened to the Cross. But there was a great difference between the eclecticism of the fourth century and that of the time we are considering, for whereas the Imperial Roman court mixed Christianity with Pagan cults from a belief that stronger charms than its old ones were required to win divine favours, the Europeans of the Age of Diffusion were eclectics because they believed that no charms were so effective that one was to be preferred over another. In an age of bitter stress such a belief might have led to despair, but it did not do so at this time. There is a great mass of religious writing by the men and women who lived then, and the most characteristic part of it is filled with an engaging good nature and tolerance and the optimism of rich people growing richer.

This happy state of mind was reflected in a complacent attitude towards patriotism and nationalism, qualities which had become so typical of that age that we find an extreme expression of them in the least likely place. The " Modernist Movement "

THEODORE HERZL

within the Catholic Church began as a revolt against the extremist reaction of the New Ultramontanes but rapidly turned into a revival of Gallicanism and attempted to teach not only the right of the individual to free enquiry, but that of States to free and natural growth in circumstances of absolute emancipation from all sacred authority. We can seize an idea of how much optimism there was in the world at the turn of the two centuries when we consider that this opinion grew up amid French clergy in the age of Bismarck. As faith faded over a great part of Europe, men insensibly fell back into that inadequate cult of the Mother City from which Christianity had rescued the Hellenised world of sixteen hundred years before. It was here that the different parties who were searching for religion met, and here that many of them, retaining an agnostic deism too vague to qualify earthly patriotism, were content to stay and worship.

There was no lack of people who found themselves repelled by so spiritless a settlement, or who in the midst of so much optimism became prophets of doom to be justified later. This we would expect. More strange was a case of divided mind: of enthusiastic acceptance balanced by suspicion, of leadership in all the cults, ideals, or fads of the time side by side with a consciousness that its ostentatious strength might conceal insecurity, of opinions, formed by conflicting experiences of triumphs and setbacks, which at last found expression in a movement both devoted and sceptical which is the subject of this essay.

The greatest beneficiaries of the age were to be found in the venerable community of the Jews. Yet from two points of view they could see their existence threatened by this same age. They alone had experience of what might happen if the Western civilisation of the nineteenth century were to become only a little less orderly, and at the same time they were peculiarly endangered by the state of mind which went with the age's stability and success. No people stood to lose more from indifferentism. On this account alone it seemed to some of their writers at this time that within a few years, within perhaps only two generations, Jewish identity might be lost in modern Europe, and, as European influence spread, might be lost for ever in the world. How to escape from this besetting nightmare became a principal preoccupation, especially in the West, of many leading spirits among the people of Israel.

Their recent history had been very curious.

From the middle ages until recent times the Jews had lived in most lands of Western Europe as a people set aside and accursed. The New Learning had eased their lot a little in the lands it reached, but the Protestant Reformation had reimposed the burden, while long before the persecutions of the Counter-Reformation, the Inquisition in Spain had opened a new attempt to destroy Israel for all time. So far as the West was concerned, the sixteenth and early seventeenth centuries were spent by most of the wandering tribes of the Jews in wandering farther in search of some place where they might eat the bread of bitterness.

In this frightful predicament the Jews of Spain and Portugal, and later those of Provence, vanished except for a fragment who escaped by pretending conversion while cherishing their faith in secret. Elsewhere in the West they seem to have survived for two reasons. The new fanaticism was not to the taste of authority, and the Papacy, the Empire, and most national princes preferred (most of the time) to maintain the older policy whereby Jewish disabilities were never so oppressive that they crushed the very life out of Jewish talent. In consequence Jew-baiting was liable to be severely punished, and by living in the shadows, by making themselves indispensably useful, notably as financiers, shippers, and " intelligencers," the Jews could come to terms, bitter, precarious, yet practical, with their enemies. This was one reason for survival. The second was that a large part of the Jews went away from Western Europe altogether to a more secure life in Poland and Russia.

In the Eastern Christian world the Jews had for long fared better than in Europe proper. They were among the oldest inhabitants of the countries bordering the Black Sea, having first gone there from Babylon, it is supposed. During two hundred years, from the eighth to the tenth centuries, they had formed an élite in that part of the world, when the Khazar Empire became predominantly Jewish by religion, (though unconnected with Jewry by race,) and the Jews remained a proselytising power in Russia till as late as the sixteenth century.

Amid the confusions and " Voelkerwanderungen " of the Slav world in the late sixteenth and early seventeenth centuries, it is possible to discern a complicated but definite pattern in Jewish affairs. The centre was in Poland where, though subjected to occasional oppressions, the Jews were for the most part allowed religious freedom, treated no worse and sometimes much better than other subjects, and given a surprising measure of autonomy. They were the backbone of the Polish civil service, in so far as any institution had a backbone in that mad state, while outside Poland, in Russia, though they were a less important minority, they enjoyed the same degree of liberty. They enjoyed a more stable life in the East than the West because their greater numbers made them easy to protect effectively, but popular feeling against them was very strong.

This feeling worked in a strange manner. During the seventeenth century an extraordinary tangle of animosities grew up. The Polish kings were often driven by enthusiasts of the Counter-Reformation into Jewish persecution so as to live down a constant accusation that they wore their relatively recent Christianity too lightly, and such policies were very naturally to the taste of many Poles who disliked Jews as foreigners and tax-collectors. But in the Ukrainian provinces of the state anti-Jewish excitement had a quite different character, for here it was the fashion of the Greek Orthodox natives to regard Jews as the very acme of everything Polish, as the symbol of the hated ruling power and of Catholic intolerance. In the Cossack rebellion of 1648 (preceded by similar horrors on a smaller scale), these feelings found a terrible outlet. The Ukrainian Jews being a weaker party than the Catholics, suffered most. There were hundreds of thousands of victims of slaughter and mass-enslavement, such as had not been seen since the Mongol invasions. The Jewish community of Poland never recovered from this havoc. A golden age of the diaspora came to an end.

For a considerable time, however, Jewish life was apparently unchanged. In Poland Government policy to the Jews remained for the most part tolerant and even encouraging until the period which begins in 1697 with the election of Augustus the Strong of Saxony to the throne. In Russia we may mark the beginning of official repression of the Jews from the short reign of Peter's widow, Catherine I. She is a somewhat mysterious queen, but it is tempting to suppose that, being a plebeian, she shared the popular hatred of the Jews in a way which was not natural to the born royalty of Poland or Moscow. She issued two anti-Jewish ukases in 1727, one prohibiting Jews from taking part in the hotel trade, another expelling them from Russia as Edward I had expelled them from England, and forbidding their return. Neither of these edicts could be put into operation, and Catherine's example was not followed by most of her successors in the eighteenth century; but the example was there, was not repudiated, was occasionally exceeded. It expressed the grim reality of the times ahead. By stages which were little noticed but which continued unchecked, the Jews of Poland and Russia began to sink, after 1648, to the position of an inferior caste, but owing to their great numbers, swollen by ancient proselytism and recent immigrations from Germany, and owing to their proud traditions, they sank as a whole world.

As we have noted the disposal of forces in the West had originally been much the same as in the East, but the stresses were different from the beginning. Popular prejudice had had its way most of the time. Outside the classic persecutions of Spain, the history of Western Jewry in the fifteenth, sixteenth, and early seventeenth centuries, was for the most part the history of Ghettoes, occasionally oppressed by rulers, usually inadequately protected by them, and frequently invaded by mobs.

In the later seventeenth century, however, there came two important changes which decisively affected Jewish prospects. After the Thirty Years' War the taste for religious persecution was weakened for a long time in Europe. The history of the Ghetto becomes less bloody after the Peace of Westphalia in the fateful year 1648: atrocities were not unknown but they became markedly rarer. Nothing is more significant of the new temper than the conduct of Louis XIV on becoming sovereign of Alsace and Lorraine and thus of one of the largest of Western Jewish settlements. The inclination of the King was to expel and persecute in the spirit of the Revocation, but he accepted moderate counsels and allowed his Jewish subjects to remain under a penal code which was only partially observed. Such was one great change in custom and ideas: the presence in religious affairs of that general weariness with violence which we may suppose helped to give rise to the later supposal that the Age of Faith belonged to a distant past.

The other change was of an entirely opposite kind. With the growth of Presbyterianism there arose sects who from reading the Bible began to cherish the people of Israel among them. In the middle years of the century certain of these went so far in their cult of Judaism that they tried to live according to the strictest Levitical Law, and conversions from Protestant Christianity to Jewry were to be met with. These Judaical sects were of political consequence in Holland because they could rally the Anti-Spanish sentiment, and one result of their influence was that in Holland a great part of the Spanish Jews were allowed to settle on liberal terms unknown elsewhere in the Western world. Similar results were obtained later by the same influence in England. During the brief Puritan heyday of the Commonwealth the Judaical sects made vigorous efforts to obtain the readmission of the Jews. Cromwell, no extremist himself but anxious to steal Jewish trade from Holland, endeavoured to use the extremists for this purpose. He invited a Dutch-Spanish Rabbi, the famous Manasseh ben Israel, to plead the Jewish cause in England, and with the Rabbi's help, and after many difficulties, Cromwell got what he wanted.[1] The same policy

---

[1] The story of the readmission of the Jews into England is extremely complicated, like that of the origin of the Marranos, and no attempt is made here to do more than indicate those events. The interested reader should consult Lucien Wolf's *Manasseh ben Israel's Mission to Oliver Cromwell* and Mr. Cecil Roth's *New Light on the Resettlement*.

was continued by Charles II. We shall see later how the original Judaical impetus of these movements persisted, but what we need to note here is that in the same years which saw the freedom and happiness of the Russian and Polish Jews entering a long eclipse, indifferentism and enthusiasm combined to bring fresh air into the Ghettoes. Of the two forces indifferentism was the greater, and as a natural consequence the move from persecution to emancipation was slow and occupied the hundred years from the late seventeenth to the late eighteenth centuries.

We hear so little about the Jews of the West during the eighteenth century that it is tempting to suppose that they lived in contentment, or else more people would have voiced their wrongs. This is true if we remember at the same time that they had to accept paltry standards of contentment. In an age of patronage they lived as the object of no one's solicitude. In an age of autocracy they were at the mercy of sovereigns, some of whom were enemies. Their security lay nowhere in the law but in the spirit of the times which was beginning to venerate the notion of Progress. One incident may show what was happening in that respect. Giving way to an untypical impulse of brutal folly, Maria Theresa ordered the expulsion of all Jews from Vienna and Prague, but she revoked the edict because her allies protested in what seems to have been an entirely disinterested spirit. In the eighteenth century the penal codes existed everywhere but the people in power, especially during " the repentance of monarchy," tended to look on them as antique and even harmful absurdities. Magistrates often ignored them in keeping with the practice of an age of tolerance.

Nothing of this sort happened in the East. On the contrary, between the seventeen thirties and sixties there were revivals of the Cossack Fronde in which brigand armies called " the Haidamaks " terrorised the Ukraine fired by the old confused hatred of Pole, Catholic, and Jew. The bloodshed was as ghastly as before: twenty thousand Jews were reported killed in Uan alone, and this was only one of many such crimes. The tide of

Jewish immigration had long since ceased to flow from West to East and now came the other way. Russian and Polish Jews settled in Germany in great numbers. But these numbers were not so great as to alter the old dispositions whereby the Western Jews were a collection of relatively small communities who sought accommodation with their neighbours, and the Eastern Jews were a state within the state. The West and the East were turning into two different worlds, the East a failing world which was becoming not only a state within the state, but an ancient time within a modern time, the West a place of hope. Emancipation finally stressed this division.

It had been foreshadowed by some liberal acts of Louis XVI's Government, then came as a sudden transformation of the old order with the Revolution and the conquests of Napoleon. We must be careful, however, not to see in this too neat an instance of cause and effect. Great as was the influence of French civil equality on the fate of the Jews, another stronger influence joined to shape their destiny.

Before the Revolution, there existed in the German-speaking world small groups of rich or influential Jews who were accepted as members of cultivated society. Occasionally their anomalous position was regularised. A class of " Court Jews " grew up, and under them another class was regularised and known as " Schutz-Juden " or "Protected Jews," which meant that they were excused the burdensome and insulting taxes of the penal codes. Among these strangely-placed people in the middle years of the eighteenth century was a scholar called Moses Mendelssohn. He came of a Rabbinical family and lived in Berlin protected by Frederick the Great. Mendelssohn had no wish to be a hero of his people and probably only became so because he was forced into a public declaration of his faith by an accidental circumstance.

This is what happened. In 1767 he became famous by the publication of his " Phaedon." Then, in the year 1769, his friend Johann Kasper Lavater published a German translation of Bonnet's essays on Christian evidence. In the introduction Lavater asserted that it was impossible to read the essays and not be converted to the Christian religion, and he challenged Mendelssohn to refute Bonnet or " do what wisdom . . . must command him to do." This friendly but embarrassing invitation to become a Christian forced Mendelssohn, against his inclinations, to throw off the shyness of Western Jewish practice and enter into a public controversy, and this redirection of his life awoke in him a noble sense of his duties to the less happy. He became the first agitator for a general emancipation of his people. The spectacle of an eminent scholar and philosopher, the admired friend and associate of Lessing and Kant, who also proclaimed his pride in his Jewish race and religion, filled his contemporaries with wonder. As a result he made an impression on the Gentiles of his own age, and on the Jews of his own and the subsequent age, which can hardly be exaggerated.

Moses Mendelssohn was not of the company of the martyrs. He was a cultured gentleman whose opinions enjoyed more respect than opposition, but for all that his path was not without distressing obstacles. As with other reformers, he found those for whom he worked reluctant at first to enjoy the novelties of freedom. He found at first that the Gentiles were more willing than his own people to hear him. There was a certain cosiness in the ghettoes which Jews did not like leaving. More than that, the Rabbis feared that emancipation from their life of narrow acquaintance and extinct ambition might finally disperse them by putting them into circumstances where, choked with the cares of this world, they would at long last forget Jerusalem.[1] The Rabbis opposed Mendelssohn throughout, but the astute scholar outmanoeuvred them. He taught Jews to take a pride in the German language. The master stroke of his work for liberation was his translation of the Pentateuch. It is the belief of most Jewish authorities that this had a decisive effect on the Jews of Germany and Austria, and that through it they came to feel that they were part of the German people. The Rabbis

[1] Even so late as 1795 the Jews of Amsterdam refused an offer of complete equality from the Dutch government on the grounds that it might damage their religious observance.

forbade Jews to read the translation on pain of excommunication, but their disapproval did not have much effect.

It will be readily seen that Mendelssohn's teaching was not in any way typical of Jewish tradition, but did belong closely to the Age of Enlightenment. An eighteenth century character informed his mind; he did not demand emancipation as an act of reparation so much as an act of reason and part of a general system of tolerance. He made the liberation of the Jews a test of the age's sincerity and so, in a manner of speaking, he made his people part of the modern world. The conquering French found in Germany Jews who were enthusiastically familiar with French ideas.

During the fifty or sixty years which followed Mendelssohn, while the Jews of the East suffered their long decline, the Jews of the West passed through a bewildering succession of experiences, leaving them at last in a position of unaccustomed prominence. From being forgotten, they became the most talked-of people in the world. From being reduced to seeking the protection of their persecutors, they rose to being closely associated with the ruling power. But their position was nevertheless precarious and to understand why we may consider the outline of their complex and inconsistent history between the days of Moses Mendelssohn and those of his great-grandchildren.

In the early nineteenth century there was a natural Jewish sense of gratitude to Napoleon. As a result the restored sovereigns became aware of a grievance against the Jews after 1814, and with almost incredible silliness they revived the penal codes in Prussia, Austria, the German kingdoms and principalities, and in the Papal States. The persecution which followed, and which was not free of violence, revolted the best spirits of the time, was doomed to failure, and yet, for many years, was nowhere mitigated except in the principality of Hesse. Between 1815 and 1847 twenty-one laws were instituted in Prussia alone to restrict Jewish liberties, and in Austria, the young Francis Joseph, on becoming Emperor in 1848, sought popularity during the first ten years of his reign by intensifying the persecution of his Jewish subjects.

But, as in the eighteenth century, the laws against the Jews were not thoroughly operated; the character of the Jewish period between Waterloo and the middle of the century tells us that very clearly. In Germany the influence of Moses Mendelssohn and his followers remained strong: the passion to be part of the civilisation of the West was more powerful among German Jews than any sense of anger or embitterment. This passion at last found expression in the very heart of the Jewish nation. In 1845, at a period when the anti-Jewish laws had been repealed nowhere except in Hesse, a historic meeting of Rabbis assembled at Frankfurt-am-Main with the object of adapting Jewish ritual and theology to the needs of the nineteenth century. The Jews were faced with a Modernist crisis fifty years before the Catholics.

The programme of these Frankfurt Rabbis was optimistic, humanitarian, and eclectic. It renounced the idea of a restoration of Israel to Palestine and the hope of a personal Messiah. It wanted synagogues to conform with Western fashions and to approximate to churches, and it wanted the vernacular used at services instead of Hebrew. Its main theological proposal was that the Jews, instead of waiting to be redeemed by a Messiah, should themselves redeem the world. What was said of old concerning a saviour must be taken now as applying to a Jewish mission, and the scattering and persecution of the people must be accepted as part of a divine plan signified in the words of the Book of Deuteronomy: " And the Lord shall scatter thee among all people from the one end of the earth even unto the other," and yet more clearly in the words of Daniel: " And I heard the man clothed in linen, which was upon the waters of the river, when he held up his right hand and his left hand unto Heaven and sware by Him who liveth for ever that it shall be for a time, times, and an half; and when he shall have accomplished to scatter the power of the holy people all these things shall be finished." To further the will of God Jews must not think of huddling into a community once more but rather of dispersing still further into every land in the world till every nation should acknowledge one God alone, in the pure terms of the Jewish tradition. Thus, they declared, would the Scriptures be truly fulfilled.

It has often been said that these Rabbis of Frankfurt were men of poor spirit anxious to make terms with the Christians at the expense of their heritage. They were more than that. They sincerely looked on themselves as teaching the only remedy for the great new danger of Jewish extinction which now began to appear to many minds in formidable shape. Following an ungrateful human habit, many Western Jews in the nineteenth century began to look on the synagogue not as a source of strength but as a reminder of old wretchedness, and this disposition gave rise to a willingness, even an enthusiasm, to change their faith and so identify themselves as closely as possible with the successful Christian world. The leaders set the example. Three of the six children of Moses Mendelssohn were baptised, and in the next generation the most famous of this great family, Felix Mendelssohn the composer, was brought up as a Christian from his childhood. It has been calculated that about a hundred and thirty thousand European Jews adopted Christianity in the course of the nineteenth century. Most of these entered the Bible-loving Protestant communions, but a later generation was ready to exchange Jewry for fashionable unbelief. It was from this last tendency that the Frankfurt Rabbis set themselves to reconvert their people, and whether or not they set about their task in the best way, there can be no doubt that they had a lasting effect. They could not capture majorities, but they did express, as the Unitarians did (to whom they may be compared), the inner beliefs of far more people than openly joined them. They exerted a strong influence over many of the chief actors in this story. By what they did they stressed anew the separation of the Eastern and Western worlds.

The year 1871 marks the height of the good fortune which surrounded Western Jews. They had triumphed over the reaction of the Holy Alliance. They had broken their shackles for ever, it seemed. In Germany one of the first acts of Bismarck as Imperial Chancellor was to grant them complete equality throughout the new Empire, a deed by which he confirmed the liberal policy of emancipation which had been going forward throughout the German independencies, and the North German Confederation, since 1848. In Austria the inept Francis Joseph had long since relinquished his Anti-Jewish campaign. In all the important countries of Western Europe, the once dreaded existence of the penal codes was only faintly visible in one or two amusing legal oddities. Furthermore, Jews could be found holding positions of influence or distinction in an extraordinary variety of occupations, and as though to crown their amazing achievement, there stood the figure of Benjamin Disraeli, the leader of a great political party and soon to be in supreme charge of affairs in the most powerful European country of that time. He was in many things typical of two generations, belonging to a family which had become Protestant in the early years of the century. Then, shortly after 1871, the anti-Semitic movement broke out after some years of smouldering, and the scene changed.

The origin of this renewed agitation against the European Jews is obscure. The unimaginable violence of the climax has influenced a great majority of modern writers on the subject, both Jewish and Gentile, to conclude that anti-Semitism was an impulse of great antiquity. In a sense, of course, that is true, since it could hardly have maintained itself as it did without the support of historical traditions. It seems a mistake, however, to conclude that between the old Jew-baiting associated with the penal codes, and the anti-Semitic movement there was an uninterrupted continuity.[1] The evidence suggests that the new movement, that tremendous act of fanaticism and mass-folly, began

[1] In this outline of anti-Semitism the writer is chiefly guided by Lucien Wolf and Bernard Lazarare. These brilliant Jewish writers gave clear and unbiased records of anti-Semitism throughout the world, and in spite of the fact that they wrote respectively ten and twenty-five years before the foundation of the Nazi party, they showed much greater understanding of this malign movement than any writer on the subject to-day. They have grown unfashionable, in the case of Lucien Wolf partly because he had an anti-Zionist bias, and partly because he took an altogether too simple and now discredited view of racial questions.

in nothing more profound than the emotional nonsense of party politics, against whose dangers subsequent rivers of blood should be an eternal warning.

Events had tended to give Jews a distinct position in parliamentary states. The emancipating influence of the French Revolution and the stupidity of the restored sovereigns, combined to make European Jews sympathise with Liberalism and Liberal parties everywhere. (In this respect Disraeli was very much an exception.) This association was made easy by another circumstance. The Jews were most prominent in that class from which most Liberals came. They were international; they were unconnected with fuedalism; they were the most "bourgeois" of all distinguishable groups.[1] It followed inevitably that their good fortune might be threatened by any great reaction against the triumph of the Bourgeoisie, coming either from a conservative aristocracy who wanted things as they used to be, or from extreme progressives who wanted all things as they had never been, and who about this time were being taught by a host of theorists to see in bankers, financiers, and kindred bourgeois types enemies more frightful than the tyrants of old.

The mutual antagonism of Left and Right no doubt made the Jews believe that they had little to fear from these extremists, but things so fell out that suddenly they were threatened by both enemies at once, the old-fashioned and the new-fangled.

In 1873 Germany and Austria were both faced with a false economic prosperity which suddenly leaped into being in the style of the South Sea Bubble. Trade expanded with extraordinary violence, so that in Prussia alone one thousand eight hundred and fifty-seven new companies were established between 1870 and 1874, raising the invested capital of such undertakings from three to seven and a half milliards of marks, staggering

---

[1]Jews very rarely became respectable members of the working classes. This was, in all likelihood, because their separate way of life was less understood in uneducated society than in bourgeois society, but the reason has never been clearly established. In London, according to Patrick Colquhoun's *Treatise on the Police*, 1795, the majority of the very poor Jews, of whom 2000 were old clothes men, made money by criminal activities. Dickens's portrait of Fagin is a melodramatic exaggeration of this situation.

figures for those days. Fools and knaves dashed into what looked like a speculators' paradise. The first warning of disaster was heard in the Prussian Diet in January of this year and came from the Liberal statesman, Edward Lasker. The inevitable crash occurred in almost the precise terms he prophesied during May. There followed the usual investigations, disclosures, scandals, disgraces and so on, such as attend these melancholy occasions. It was found that no small number of Jews were guiltily involved, and also that a celebrated Jew, Bethel Henry Strousberg, was not only involved but had been the principal mover. These discoveries provoked an idea that there had been some horrible Hebraic plot behind all this ruin, and because this was a dramatic idea, supported moreover by remarkable evidence, it caught on when it was used by party politicians of both sides to rouse anti-Liberal excitement. The fact that Edward Lasker was himself a Jew made by comparison very little impression.

The commotion might have passed over in a few months had it not been that the sudden feeling against the Jews attracted attention to a little-known body of second-class theorists and philosophers, the pioneers of popular anti-Semitism. Pre-eminent among them was a purveyor of impressive bosh called Wilhelm Marr. He wrote an alarmist pamphlet which appeared just after the crisis, with the title " Der Sieg des Judenthums über das Germanenthum," which can be translated as " The Victory of Jewishness over Germanism," and he became famous thereby in a few days. His book was a hotch-potch of half true history, of careless and emotional studies of Jewish law and theology, and of violent denunciation, but closely held together by an exciting theory expressed with that weighty portentous-ness for which the German language in its lower flights is peculiarly fitted. " Ja! " exclaimed Wilhelm Marr in a key passage, " I am convinced! I have spoken out loud what millions of Jews ponder *im stillen*: ' To the Semite belongs the mastery of the world! ' " He saw Germany being gradually turned into a " New Palestine in the Land of Sunset," and he did not mince matters when he came to suggest practical remedies: "They (the Jews) use religion as a pretext. Shall we not then exploit the example of the 'Crusaders of Christ'? Let the people cry 'Hep! Hep!'" (This was the traditional howl of the German medieval mob on attacking ghettoes.)[1] He ended his little book with a warning of what might happen if his words were ignored. "We will find ourselves confounded by an Inevitability, if we lack the power to curb its force. And this inevitability is called: Finis Germaniae."

Marr's pamphlet had an important sub-title which is part of its claim to be considered as the precursor of the new, rather than as a survival from the old. He called this stuff: "Vom nicht confessionellen Standpunkt aus Betrachtet." This is: The Victory of Jewishness, etc., "regarded from a non-denominational point of view." Up to now disapproval or dislike of the Jews had always had a theological impetus. Wilhelm Marr is important for one reason: he was the first popular writer to put forward reasons for persecution which were exclusively concerned with politics and were suited to the age of unbelief.

From 1873 onwards anti-Semitism, as this movement was now ridiculously called, became a considerable force in the world. Though its progress was often impeded by the low mental and moral class of its champions, men like Ahlwardt for example, who brought it into complete public ridicule, it was not confined to their clumsy hands. Wilhelm Marr and his sort were the "vulgarisateurs" of opinions which had for some time been formed by learned men and leaders of thought not only in Germany but throughout Europe. From its beginning anti-Semitism had the power to attract to itself men of high talent such as Eugen Duehring, Houston Stewart Chamberlain and Heinrich von Treitschke. In Richard Wagner the cause was early associated with the greatest genius then living in the world. It enjoyed a triumphant progress. From providing a political argument against toleration of the Jews, anti-Semitism went on

---

[1]Supposedly formed from the initial letters of the phrase "Hyerosalem est perdita" (Jerusalem is lost).

to obtain what seemed to many people strong philosophical and scientific arguments in addition. We do the Germans and their followers a grave injustice if we think of anti-Semitism as being a mere mob movement or a simple outbreak of cruelty. It was far more than that. It succeeded as part of a burning idealism, part of the search for religion which marked this age.

The idealism in question was the cult of the all-conquering Western white man and was sometimes called " Aryanism " for short. We have come to know this thing with such distressing thoroughness in the last twenty years that a writer has incurred an obligation not to inflict more of it on his readers than is strictly necessary to the purpose in hand. To follow this strange story, however, the reader should know what was the shape of this movement at the end of the nineteenth century when Aryanism stood some way above the savage mania into which it degenerated fifty years later.

The origin of the cult was in the writings of Hegel, though whether or not these were rightly interpreted by the Aryanists must be doubted. It was certainly a crude form of Hegelianism which resulted, but then it may also be noted that the practical objects of Hegel's admiration were indeed crude by contrast with the exquisite subtlety of his thought, and so the crimes and follies of the anti-Semites may after all have been an accurate reflection of the more earthly of the master's ideals. The state was the object of worship. The love, passion, and self-forgetfulness which had aforetime been devoted to God were transferred with little loss of intensity to nationhood, and since nationhood thus became the first of all preoccupations and was believed to be the supreme manifestation on earth of divine or cosmic will it seemed important, as it had never seemed before, to maintain the composition of the state in all purity and all unity. It was here that the teachings of Gobineau on the Aryan migrations came in with remarkable appositeness. A theory of race which suited a long tradition of patriotic German teaching was evolved from his writings. This theory was finally classified by Houston

Stewart Chamberlain twenty-five years after the fatal 1873,[1] and in his work we can see the sort of ideas which animated the most progressive German thinkers during the last quarter of the nineteenth century. These ideas revolved round an idolatrous admiration of recent German achievement. European history was considered afresh: it was argued that the fall of the Roman Empire through the invasion of Teuton tribes, an event deplored through ignorance, was rather a matter for joy, since it meant that by the operation of a vast historical process covering many centuries, a primitive form of the state was superseded by the highest imaginable form of this highest imaginable human accomplishment. Chamberlain called the Roman Empire " that monstrosity, a state without a nation, that empty form, that soulless congeries of humanity, that union of mongrels," and by contrast, and following many predecessors, he extolled in terms which belong to hysteria the rise of Germany under the God-given shadows of Frederick and Bismarck. This event was considered to be the ultimate flowering of the carefully nurtured and cruelly but therefore gloriously tested genius of the German Indo-Europeans, that chosen race who carried with them the mysterious and everlasting wisdom of the ancient Aryans. Racial purity had allowed these people to pass unscathed through the fires, and alone to preserve the capacity to pass on this wisdom to future generations. Fantastic as much of this may appear now it must be remembered that in the age of final Western expansion, the untested Aryan theory provided ideas wherewith to explain something which for size and completeness was without any parallel in history. It can be readily seen too that, for people who believed such things, the presence of the largest Western Jewish population in the midst of their all-hallowed Germanic state constituted a grievous irritation. Yet, in the first phases of their movement it was believed by the earlier leaders of German

---

[1]In his *Foundations of the Nineteenth Century*, in which he assembled the ideas of the leading and most interesting of the anti-Semites. The book, while based on fallacies, is not the brutal absurdity which has been made out by propaganda. He had an unpleasant but honest mind and he took his arguments to their logical conclusion. His ultimate objection was to dark hair.

anti-Semitism that it was possible for the pure-bred Teutons to compromise with the Jews. They were still under the influence of theological anti-Judaism and believed that a general conversion to Christianity or some other religion acceptable to Aryanism would solve the problem. Wagner thus addressed the Jews: " Bear your part undaunted in this work of Redemption, gaining new birth by self-immolation whereby we shall then be indivisibly one," but adding with characteristic Germanenthum: "Remember that there can only be one release from the curse that rests upon you: the release of Ahasuerus—destruction!" When the movement was more fully developed such words as these appeared dangerously tolerant among believers.

By the eighteen-eighties anti-Semitism was firmly established as a major factor in German political life. In the place of Wilhelm Marr it had found a far more useful popular leader. This was Adolf Stoeker, a Protestant clergyman of advanced Socialist views. He was a man of commanding position in those days. He had a large following in the working class. He was a court preacher. He was a leading member of the Prussian Diet, where he was able to use anti-Semitism to bring about a repulsive alliance between Socialists and Conservatives. He had admirable luck, for at the same time, around 1880, another large and influential party joined the anti-Semite host under his banner. These were the New Ultramontanes. They had some excuse for their action. The Liberals and their Jewish supporters in the political world had been Bismarck's allies in the Kulturkampf and this movement of revenge followed more or less inevitably.

When the Jews were thus isolated with the German Liberals (but far more isolated for no-one had invented a racial prejudice against Liberals), and when their weakness was apparent, the anti-Semitic movement passed over from its preliminary phase of pamphleteering, speechifying, and political manœuvre, to that of action. Scenes of physical Jew-baiting became, if not common, things that were often to be found reported in German newspapers. Lives were lost in duels. A strong effort was made

to get Bismarck's approval[1] for a new penal code on the lines
of the recent Austrian one.[2] The air was heavily charged with
hatred, and many things pointed to a new German relapse into
organised persecution, when in the year 1881 the whole of
Western anti-Semitism was shocked into moderation.

On the 13th of March that year the Emperor Alexander II of
Russia was murdered. A little more than a month later there
was a riot in a small town called Elizavetgrad in which the
Jewish quarter was sacked. This riot was followed by greater
riots at Kiev. It had been suspected at Elizavetgrad and it became
quite clear now that the ringleaders were agitators in Government service. There was bloodshed and loss of life and two
thousand people were made homeless. This great riot was
instantly followed by others throughout South-West Russia. It
is calculated that these pogroms, as they were called in the
Russian langauge, occurred in a hundred and sixty-seven places
during the rest of 1881, and any remaining doubts as to the
Government's responsibility were removed. It was evidently the
official aim to rally the people of Russia with emotional violence.
It was never pretended that the death of Alexander was in any
way connected with Jews.

Many people who in Germany, Austria and France had
listened to the magniloquent vapourings of the racialists saw
now for the first time what anti-Semitism really was.

Russia was its most natural breeding ground. In the East
the traditions of Government which had afforded strong protection to Jews had by now been lost for more than a hundred
and fifty years, and opposite ones had been slowly growing up
in their place. One of Catherine II's first deeds on taking charge
of the majority of Polish Jews after the partition of Poland had
been to establish the Pale of Settlement in 1791. This was not
intended to be, nor was it in effect an act of oppression: the

---

[1]Bismarck's guilt or innocence in anti-Semitic affairs is still a matter of doubt. There
is evidence that he was the hidden driving force behind the second onrush of the movement in 1879, but if so he kept the matter secret, and this was very unlike the way of
the Iron but garrulous Chancellor. He made some suggestive anti-Jewish remarks, but
they cannot be taken as conclusive evidence.
[2]See page 121 above.

area was vast and the restriction on movement injured no accustomed freedom, but the mere formation of the Pale gave the Russian Imperial House a new and delicious taste of power. Even so, it is a mistake to suppose that by the late nineteenth century the Russian throne had a long tradition of Jewish persecution. Catherine, Paul, and Alexander I conducted moderate Jewish policies. Nicholas I is usually considered as the first great modern persecutor, but this may be a misjudgment. By his " fundamental law " of 1835 he ordered Jews to adopt Russian names and abolished the autonomy of Rabbinical courts. He introduced the insufferable regulation whereby Jews were forbidden to live within fifty versts of the Western frontiers. He was guilty of thousands of forcible baptisms of the Jews in his army, and dreadful stories were told of the kidnapping of Jewish boys for this purpose, and of lifelong separations from home suffered by recusants. On the other hand, it was Nicholas who abolished the trade-bans against the Jews, allowed them into Universities, and permitted Jewish holders of degrees to live where they chose. His policy bears some resemblance to Napoleon's and may have been influenced by it, but the difference between the two was decisive. The Jews of France were attached by the genius of Napoleon to the national interest. Nicholas failed utterly. The Jews of Russia remained a world apart from their fellow-subjects. They spoke a different language, German or Yiddish; their preoccupations, their hopes, their desires had little in common with their neighbours'. In the withdrawn world of the Catholics in eighteenth-century England or of the Protestants in eighteenth-century France, we can catch but the feeblest image of the enclosed life of the Russian Pale, thrown on to its inner self by the murderous hatred of those who surrounded it.

There was a brief period under the mild rule of Alexander II when it looked as though the Jews of Russia might follow a line of development similar to what they had found in Germany, France and England. The liberal Emperor allowed the Anti-Jewish code to fall into disuse, while on the Jewish side there grew up the " Haskalah " or " Enlightenment " movement, founded on the teaching of Moses Mendelssohn. The idea that the good Jew ought to be first and foremost a good Russian patriot became fashionable, and such extravagances of Jewish life as " Hassidism," the pietism which seems to have grown up as a response to the Cossack Fronde, were laughed out of existence.

But this Jewish assimilation and Russian mildness were short-lived and without great subsequent influence. The trouble with Grand Monarchy is shallowness. Alexander's efforts to temper the lot of the Jews were treated as court fads and did nothing to change the popular habit of mind. Throughout the huge wretched Empire of the Romanovs the Christian Slav continued to honour his Saviour by spitting on the Jew, and laying to his charge the economic calamities of the hour, especially when these grew serious after the muddled manumission of the serfs in 1861. Thereon anti-Jewish feeling increased, and in this question the generous Russian soul seemed to find no room for compassion. In literature Tolstoy alone among the giants of that golden age contrived pleasing descriptions of Jews. Turgenev and Tchekhov only mention them in terms of contempt. Dostoyevski was a violent anti-Semite. When the ministers of the new Tsar decided to promote unity by a policy of Jew-baiting they showed that they understood the psychological state of their country.

In their successful endeavour to associate the autocracy with mob-passion the men of 1881 did not only rely on the old Jew-hatred which had given impetus to the Cossack Fronde and was kept alive by worthless priests and religious charlatans; they drew additional strength from some of the Western influences which had been able to enter Russia during the easy days of Alexander II.

The Pan-Slav movement was largely an adaptation of the modern Hegelianism of Germany; it thought about the Slavs in the same terms of self-praise as Treitschke and his imitators thought about the Germans, and as German Hegelians were for ever searching for unadulterated Germanenthum, so the Pan-

Slavs aimed to restore the old " pure " Russia of pre-Petrine days. Pan-slavism was productive of monstrous works of sham Byzantine architecture, blood-curdling historical pictures, and some great masterpieces in music and literature. In morals it saw itself as the promoter of what Oscar Wilde was to call " that beautiful white Christ which seems coming out of Russia," but what it unquestionably did do was to impart fresh vigour to the abominations of Alexander III and his advisors throughout the pogroms. In this bloody field the worst of the old and the worst of the new met " and held high festival."

In an age which was getting tired of peace the horror with which the pogroms filled the world was not long-lived or deep enough to turn back the progress of anti-Semitism. By the middle of the eighteen-eighties the movement, in spite of disgust at the massacres, was again spreading over an enormous area of Europe, delighting the intelligentsia by supplying a learned form of patriotism, and the masses by a return to some enjoyable and half-forgotten superstitions. The fantastic legend that Jews crucified children and used their blood in the making of un-leavened bread was revived on many occasions, and despite a celebrated legal trial, the once famous Tisza Eszlar affair, which not only proved for all time the absurdity of that accusation but covered the anti-Semites of Hungary with contempt, a strong and avowedly anti-Semitic party was formed in the Empire. Both from the German-speaking world and from Russia the anti-Semitic poison flowed into the Balkans, and we can grasp the raging madness of the cult when we find that the Rumanian anti-Semites,[1] who were conscientious and learned Hegelians on the strictest German pattern, considered that their main grievance against the Jews was that they introduced into the sacredly pure state and race of Rumania an alien element of Germanenthum.

One important reason for the spread of anti-Semitism was

---

[1]According to Bernard Lazare the Rumanian anti-Semites were unique because most of them were drawn from the Liberal bourgeoisie, rather than from aristocratic or radical circles as in Germany, Austria and France. As in Germany they were largely run by universities. See the article on Rumania in *The Jewish Encyclopædia*.

that a large part of the Catholic clergy had slid into it through opposition to Liberal anti-clericalism and Freemasonry. Some foolish priests were to be found preaching the " blood-accusation " and kindred stuff; other bad-minded ones, like the Abbé August Rohling of the University of Prague, wrote skilful pamphlets in support of the extremists. None of these was publicly rebuked. Modern racialism was hardly known in Italy, and the advisers of Leo XIII do not seem to have recognised that there had grown up this fearful heresy which was inciting to murder and rape in the Russian Pale, and in Germany was repudiating allegiance to Christ on account of his un-Teuton origins. There was no Papal act of leadership away from this new seduction of the mind, while some careless Papal acts, such as Leo XIII's political support of Prince Liechtenstein, the Austrian anti-Semitic leader, were not publicly put right. Church influence was among the agencies which facilitated the spread of the mania westward into France. In that country it found irrigated soil, as we shall see later.

To sum up, we may say that from the reactions against Liberalism, the teaching of German professors (then at the height of their reputation) and supposed Church approval of what they said; from the intensification of Western patriotism, and the marriage of this with Russian barbarism, it came about that towards the end of the nineteenth century anti-Semitism was a thoroughly familiar thing in most lands of the West and throughout the Greek orthodox world. The exceptions were the Mediterranean countries (apart from France), where the new racial teaching was not easily understood or enjoyed, the outlying countries of the north, where Jews were almost unknown, and England.[1] We must now see what action was taken by those who were imperilled by the new movement.

[1] Anti-Semitism was not unknown in England but it never became of much importance. T. P. O'Connor's strictures on the Jews in his *Lord Beaconsfield* are among the very few serious English attempts to give history an anti-Semitic complexion. For the most part it was confined to music hall humour and a form of upper-class joking such as can be studied in the short stories of ' Saki.' There was danger of it at the time of the South African War when an idea was put forward, unfortunately for the reputation of certain eminent writers, that the war was the result of a Jewish big business conspiracy. The

Two Studies in Virtue

The reader of Jewish history may easily imagine that throughout Russia and the Western world, the time we recall was one of dark Jewish tragedy. We can imagine happy lives suddenly clouded by fear and embittered by a mass-sense of deprivation; we can imagine the people brooding over the freedom which had been longed for, was obtained, and was now dashed away. Such a picture may be true of many who lived in the Russian Pale, but even there the " Enlightenment " movement continued till the end of the Romanov Empire. In the West we must forget such a picture altogether. The ferocious exhortations of Treitschke, or such episodes as the 1892 resolution of the All-German Conservative party to withdraw its protest against the pogroms, all these dreadful writings on walls had surprisingly little effect on those who stood in danger. Even the Russian massacres did not perturb Jews as much as we might suppose, and for a simple reason. These things were not the prime concern of the Age of Diffusion, and the great majority of Western Jews were so preoccupied with their part in the successes of that age that they treated the events of Germany and France, for all their bloody-minded character, as violent but essentially unimportant outbursts of excessive party zeal, while as for Russia, this was understood by the West to be a land of perennial horrors. (How many Christians wept for the Christian exiles in Siberia?)

In his last years Disraeli paid no attention to the anti-Jewish revival in Germany, though he lived during the first nine years of it.[1] He had vaster and more delectable interests.

But while the majority of the Jews were either too engrossed by their splendid prospects and fortunes, or too gifted, too selfish or too proud to busy themselves with the partial science and squalid butcheries of their enemies, minorities rose up to vindicate their rights.

most remarkable proof that anti-Semitism never obtained a footing in England is contained in the fact that without a knowledge of French and German it is literally impossible to study the movement at all closely as so little of its literature has been translated, and even less of anti-anti-Semitic literature, Monsieur Jean Paul Sartre's ridiculous and inaccurate *Portrait of an Anti-Semite* being very much an exception.

[1] His death in 1881 occurred just before the news of the first pogrom at Elizavetgrad was known.

From the year 1881, for many years onward, the roads leading towards Western Europe were crammed once more with crowds of refugees, as they had been in the seventeenth and eighteenth centuries at the time of the Cossack uprisings, and as it was supposed they never would be again.

Their reception by their fellow-Jews in the West showed a curious mixture of embarrassment, alarm and delight. There was embarrassment and alarm at their great numbers because this meant that the several communities would now have poverty-stricken lower classes to deal with and thus, so it seemed, the assimilation of Jews to Western nationalities (a process which went on without interruption during the whole of the first anti-Semitic period), would be beset with difficulties.

For that very reason the refugees were welcomed by certain ardent spirits among the devout. They saw a purifying influence in these people who had never been corrupted by contact with religious indifferentism, whose learning and thought and habit of life were based on the Talmud, who went to the synagogue three times a day, heard the Law read to them with solemnity every Monday and Thursday; who sat shoeless on the Day of Ab bewailing the vanished glories of Israel; who left an untended patch on one wall of every Jewish house for the sake of Jerusalem, and among whom the bridegroom at the wedding feast crushed a glass under his right foot as a show of grief because even in this hour of delight he would not forget that he was a stranger in a strange land who mourned with God for the destruction of His temple. In people whose lives were regulated by such practices the devout saw a hope of liberation at last from that besetting fear which never left them from the time of Moses Mendelssohn: that of engulfment and disappearance in the ever-expanding and apparently invincible European world.

Among the Eastern Jews there was a movement which came partly from the influence of Western writing, but more from ritual and tradition. In Hebrew it was called " Hibbath Zion," meaning " The Love of Zion." It was known throughout the Russian Pale of settlement and in Jewish communities of the neighbouring countries.[1] Though of ancient origins, it was of very recent formation. It seems to have taken shape, like so many movements of the time, from the preoccupations of the Industrial Revolution.

With the coming of the railways and the modern mastery of nature (nowhere more exciting than in the slow changing Russian Empire), the Jewish belief that the kingdom would be restored in Palestine began to take on an unwontedly practical shape; it was widely speculated among the Russian Jews that since the physical impediments were less than they had ever been, now might be the appointed hour. The " Hoveve Zion " or " The Lovers of Zion," as the followers of the cult were named, found that their beliefs were reflected in a Western school of Jewish literature which the learned among them came to know. Joseph Salvador, a French Jew of the reform school, and a man much esteemed in his day as a historical thinker, had written a book in 1860 called *Paris, Rome, Jerusalem*, in which he asserted his belief in the necessity of granting a national status to the Jews of Europe.

Two years later, Moses Hess, a German Jew living in Paris, published a book which he called *Rom und Jerusalem*. Hess had been stirred to write his book by disapproval of many of Salvador's ideas, notably his " fusionism," a proposal that all religious creeds should be united under Jewish management. But for all his disagreement, Moses Hess shared the other's extravagant faith in his age and the beneficence of all progress, and above all he shared Salvador's Jewish nationalism. Both these writers influenced their admirers in the same direction.

A little before *Rom und Jerusalem* another book largely devoted to Jewish irridentism had been published in Paris. It was called *La Nouvelle Question d'Orient* and was written by Napoleon III's private secretary, a Gentile called Ernest Laharanne. In this fiery and thoughtless work Laharanne suggested that it would be

[1]The best descriptions of how the Jews lived under Imperial rule in the later stages of the Russian Empire are to be found in the opening chapters of Dr. Weizmann's autobiography *Trial and Error*, in the autobiographical works of Shmarya Levin, and in Israel Cohen's *Jewish Life in Modern Times*.

both practical and easy for the Jews to establish a kingdom extending from Suez to Smyrna. In the year of *Rom und Jerusalem* an East Prussian rabbi, Zebi Hirsch Kalischer, had produced a book in Hebrew belonging to the same category as those of Salvador, Hess and Laharanne. It was called *Drishath Zion*, or *The Quest for Zion*, and the author asserted among other theological opinions and with the weight of an enormous rabbinical learning, that the Jews not only had the right but the duty to return to Palestine by way of self-reliant action and without the need to await the Messiah. In 1873 Perez Smolenski, a Jew of Russia, echoed many of these ideas in a book written in Hebrew and published at Prague.

With the possible exception of *Drishath Zion* and Smolenski's *Am Olam*,[1] these books cannot be admired except by a pre-judiced reader. They share some main faults with anti-Semitic literature: they are full of careless and emotional history, sham science, and propaganda artfully disguised as the result of honest research. There is an element of sly anti-Christian propaganda in Salvador and Hess which is extremely repulsive, and one cannot respect the judgment of men who lavished praise without any reserve on those very excesses of nationalism which were already introducing a new age of persecution.

But for all their imperfections these writings formed the mind of Hibbath Zion.[2] Their influence though not widespread was very deep. It is not hard to see why. The trend of modern Jewish leadership from the days of Moses Mendelssohn had been towards a denial of the undeniable identity of the Jewish people, and Salvador and Hess reasserted the truth that the Jews are a nation, and not only a nation but a unique one in the whole of mankind. However wild their ideas of history in general, they understood their own people thoroughly, and however little they understood the nationalist age, they did foresee the possi-

[1] The present writer has been unable to find a translation of either of these Hebrew books into any language. *Drishath Zion* appears from accounts to be a highly specialised work.

[2] There is some difference of opinion among authorities as to the extent of this influence. Dr. Weizmann is followed more than others at this point, since his account, though distantly remembered, is a first-hand one.

bility of an approaching catastrophe of anti-Semitism. Thus it came about that, though they were not wise men themselves, they could fulfil certain functions of the wise. In a world that looked peaceful these men sounded an alarum. Twenty years later, when the pogroms were under way, in 1882, there occurred a very remarkable though not much noticed episode in the career of Hibbath Zion.

Dr. Leon Pinsker, a Jewish medical man practising in Odessa, added an anonymous book in German to these new Jewish scriptures. He called it *Autoemanzipation*. Though Eastern Jewish by birth and loyalties, he was thoroughly Westernised in mind. True to the style of Hess, Laharanne, Salvador and their imitators, he crowded his pamphlet with fashionable nonsense, not least in a passage which anticipates much psychological stuff of a later time, where he asserts that anti-Semitism belongs to our inborn night-fears since in the Jews men fancy they see a ghost of the dead civilisations of antiquity stalking through the living world; but in one respect he was the author of a book more significant than any of its predecessors. He proved in an unexpectable manner the strength of the oldest Jewish ideas.

Pinsker was an extreme modernist. His main purpose, apart from his wish to excite the nationalist ardour of his people, was to dissuade them from setting forth in pioneering bands to Palestine. He objected that such enterprises could only be run by philanthropists and thus could not redeem the Jews from their habit of dependence, but over and above such considerations Pinsker wanted the Jews to turn their back on " ancient Judea " just because that land was ancient; he wanted them by a tremendous modernist act of mass-will to move in irresistible numbers towards America and found a new Jewish State in the new world. He wanted them to forget Jerusalem with everything else belonging to the past. He had a considerable effect on Jewish thought in Russia. An extraordinary consequence followed. While Pinsker's nationalist enthusiasm was sincerely imitated, his novel opinions about Palestine were not only ignored but, as it were, reversed by his followers. Inspired by this anti-Palestinian agitator yet more Jews left Russia for the Promised Land. We shall see later on in this story that many people, both Jews and Gentiles, who took a leading part in this national revival underrated, to the very end, the intense force of the Jewish tradition. Nowhere was this force stronger than in the Pale. Dr. Weizmann relates that as a child he once saw a man, one of these very pioneers of Hibbath Zion, who was about to set forth on a journey to Jerusalem, and he recalls how he gazed in awe and wonder at this being whose hands and feet were destined to touch hallowed soil.

The cult of Hibbath Zion spread quickly over the Diaspora, to all the countries of Europe and to the United States. If history were neat we might expect to find that the grain of mustard-seed, planted thus in the Pale, grew to power. But the development of Jewish nationalism became complicated at this juncture. In the eighteen-nineties, shortly after the term "Zionism" had been invented by Nathan Birnbaum in Vienna, and shortly after the first pioneers had sailed to the Sanjak of Jerusalem, the whole shape of this enterprise underwent a change. The centre of Zionism (as we may now call the movement) shifted from the slatternly provinces of Russia to the Queen of European cities, from Elizavetgrad to Paris.

In the year 1891 Theodore Herzl was appointed correspondent in France of the Neue Freie Presse, the principal Viennese newspaper and the most influential one to exist at any time in the German-speaking world. He had already acquired a little reputation as a writer. His tall majestic appearance, his black hair and his long beard, became a familiar spectacle in the smart literary society of Paris. A dramatic picture has been drawn of this well-to-do journalist reporting to his paper the court martial of Alfred Dreyfus and suddenly recognising from the chance utterance of a colleague that he was witnessing the attempted murder of his race. This is a pleasing fantasy. Herzl was entirely deceived by the Dreyfus conspiracy. He did not suddenly change his mind on its account, but rather did he regard the hatred it let loose as the last of a long succession of incidents which drove him to abandon his pleasant position in the world, and to labour for the Jewish cause.

In his Viennese youth he had met the anti-Semitism of Wilhelm Marr. He had seen his fellow-undergraduates of Vienna mourn the death of Richard Wagner in 1883 by an anti-Semitic demonstration. He knew Eugen Duehring's poisonous writings, and the utterances of the well-named Karl Lueger, the anti-Semitic mayor of Vienna. When he reached manhood Herzl had an unmistakably Jewish appearance which easily attracted attention, and in Germany he had occasionally heard the national screech of " Hep! Hep!" cried after him. But though these incidents were such as to turn his sensitive mind to his position as a Jew, and to the Jewish question, they did not seriously alter his outlook on life. We may see this in the fact that although his friend Hermann Bahr, the poet, had been the leader of the Wagnerian demonstration aforementioned, their friendship continued undisturbed.[1] We can imagine him looking on the anti-Semitism of the German world as an absurd relic of an absurd past, and not to be reckoned among the great forces of the future. Life in Paris awoke him to the fact that it was a vaster and more terrible thing than he had supposed.

French anti-Semitism was of a peculiar kind. As in Germany there was a long tradition of theological anti-Judaism largely run by clergymen. This had only indirect influence on ordinary opinion. Of far greater moment, so far as immediate things were concerned, was a tradition of historical writing which had begun in the last years of the eighteenth century in the works of the Abbé Barruel. This man, whose name was once famous in Europe, was not an anti-Semite but he wrote a book which opened a way to anti-Semitic thought. It was called *Memoires pour servir à l'histoire du Jacobinisme*, and with great and convincing skill he put forward the fantastic theory that the French Revolution was the result of an enormous secret plot engineered by Freemasons. Barruel was followed by a number of writers

[1]Bahr's anti-Semitism was no more than an undergraduate phase. In later life his feelings were very much the other way. He was to be one of the contributors to the Herzl memorial volume.

who applied his notion of world-wide secret conspiracies to explain revolutionary events, and from the fact that Masonry loves to deck itself in Judaic symbols they soon came to describe this unseen power as of Jewish origin and organisation. The Freemasons were much associated with Jews and Liberals, and both of these were associated with extreme anti-clericalism, so giving a semblance of truth to these opinions. We should remember, too, at this point the skill in intrigue and the subtle cliqueishness which many Jews retained from their Marrano past.

Belief in secret Jewish plots had something in common with "the Conviction" of Wilhelm Marr,[1] but it led to a different type of anti-Semitism, for though the racial argument was hotly represented in France, it had no great consequence. Gobineau's work never enjoyed a wide success in his native country, nor did Frenchmen in the age of Bismarck relish the thought that Germanenthum was the best the universe had to offer. But any failure of racialism was amply compensated by the especial violence of this French brand of political anti-Semitism, in which exasperation at a hideous phase of French life found means to express itself. In the financial outrages which disfigured public affairs from the beginning of the Third Republic and reached a climax in the Panama scandal, Jews were involved. At our distance from these events it is not difficult to see that what was amiss with the country was the arrival of an era of enormous commercial opportunity and expansion, what we have called the Age of Diffusion, among a people shaken to the soul by national defeat; but at the time, when scapegoats were in fashion, and when the Jews were not only prominent in politics and finance but among anti-clericals and freethinkers, and in literature among anti-Christian propagandists, it was easy to say " Ah, there is always a Jew at the bottom of it," and to suppose

[1] It seems impossible to find evidence that Marr was indebted to the French Barruel school for his ideas. There may have been an indirect process. The anti-big business Socialists of Orleanist France were prolific of anti-Jewish (not anti-Semitic) literature and their works were known to German radicals at a time when there was little anti-Jewish literature in Germany.

that this explained everything. A journalist of high ability, Edouard Droumont, set himself to make this kind of idea popular.

He made a promising start in a book called *La France Juive*, published in 1886, by which he explained a financial disaster of four years previously, the collapse of the " Union Generale," along simple anti-Semitic lines. Three years after this publication there occurred General Boulanger's failure in 1889. This served to increase anti-Semitism in the non-Liberal world because his ruin was to some extent the work of a Jew, Joseph Reinach. The reappearance of the Reinach family in the Panama disaster three years later seemed, among Royalists, Bonapartists and certain radicals to add a final proof to the idea that Jews were set on destroying Church and State. By this time Barruelism, from being a set of complicated ideas known only to advanced thinkers, had become an ordinary mental exercise practised by a great number of ordinary Frenchmen, and thereafter anti-Semitism began to enjoy a progress in France even more remarkable than among the racialists of Germany and Austria. The anti-Semitic League established branches throughout the country; Droumont's newspaper *La Libre Parole* kept the excitement at concert pitch; the anti-Christian propaganda of Jewish intellectuals drove more and more of the clergy into the anti-Jewish camp; in the army aristocratic officers, under the influence of such men as Morès, took to provoking Jewish officers into duels, some of which ended in death. Against such a background there was enacted the trial of Dreyfus in 1895, a little over two years after the Panama scandal.

When the supposed facts had been reported in January and Dreyfus publicly cashiered, aristocratic loyalism on the right wing, and hatred of the Jew-infested bourgeoisie on the left, gradually united to produce the most violent outbreak of anti-Semitism which had been seen in modern Europe outside Russia. The day of massacre in this land to which for a hundred years every Jew had been accustomed to look with gratitude, seemed not only possible but close.

Immediately after the trial, Theodore Herzl, while still quite unaware of the man's innocence, wrote a short book. When he had finished it he was astounded at his boldness, and showed the manuscript to a friend. The latter had read but a short way when he burst into tears and pronounced Herzl insane; but another friend, Max Nordau, asserted that here was a work of the very first importance. The book was published in Vienna in February of 1896. It was called *Der Judenstaat* or *The Jewish State*.

We should briefly pause at this point in the story to consider this odd little book and the man who wrote it.

To the student of Zionist literature who has waded through the turgid prose of Salvador and Hess, the first impression made by *Der Judenstaat* is that there is little originality in Herzl's ideas. They are all to be found in his predecessors, sometimes expressed in terms much the same as those he used. But in truth Herzl had a highly individual outlook, and we can gain some notion of the obscurity of Hibbath Zion and its attendant spirits by the fact that this Jewish man of letters had never read any Zionist literature, knew the names of no Zionist writers, and was hardly aware that others had been labouring in this vineyard before him.[1] We can also gain an impression of how widespread Zionist ideas had become since they had all found their way unrecognised into Herzl's mind. They suited the neo-Hegelian philosophy of which he had drunk deep in Austria and which gave him a preference for group-rights over personal ones which he took to the farthest extremes. "I do not regret its disappearance," he could say of individualism. "Whatever is unfit to survive can, will and must be destroyed," and with this Prussian faith in the superior claims of nationhood he proceeded in an arresting and dramatic journalese to demand a full measure of national rights for his people.

Like Leon Pinsker (of whom he had never heard), Herzl was somewhat abnormally attracted towards novelty and progress. He had Pinsker's same vision of the Jews discovering salvation

---

[1] "Seldom has a movement owed more than did Political Zionism to the fact that its founder was totally ignorant of his predecessors." Israel Cohen in *The Zionist Movement*.

in a world sustained by the elements of a new age and cut utterly
free from the entanglements of the long Jewish past. There were
at that time two Jewish enterprises for settlement on the land:
the Palestine colonies founded by the Russian pioneers and then
preserved and financed by Baron Edmond de Rothschild; and
the colonies formed and maintained in the Argentine by Baron
Maurice de Hirsch. Herzl's plan was influenced by these, but
most by the South American venture. Though he was careful
not to commit himself in this matter, he suggested very forcibly
in his book that the Jewish state should be in such a new land
of virgin soil and great potential riches. But he differed from
most of his Zionist forerunners, and from Hirsch particularly, in
having no " mysticism of the soil." This townsman was too
much a modernist to admire peasant life or the cycles of toil and
play associated with the tilling of the earth. He regarded all that
as a moribund thing in human history shortly to be swept away
by mechanisation and a wholly urbanised civilisation.

Because he was a modernist, again, he attached surprisingly
little importance to the rabbinical traditions of Zionism or indeed
to traditionalism of any kind. He was thus not in sympathy
with the Zionist passion to revive Hebrew, and preferred that
his Jewish state should be managed along the language system
of the Swiss, though here again he was careful not to make
categorical assertions. In one respect only he was the opposite
of progressive. Having witnessed the depth to which France
had sunk under a democratic regime he preferred monarchy
or an aristocratic republic. He differed here from the Eastern
Jews and their sympathisers who had come to execrate all royal
and aristocratic power. However he was a very adaptable man
and before the end of his life he changed many of the views he
set forth in *Der Judenstaat*.

The Jewish " question " was the most debated matter in
Europe: France was rent in two by " the Affair "; the accession
of Nicholas II had brought no relief to his wretched minorities;
it is not surprising, therefore, that Herzl's book caused much
commotion, unlike the similar productions of Salvador, Hess,

Kalischer or Pinsker, which had appeared in calmer moments or obscurer circumstances. To the Jews, especially to the Jews of Russia (when it reached them by the usual roundabout methods), Herzl's optimistic vision of a brave new world redeemed from strife, tyranny, licence, injustice, and poverty, wherein joyful citizens dwelling in exquisite maisonettes, and protected by the most orderly of armies, owed allegiance to a flag adorned by seven golden stars, symbols of the seven working hours of a life from which the curse of Adam had been conjured away; to people who lived as the victims of Russian spite and stupidity, and to many luckier ones who sorrowed for them, this picture, for all its exaggerations, inaccuracies and crudities, became an inspiration for life, and more precious than life. Henceforth Zionism, though often weak, though often defeated, was a force in the politics of the world.

The author of the book which brought about this result was a curious mixture of strength and weakness, of greatness and limitations, of masterful intellect and absurd sentimentalism. From that Darwinian passage alone on the worth of individualism which we have quoted, and from many others in his book, one can rightly guess that he suffered and gained from a characteristically German disposition, and it was inevitable that in time he should have come into conflict with Jews of a different mind from the East. The impressive thoroughness of the Teutonic character was in his own, and whenever he made up his mind he did so with the most definite positioning or change of direction. We see this in the great crisis of his career. When he learned that many of his ideas had been expressed before he declared that had he known this earlier he would have written nothing. He made no effort of his own to become the Zionist leader, but when this responsibility was thrust upon him he became the absolute and complete leader, putting forth all his energy to fulfilling that task and taking command in the fullest sense. As a result he dominated the Jewish world as no one had done since the remote past, and by exerting a formidable gift of leadership he roused an enthusiasm that fortified anew, perhaps to its hurt, the gigantic strength of Jewry.

He is difficult to judge as a human being because no one ever knew him very intimately, even in his own family. He was an affectionate but distant father, a conscientious unhappily married husband. Circumstance and temperament forced him to give the whole of himself to his public life. Yet for all the simplicity of his fate he was never simple. Under his calm appearance there raged a stormy emotionalism which he held in tight check. It is reasonable to suppose that by this constant feat of his inner strength he not only debarred himself from private joys but imposed on himself his extreme habit of self-importance. " When Dr. Herzl says something, he is always in the right" was a woefully typical utterance. From numerous records of him there appears at moments a disconcerting picture of a preternaturally pompous person who attached an extraordinary significance to correct costume and high rank. It is not difficult to agree with some strictures which have been passed on this autocratically minded Germanic figure. But such criticisms, even if deserved, are essentially trivial, because, whatever we may say of Herzl, there always remains before us the figure of a man who was great for a great reason, who was consumed by an idea of indescribable power. " I know," he once said,[1] " that in this struggle I myself shall die, but I too can no longer help myself, and I cannot hide from it." Like a great scientific discoverer he saw an essential truth about his own people and proceeded with all his vigour and courage to prove it by practical tests. His short Zionist career was in the nature of a first, very imperfect, but entirely needful experiment. Clemenceau knew him as a journalist colleague at the time when he wrote Der Judenstaat, and he thus described him twenty-five years after: " He was a man of genius, not to be confused with a man of talent. The Burning Bush and Revolutionary Sinai took shape in his appearance. There was a breath of eternity in that man."

His work is divided into two parts, both of them so well

[1] To Maria delle Grazie

known now that we need only give their outline. Let us first
define them. He interviewed as many of the leading statesmen
and rulers of the world as he could in an endeavour to organise
influential support for his project; this was one half of his work.
With his own people lay the second half, in the establishment of
the Zionist congresses. We may deal with his mission to the
rulers first, as it began some time before the other, but first we
should note a very strange influence on it which was of considerable importance to the Jewish national revival. This
influence we may call Gentile Zionism.

We have already come across an offshoot of this in Ernest
Laharanne, and we call him offshoot advisedly because as a
Catholic he was quite untypical. Gentile Zionism was best
understood by and most widely known to the Protestant world.
It was to be found all over the Continent, but without question
its most fertile breeding ground was Protestant England, and
we should look at its development there.

The first English document of such a movement to make a
commotion in the world belongs to the reign of James I: a
pamphlet written by an eminent lawyer, Sir Henry Finch, and
entitled "The World's Great Restauration or the calling of the
Iewes, and (with them) of all the Nations and Kingdomes of the
Earth, to the Faith of Christ." Finch has been described as a
forerunner of Zionist nationalism, but this is foolish, for though
he liked to contemplate a golden future for the Chosen People,
he wanted such a development conducted along harshly Christian
lines. In the "Epistle Dedicatory" of his strange work he alleged
of the Jews that no nation was "so contemptible and abhorred
in the sight of God and men. And that worthily; for in thee is
found a sinne of all that ever were in the world the shamefullest.
To murder Him that created thee, that by his word and workes
did magnifie thee, and make thee so famous. . . ." Then in the
paragraph following these scoldings Finch put forward his main
proposition: "But the days of this thy sinfulness, God winking
at, doth now every where, and by all meanes, invite thee to
repentance. Out of all the places of thy dispersion, East, West,

North and South, his purpose is to bring thee home againe, & to marry thee to himselfe by faith for evermore." The book consists of numerous illustrations, especially from the books of Psalms and prophecy, showing that the Divine Plan for the Jewish people was such as he described, and that compliance with it would give them among many other blessings complete temporal dominion over the whole world. Finch's book brought great trouble to its author: the proposal that the King of England should be under the direction of a Jewish Emperor in Jerusalem put James into so fearful a " taking " that he ordered Finch's arrest, and he only liberated him after receiving suitable apologies and disclaimers. But Finch had done more than he knew. The King's action was fruitless, the book became a classic. It was to set a pattern for at least three hundred years, perhaps for longer.

We have already noticed the Judaic sects of the Protectorate, which, during Cromwell's rule, occupied the middle of the stage. When Puritanism went down at the Restoration, they went down with it, but with it stayed on to become an abiding influence on English life and ideas, profuse of sermonising and the printed word. Many pamphlets published in the eighteenth century tell us that their particular form of millennial tradition was still flourishing lustily in the hostile atmosphere of the Age of Reason. The title of one such work[1] runs as follows, and tells us everything we need to know: " Full and Final Restoration of the Jews and Israelites, evidently set forth to be nigh at hand: with their happy settlement in their own land, when the Messiah will establish his glorious kingdom on earth and begin the Millennium: with some hints that the late Act for the Naturalisation of Jews,[1] may contribute towards their more easy and speedy departure. Addressed to all Christians as well as Jews."

With Evangelicalism, that second spring of the Puritan genius, Gentile Zionism became prominent in England once more, and in the course of the nineteenth century developed into

[1]Quoted by Mr. A. M. Hyamson in his *Palestine under the Mandate*.
[2]This refers to Pelham's bill of 1753.

two distinct schools: the old-fashioned millennial type chiefly run by clergymen, and a new type which had a dual interest in the subject, religious and political, and which was for the most part the concern of laymen. In Lord Shaftesbury we can see both schools combined in one person. It was he who in 1838 persuaded Lord Palmerston to appoint a British vice-consul to Jerusalem, and further to charge this official with " protection to the Jews generally." In this action Shaftesbury was prompted by Evangelicalism, but we may suppose that Palmerston allowed himself to be guided by his step-son-in-law for Imperial reasons, and that Shaftesbury knew this.

The establishment of a British Consulate in Jerusalem was without question of moment to the Jewish national cause, but it is easy to over-estimate what this meant in history. Zionist writers have liked to see the growth of a mustard-tree here, but in fact, though Palmerston's instructions remained in force so long as the Consulate remained in existence (that is, until the First World War), the Zionist origin of this place was gradually forgotten, and no Zionist tradition was established in British policy. Nor did the fact of occasional Zionist representations, Jewish and Gentile, being received at the Foreign Office mean, as some apologists pretend, that the British Government became committed to any cause.

Much has been made also of the great number of English enthusiasts for some form of Jewish revival in Palestine who wrote the literature of the political school. Laurence Oliphant was the most courageous, energetic and amusing of these people, but George Eliot was the only Gentile writer of great distinction who can be claimed without hesitation as a member of the literary wing of this unorganised Gentile-Zionist party. Most of them were religiously minded eccentrics, or men of the stamp of Colonel George Gawler, the least competent Governor to be inflicted by the Mother Country on South Australia, who sought to bury his grief at manifold disappointments in this wondrous excitement. To the historian the lasting importance of this strange procession of mystical politicians and military men in retirement is not that they instituted an Apostolic succession, but that they came to express a wholly secularised version of their cult, such as was congenial to the Age of Diffusion.[1] Among Gentiles at large this new non-religious Zionism belonged as a force to the future. It can be said that the Gawlers and Oliphants and the rest exerted no influence on the course of events beyond keeping the fact of Jewish national aspirations known to the readers of their works. We may even say this of George Eliot.

Ecclesiastical Zionism, on the other hand, was destined now to produce a distinct effect beyond its own limited and accustomed circle. There is no need to recall the long list of English divines who contributed to millennial literature in the nineteenth century. It is only necessary to recognise that the Zionist tradition in such writing was never lost since the days of Finch. We may remember our old friend Richard Sibthorp again. In his correspondence with Dr. Bloxam during his last years there occur (with Sibthorpian frequency) millennial-minded references to the Holy Land. "We little know His purposes," he wrote in 1876, "except as prophecy gives us glimpses. Of one thing I am sure therefrom, that the present state of Palestine and Jerusalem is not to continue for ever. The seed of Abraham is to possess the land promised to him." This kind of thing was rare among Catholic priests, such as he then was, but a thousand

---

[1] Two quotations may (with the reader's indulgence) illustrate the transition. In a book called *Mount Lebanon*, published in 1853, the author, Colonel Charles Henry Churchill (another highly esteemed Gentile Zionist), urges the annexation by Great Britain of Egypt and Syria. The British Empire, he says, must make "imperative, though not exclusive claims upon her national feelings and sympathies. I say not exclusive, and advisedly; for the East, to an important portion of which I now invite public attention—the East, whose shores are washed by the Mediterranean Sea—the East of rock-hewn cities and colossal tombs, of heavenly poesy and gigantic art, of Jacob's might and Ishmael's wandering power, of David's lyre and of Isaiah's strain, of Abraham's faith and Immanuel's love,—where God's mysterious ways with man begun, and where in the fulness of time are to be accomplish'd,—this East, which may yet become the seat and centre of universal reign!—it also has claims on England's watchful vigilance and sympathising care." In this mingling of sacred and profane interests the latter use the former as an excuse, but by the time of Laurence Oliphant at the end of the century political considerations needed to pay no attention to holy ones in the view of the followers of this school. He even went so far as to say that: "It is somewhat unfortunate that so important a political and strategical question as the future of Palestine should be inseparably connected in the public mind with a favourite religious theory."

English parsons exchanged letters in such language every day. The type was commonly known.

Of such men a formidable example was to be found in Vienna in the eighteen-nineties. He was called William Hechler and for some years had held the post of chaplain to the British Embassy.

He had spent a great part of his life since ordination in studying the Millennium and the signs and wonders connected therewith. He had acquired a certain fame in Austrian society on account of a lecture on Ancient Egypt which he delivered in 1891. Of this he published an English translation called " The Oldest History of Man in the Light of Recent Researches," and one characteristic passage may give us an idea of this man's style of thinking. He said: " I have been asked the question: Did the Patriarchs really live such a length of time? I can now answer this question in the affirmative and in order to give it a thoroughly scientific investigation, I have attempted the construction of a calendar for the year of the Deluge." In 1884, seven years before this lecture, he had published a broadsheet called " The Restoration of the Jews to Palestine," which he distributed from his parsonage in Kilburn. It set forth a proposition exactly similar to that of Finch.

Unlike many other Gentile millennianists, Hechler had some experience of Jewish life. He was not an idle well-wisher of the people whom he loved so passionately. When the pogroms broke out he busied himself with philanthropic undertakings; he collected money for the settlement of Jews on to land in Palestine and he travelled there to help in the work. He was a man who got to know those whom he wanted to by exerting the charm of a mild but impressive personality. In the year 1882 he carried a personal letter from Queen Victoria to Abdul Hamid II. This was one of several missions. But though his life was fuller and busier than that of most Embassy chaplains, he never lost sight of his first passion. In 1896, when he had reached some final conclusions, he read *Der Judenstaat* after its first appearance in Vienna. He was amazed at a similarity between the date of its publication and the result of his most recent assessments, and he determined to discuss the matter with the author. Herzl recorded their meeting in his diary.

March 10th 1896

The Reverend William Hechler, Chaplain of the English Embassy here, came to see me.

A sympathetic, gentle fellow, with the long grey beard of a prophet. He is enthusiastic about my solution of the Jewish question. He also considers my movement a 'prophetic turning-point'—which he had foretold two years before. From a prophecy in the time of Omar (637 C.E.) he had reckoned that at the end of forty-two prophetic months (total 1260 years) the Jews would get Palestine back. The figure he arrived at was 1897-98.

When he had read my book he ran at once to Ambassador Monson and said: 'The prophesied movement is here.'

Hechler had a great feeling for royalty. So had Herzl. These two devised a plan: namely, that Hechler, who had an extensive court acquaintance, should arrange a meeting between his new friend and the Grand Duke of Baden. The latter was uncle by marriage to Kaiser Wilhelm II, on whom he had some influence, and it was hoped that he would persuade his nephew to adopt the role of Cyrus. A little over a month after the first meeting between Herzl and Hechler, the English Chaplain was in Karlsruhe at the same time as the Kaiser was paying a visit to his uncle, and he seized the opportunity of explaining Jewish irredentism to both potentates. A few days after, Herzl arrived from Vienna and was received in audience by the Grand Duke. "Hechler asked me whether I would put on a frock coat," he related in his diary. "I said no, because too festive attire on such an occasion might also be considered tactless. The Grand Duke wanted to speak to me, as it were, incognito. I therefore put on my well-tried redingote."

The Grand Duke had leanings towards Protestant Zionism,

and Hechler, by the deft use of his quiet charm and a disquisition on his prophetic discoveries and also by touching on the death of the Grand Duke's son, had been able to persuade him to take a sympathetic interest in Herzl's project. At the audience Herzl made a remarkable impression. He won his object. Though the Grand Duke excused himself from making a public declaration in favour of Zionism, he occupied himself whole-heartedly with this prophet's plan to meet the Kings and rulers. From this audience, which was followed by others, began Herzl's spectacular diplomatic career.

Hechler remained a faithful disciple to the end; he helped Herzl in many small ways but not again, after this, in a great one.[1] He represented the first meeting between Gentile Zionism and modern Jewish Zionism, a meeting which was to be repeated nearly twenty years later with great and decisive effect.

Herzl's adventures in the courts and ministries of Europe and the Turkish Empire seemed at the time to form a melancholy record of frustration. Kaiser Wilhelm was at first delighted with the prospect of his new part, but in the course of his famous trip to Palestine Buelow alarmed him out of a pro-Jewish policy. The dream of a German-protected Zionism vanished. Abdul Hamid was tempted by Herzl's design of enormous Jewish financial help to the Ottoman Empire in exchange for the Promised Land, but in the end he refused to concede Palestine on any terms. Instead, and most strangely, he offered facilities for Jewish settlement in Mesopotamia, Syria and Anatolia. Herzl refused these as he had long since recognised that Zionism without Palestine had no meaning. The King of Italy gave him his good wishes, and when Herzl met Prince Ferdinand of Bulgaria (the ruler of a land disgraced by anti-Semitic atrocities), the latter expressed himself forcibly as a friend of the Zionist ideal. Both the King and the Prince exchanged signed photographs with him, but did not proceed further.

Herzl's belief in the value of these royal interviews was per-

---

[1]He had hopes of receiving support from the royal family of Great Britain but after several attempts he failed to engage the interest of the Prince of Wales.

sistent. From the beginning he aimed to meet the Tzar. He was badly informed about Russia and never seems to have recognised that in the matter of anti-Semitism Nicholas II was as fanatically evil-minded as his father, if not more so. He went to St. Petersburg in 1903, but the desired audience never took place. Instead Herzl had to be satisfied with meeting the Minister of the Interior, von Plehve, and the Finance Minister, Count Witte. The latter treated him with a revolting jocularity before which he recorded his indignation, but von Plehve, who bore a hideous measure of guilt for the policy of Nicholas whereby the massacres had been revived and intensified, was a person of finesse, and by playing on Herzl's predilections he succeeded in taking him in. Nevertheless, in the light of history Herzl's Russian journey was not a failure for his cause. He left the country by way of Vilna, where he was received by an immense crowd of his people, some of whom had travelled there from far away. The effect in keeping enthusiasm on fire was enduring.

Herzl's last meeting with a European sovereign was with Pius X. This was the most interesting though least noticed of these interviews, and it is worth recalling the principal remarks made by the Pope and his visitor on this occasion because they have some later importance.

The meeting was not smooth. After the usual courtesies of such occasions, Herzl opened the discussion by describing his plan for according extra-territorial status to the Holy Places as part of the wider Zionist policy which was to relieve the pressing need of the Jews without reference to the religious interest. The Pope heard him coldly, and replied as follows:

" There are two possibilities: either the Jews retain their old belief and still expect the Messiah, who for us has come already, in which case they deny the Godhead of Jesus Christ, and we cannot help them; or they wish to go to Palestine as a people without any religion at all, in which case we can favour their doing so even less. The Jewish religion is the basis of our own, but this religion was superseded by the teachings of Jesus Christ, and for that reason it is not possible for us to give more support to the Jews than we have done.[1] They who ought to have been the first to acknowledge Jesus Christ have not done so up to this day."

Herzl struggled with a temptation to counter-attack with an angry witticism, but in the end he gave this telling reply: " Calamity and persecution were not, I think, the best means to convince our people."

These words roused the Pope to a spirited defence. " Our Lord came without power." he said. " He was poor. He came *in pace*. He persecuted no one. He was persecuted. He was abandoned—even by His apostles. His power grew after His time. Only then. Not for three hundred years from her foundation was the Church fully established as a power. The Jews had all that time in which to recognise the Godhead of Christ. But they do not do so even to-day."

Though he was bitterly anti-Catholic, more so than was usual even among the Jews of this time, Herzl, according to his own record, was moved by the majestic simplicity of the Pope's utterance.

After some further discussion, Herzl attempted, for the last time, to divert the conversation from theology, pressing on the Pope the terrible social and political situation of the Jews, and at this point we find curious evidence that, living in the cleaner air of Italy, Pius X, like his predecessor, had little idea of how frightful a thing modern anti-Semitism had become in Central Europe, France and Russia. Pius had been Bishop of Mantua for nine years and he obstinately believed that his experience of

---

[1]This is presumably a reference to the occasions (referred to above) when the Papacy had intervened to rescue Jews from the persecution of zealots, notably under Calixtus II, Gregory IX, Innocent IV, Gregory X, Martin V, and Paul III, and to the numerous bulls and official pronouncements discouraging belief in the " Blood Accusation " of ritual murder. (See Menasseh ben Israel's account of Papal protection in *Spes Israelis*.) The most famous of these Papal interventions is connected with the name of Clement XIV (1758-1769). He was appointed by Benedict XIV to examine the " Blood Accusation " in the light of an anti-Jewish movement in Poland. His report published under Clement XIII exonerates the Jews without qualification. This document has often been the subject of Jewish gratitude but in the first anti-Semitic period was unknown to or ignored by the anti-Semitic wing of the Neo-Ultramontanes. It was a peculiarity of this party that, while desiring Papal infallibility to be accepted more widely than is tolerable to theologians, they never scrupled to ignore Papal direction when this proved uncongenial.

the large Jewish colony there was sufficient for him to form a judgment. He refused to enter into any detailed discussion of the modern Jewish disaster, and (yet more surprisingly) Herzl did not press the advantage offered by the Pope's apparent ignorance. Pius concluded by reiterating his views. The Church prayed for Jewry, he said, and " this very day (January 25th) celebrates the feast of an unbeliever who on the Damascus Road was converted to the true faith in a marvellous manner. I can only tell you that if you succeed in settling your people in Palestine, we, on our side, shall prepare churches and priests to baptise you."

The audience terminated with a curious comedy. A certain Count Lippay, who had helped to arrange it, was ushered into the room. He seems to have been ill at ease at having introduced a non-Christian to the successor of St. Peter, and in a courtier-like effort to smooth matters he told the Pope that Herzl " was one who often spoke with approbation of Jesus Christ and His many fine qualities," the while Pius took snuff and wiped his nose with an enormous red cotton handkerchief. Herzl followed this unusual scene with interest, and was gratified when the Pope interrupted Lippay by saying: " No, no, on the contrary—I am delighted to have met the Signor Commendatore." When it was time to go, the Count knelt and kissed the fisherman's ring. Herzl had not performed this ceremony at the beginning of the interview, and although as a non-Christian he had thus followed correct procedure, he believed that the harshness of the Pope's words was due " to that missing kiss on the hand." Pettiness of this kind is at variance with everything we know of Pius X's character, but Herzl fancied that he detected an expression of extravagant joy on his face as Lippay did what he had refused to do. " I shook hands and bowed," he recorded of himself.

Herzl's interview with the Pope has one unique characteristic. The idea of a mass conversion of the Jews, once prominent in Gentile Zionism, had been lost. In the many encounters of Zionists with Gentiles of great position before 1917, this was the only one, so far as is known, in which the traditional Christian hope was mentioned, or in which the orthodox Christian objection to a return without such a hope was stated plainly to a Jewish leader. This was the last appearance of Orthodox Gentile Zionism in the story. The effect was transient.

There were, besides those we have mentioned, several meetings with rulers and princes which are not worth recalling. Others such as the famous ones with members of the British Government are more easily considered with the Congresses they influenced.

We have seen how the dispersed Jews were apt to form themselves into hostile parties; we have seen how Moses Mendelssohn was attacked and impeded not by Gentiles so much as by factions of his own people. In somewhat the same way Herzl had to contend with a multitude of Jewish enemies from the moment he became a Zionist. The two great philanthropists of the Jewish world, Baron Hirsch and Baron Edmond de Rothschild, refused emphatically to have anything to do with his project. In 1897 Dr. Moritz Guedemann, Chief Rabbi of Vienna, published a pamphlet, *Nationaljudentum*, as a counterblast to *Der Judenstaat*, and a plan that Zionist delegates from all over the world should assemble in Munich was frustrated not by the Bavarian Government but by a group of German rabbis, the " Protestrabbiner," as Herzl called them, who saw in Zionism a denial of the Messianic doctrine. These were a few of many similar reactions.

Of even greater danger to the cause was a tendency for Zionism itself to split into fragments from the inner party politics which characterised it from the beginning. The old guard of Hibbath Zion in the East and the West often resented the converts and the noise they made in the world, traditionalists turned against modernists, Eastern Jews would look down on German Jews as soft-livers who were half ashamed of being Jews, and Germans would resent the rough manners and poverty of the Russians; there were quarrels prompted by personal matters; there were outbreaks of class warfare; there were heresies and schisms at some of which we shall look, not here, but when we reach a later stage in the story.

After much discussion and wrangling and calming of hurt feelings and bringing together of the new men with the old lovers of Zion, it was decided not to challenge the Protest-rabbiner, but to hold a Jewish assembly in Basle in the August of 1897. This was the first Zionist Congress, the first authoritative assembly of the Jewish nation since its suppression under the Roman Empire. The Zionist Congresses might be challenged by many sects of the Rabbis but for all that they proceeded from within and had allegiance. Compared with such a circumstance it was of little importance that the first of the Congresses was not much noticed by the world at large, or that little interest was taken in its principal decision to found a " Heimstätte " or " National Home."[1]

The Zionist leader had taken a course which was to end in the realisation of all his dreams, and yet for some time he remained in partial ignorance of the impulse which brought people under his rule. Like most of his contemporaries, like his forerunner Leon Pinsker, he forgot the persistence of the Age of Faith, and as a result he came near to losing his position as leader. This happened after the fifth Zionist Congress in 1901, and after his negotiations with British ministers, in which for the third time[2] a British Government attempted, without success, to establish a Zionist tradition of policy.

Lord Lansdowne, Foreign Secretary in 1902, was the first

[1] This term was the invention of Max Nordau. In an article published in 1920 Nordau made a candid assertion that it was intended to deceive by its mildness and was in no sense an abjuration of the Jewish claim to a Palestinian state. He said: " I did my best to persuade the claimants of the Jewish state in Palestine that we might find a circumlocution that would express all we meant, but would say it in a way so as to avoid provoking the Turkish rulers of the coveted land. I suggested " Heimstätte " as a synonym for ' State ' . . . This is the history of the much commented expression. It was equivocal, but we all understood what it meant. To us it signified ' Judenstaat ' then and it signifies the same now. . . . Now there is no reason to dissimulate our real aim." (From the MS. of the article, lent to the writer by Mr. John Carter.)

[2] We may consider Cromwell's as the first, Palmerston's as the second of these endeavours.

British statesman to attempt a wide-scale territorial settlement
of the Jews. This came about in a devious manner. A Zionist
financial trust had been formed in London in 1898, and a Zionist
proposal had already been put to the Colonial Office that Jews
should be allowed to occupy land in Cyprus on a national scale,
when, on the Colonial Secretary's advice, Herzl as President of
the Zionist organisation approached Lord Lansdowne with a
request for his good offices. This was because the Cyprus scheme
had given way to one for Egyptian territory. It was believed
that the Wadi el Arish in the Sinai peninsula could be colonised
if water from the Nile were diverted for the purpose. Lansdowne
agreed to help and there ensued a three-cornered correspondence
between the Foreign Office, Herzl and Lord Cromer, followed
first by the despatch of a technical mission of enquiry, and then
by a personal visit to Cairo by Herzl, where he tried to engage
Lord Cromer's sympathy. We have a glimpse of these two very
different men at a hot dinner-party in the British Agency. " Do
you realise," said Herzl to the great Proconsul, " that if I wished
I could gain Palestine by conquest and bloodshed, and that if I
only consulted my predilections I should much prefer to do the
business that way? " Lord Cromer was deeply impressed, and
sceptical.

It has been supposed by some Jewish authorities that there
were intrigues on the British side which prevented the El Arish
project coming to anything, but Lord Cromer's views as they
are reported in the correspondence between Lansdowne and
Herzl are perfectly plain and in keeping with the common sense
of the man. He wished to avoid complications and risky enterprises under his jurisdiction, and said so. His word was final.

Then, by a remarkable coincidence (too subtly described as
the result of another intrigue) the Colonial Secretary, Joseph
Chamberlain, strode back on to the scene which he had opened.
He had been to Africa while the El Arish negotiations were proceeding. He now summoned Herzl to his Ministry. " In the
course of my journey I saw the very country for you," he said.
" That's Uganda. The coast region is hot, but the farther you

get into the interior (i.e. into Kenya) the more excellent the climate becomes . . . So I thought to myself: that would be just the country for Dr. Herzl." So began the famous " Uganda Project."

In Chamberlain's enthusiasm for Zionism, and it was a passionate thing with him, we must not suppose that we see another manifestation of the Millennial tradition. Here was no successor of Lord Shaftesbury, no spiritual brother of Hechler and Sibthorp. Chamberlain's interest in Jewish fortunes was financial. The money power of the Jews was at its greatest then. It was apt to be grossly misrepresented. It was exaggerated, as much by the Jews as by Gentiles, and supposed to be far more homogeneous and organised than it was or could have been; it was accused of crimes to which it could only be accessory, and its unselfish deeds, such as those of Hirsch and Edmond de Rothschild, were often forgotten; but it was as great as any financial power can be without the open thrust of Government. Chamberlain wanted to tie this force to the British Empire, and in all the written or spoken words which have been preserved from him concerning this matter no other or deeper impulse of statesmanship can be discovered. He never pretended that it was otherwise. There was nothing strange in this. What was most wonderful was the effect of Chamberlain's proposal on the Jews themselves, especially when we remember that he was making an offer of some of the best colonising land in all tropic Africa, and when we remember, too, the time at which these things happened.

The interview between him and Herzl took place on April 3rd of 1903. A few days later the Russian Government organised a fresh pogrom in Kishinev in Bessarabia, where the attack on the Jewish quarter lasted twenty-four hours, resulting in the murder of fifty people, including children, and the injury of more than a thousand. Terror spread once more. The roads from Russia were crammed anew with refugees. Later in the same year Herzl went to Russia for his fatuous interviews with von Plehve and Witte, and it was on his way back from St.

Petersburg, while he was stopping for a day at Vilna surrounded by crowds of his devoted fellow-religionists, and fellow-nationals as he now thought of them, that he received a letter from Sir Clement Hill in London renewing Chamberlain's offer in official terms. Herzl received the news with tears of joy. It seemed that his life work was accomplished and he hastened to communicate the result of his labours to his followers. A week after he left Vilna, a well-known English Jew, Leopold Greenberg,[1] read Hill's letter to the Sixth Zionist Congress in Basle.

We have the record of one of the Russian delegates, Dr. Chaim Weizmann, of the effect on the assembly: " The delegates were electrified by the news. This was the first time in the exilic history of Jewry that a great Government had officially negotiated with the elected representatives of the Jewish people. The identity, the legal personality, of the Jewish people had been re-established . . . But as soon as the substance of the offer . . . sank home, a spirit of disquiet, dejection and anxiety spread through the Congress."

Experience had taught Herzl that Zionism must not lose sight of Zion. His view and that of Max Nordau was that the horrors which surrounded Russian Jewry made some instant means of relief necessary and they explained that Kenya would never be anything but a " Nachtasyl," a halting-place in the journey towards the Promised Land. But the political instinct of the Jews saw danger here, and in the tempestuous scenes which followed the reading of the letter, in the tearing down of maps of Uganda, the collective mourning by Russian delegates, not for the slaughtered innocents of the Pale but for the loss, as they fancied it, of the historic land of the Jews, it was brought home to Herzl that compared with remembrance of Jerusalem even the perils of anti-Semitism were a small thing in the mind of his people. Among the Jews assembled in Basle for this Congress were two delegates from Kishinev. They both voted against acceptance of the British offer.[2]

[1]He was the editor of *The Jewish Chronicle*.

[2]In December of this same year a Zionist fanatic attempted to murder Max Nordau in Paris on account of his support of the Uganda project.

In the July of 1904, a little less than a year later, Herzl died at the age of forty-four. It has been ridiculously pretended that he perished of grief at the failure of the Uganda scheme. Nothing of the sort happened. He died because he suffered from angina pectoris. Nevertheless, though there was no broken heart in the case, the early end of his life had about it so tragic an air that it is often referred to as something to be mourned among the calamities of all time. This is probably a mistake. The very brevity of his life, especially in his Zionist career, added to its splendour, therefore to its effectiveness. At the time he seemed to have failed. In the Congresses he had only with difficulty prevented a division of Zionism and he could not prevent minor schisms. His meetings with royalty had amounted to nothing more than a series of glamorous social jaunts; his only fruitful interview, that with Joseph Chamberlain, had been annulled by a rebellion of his own people; but, in truth, because all his enterprises were cut short they provoked new life. He was that recurrent and tremendous phenomenon, the outside meteor whose impact with a world changes its course. None of this was visible in the early nineteen hundreds. As though hiding itself, Zionism went into a ten-year retreat in which little was heard of it, and in which those who had once heard of it, even among the Jews, became forgetful.

We should remember one of the last glimpses to be had of the movement by the outside world as it sank out of sight into withdrawal, even though this means reciting a story which has been told many times before.

The scene is Manchester in the rainy January of 1906 in the constituency of Arthur Balfour during the General Election of that year. The local chairman of the Conservative Party was called Charles Dreyfus. He was a Jew who divided his life between British party politics and the local Zionist organisation. One day Arthur Balfour asked this man to explain an event of his premiership which, he said, had utterly baffled his understanding, namely the rejection by a Zionist Congress of Chamberlain's offer. Dreyfus himself was a member of the " Ugandist " group, but he was a fair-minded man and he told Balfour that there was a member of the other party then in Manchester, who could explain to him the motive of this extraordinary denial. It was one of the most pleasing things in Balfour's character that immense immediate preoccupations such as elections, the fall of the Conservative Party, personal defeat, a campaign of calumny, could not for one moment numb his passion to study the deeper flows of human destiny. So he arranged with Dreyfus that one evening Dr. Weizmann, then a man of thirty-one practising chemistry at Manchester University, should be brought to see him " for a quarter of an hour." Dr. Weizmann came to Balfour's hotel and stayed for seventy-five minutes endeavouring to explain the foundation of the movement he was one day to lead.

" I looked at my listener," he recorded afterwards, " and suddenly became afraid that (his) appearance of interest and courtesy might be nothing more than a mask. I felt that I was sweating blood and I tried to find some less ponderous way of expressing myself. . . .

" . . . suddenly I said: ' Mr. Balfour, supposing I were to offer you Paris instead of London, would you take it?'

" He sat up, looked at me, and answered: ' But Dr. Weizmann, we have London.'

" ' That is true,' I said. ' But we had Jerusalem when London was a marsh.'

" He leaned back, continued to stare at me, and said two things which I remember vividly: The first was: ' Are there many Jews who think like you?'

" I answered: ' I believe I speak the mind of millions of Jews whom you will never see, and who cannot speak for themselves.'

" To this he said: ' If that is so, you will one day be a force.' "

As Dr. Weizmann was about to leave, Arthur Balfour made one of those simple remarks which often caused him to be misunderstood by his hearers. " It is curious," he said, " the Jews I meet are quite different." Dr. Weizmann boldly replied that

Balfour evidently knew " the wrong sort of Jews." The two men did not see one another again for eight years.

We will not relate anything more here of the main movement of Zionism during the period of obscurity. But we should briefly consider one Jewish episode which occurred between the year of Herzl's death and those of the Great War. Though this episode did not belong to the central line of Zionist history, it has a curious importance when viewed in the perspective of forty years.

This is what happened. Herzl himself had abandoned the Uganda project without any reserve as soon as he knew the mind of the Russian Jews, but his departure from the straight road of orthodoxy, though so brief, had been long enough to cause a minor schism which persisted for several years. From the defeated " Ugandists " a new party collected, and under the title of " The Jewish Territorial Organisation " set itself to find land, anywhere in the world, on which Jews might be settled in large numbers. The moving spirit in this enterprise was Israel Zangwill, a Jew of Russian origin born in London. The new party had already come very near to success in 1909 in an effort to obtain a colonising concession from the Turkish Empire. In 1912 it appeared almost certain for a moment that they would get all that they wanted from the Portuguese.

A peculiar problem had beset Portugal since her great days: here was a country too small to wage war or build great defences, which was the inheritor of Imperial possessions. Most of the Portuguese Empire had been removed by larger powers, but a good deal remained and the world's debate had been livened for more than a century by suggestions that the residue might be redistributed in turn so as to appease eminent and dangerous hungers and prolong the reign of peace. Constantly alarmed by proposals of this kind, the Portuguese wanted to increase their colonial population by any means. In the words of one of their administrators, " They welcomed colonial settlers of whom they had no cause to feel afraid." Then a man called José d'Almada, an official in the Imperial offices in Lisbon, had the idea that the Jews of Russia and Eastern Europe might solve the problem by settling in Angola. He was able to exert influence on political society and a movement for carrying out a mass-transportation of Jews was rapidly and successfully organised. As a result, in June of 1912, a Bill authorising the colonisation of Angola by Jewish immigrants received an unanimous vote from the Portuguese Cortes. By this time, however, when the proposal had passed thoroughly through parliamentary hands, it had suffered modifications especially in two respects: there was to be no mass colonisation, but Jews were to be allowed in as individuals not as a people, and secondly, the administration of Angola was to remain the business of the Portuguese Government in Lisbon, an almost inevitable provision when we remember the preoccupations of this weak and heavily endowed people.

There followed an angry quarrel. The Jewish Territorial Organisation was holding a conference in Vienna at the time, and on receiving news of the decision of the Cortes, the Committee sent a telegram whose haughty tone must be supposed to indicate a determination to get out of the entanglement. The offer was described as a deed which " softened the memory of the expulsion of the Jews under King Manoel in the 15th century," thus, as it were, placing the Portuguese Government in the position of remorseful criminals who wished to acknowledge their indebtedness. The message went on to say that in view of the unsettled state of Angola it could not recommend Jewish people to accept the Portuguese invitation without further guarantees of protection from the State, and without the greater powers of self-protection which would have gone with a greater degree of autonomy.

The Portuguese considered this response to be ungrateful and insulting, and the sense of the Cortes turned against the Jews. A feeling of hostility might have spread to the country at large, had it not been that no final action was taken by one side or the other; the matter was allowed to linger and quietly disappear. But there remained the impression of an inexplicable event: the Portuguese from an impulse which though self-interested was generous, had made a magnificent offer to the Jewish Territorial Organisation, and because they could not meet the latter on all points, they suddenly found themselves treated as though they had committed an atrocity. All they had done was to offer land, and all the result for them was to be held up to the world as anti-Semites. They had made the mistake, especially easy in a period when material success seemed to be an infallible sign of the ascent of man, of supposing that because the Jews were the subject of pillage and contempt they were easily disposed of.

It seems that none of the leading politicians of the world noticed this strange incident, and it is certain that none of them remembered or examined it when they should have done so five years later. As a whole Zionism was once more a movement without fame. Among Gentiles the fulfilment of Jewish aspirations was once more the concern of people of whimsical mind, and very few others.

Let us now consider August, 1914.

The outbreak of war might have been expected to set difficult problems before the Jews of Europe. Treachery, it might be conjectured, could tempt them in that hour, in a fair disguise. The German Jew had grave reasons for qualifying his patriotic loyalty, the French Jew could remember the Dreyfus conspiracy, and the contented English Jew was not likely to be so distressed by news of the battle of Tannenberg as his Gentile fellow-subjects.[1] Nowhere could the struggle engage his enthusiasm; so it might have seemed to a logical observer. But in the event the Jews of Europe (outside Russia) were not principally moved by logical consideration of their wrongs. The reason is not hard to find. Once more we must remember their joyful interest in the triumphs of that age. This was so much greater than their grief at its misdeeds against themselves that in Germany and

[1]There was not a little anti-Semitism in popular English propaganda of the first war. It was mainly directed at their alleged prominence among the "profiteers," and at German origins.

Western Europe the Jews naturally followed popular patriotic tendencies.

In America it was somewhat otherwise. The presence of a great host of refugees from the pogroms impressed Jewish opinion more violently than the same thing did elsewhere, and the New World was thought of as the antithesis of ancient Slav unredemption. In the first part of the war, Jewish influence in America tended towards neutrality coloured by hopes that Germany would destroy the Romanov Empire. This Jewish disposition was destined to have results of the greatest possible importance.

In the crisis of 1914, the chiefs of the Zionist movement did not attempt to impose their own leadership. Their headquarters had for some years been in Berlin. From here they opened a branch office in Copenhagen whence they communicated with their followers on both sides, and one of the first tasks of the Copenhagen office was to inform Zionists that the Executive considered itself neutral. Such a policy was inescapable and (as appears later) very wise, but being in contradiction to the feelings of most Jews it cost the leaders their authority. This was in any case slight. The political fortunes of the movement were low in 1914, and one reason why its followers were unmolested by any of the warring Governments in Europe[1] was that they were noticed by so few people at the head of affairs. Nevertheless, to this obscurity in high places there were exceptions of a curious kind. They were to be found in England. In the early part of the war Zionism became prominent in the minds of several British ministers and public men. In this country, a resplendent false dawn once more illuminated the Jewish Cause for a little while.

There was no member of the Zionist executive in England in 1914, and so, in spite of discouragements from Copenhagen,

[1] The Turkish Government alone took official action against Zionists. Anti-Jewish atrocities continued in Russia till the end of Nicholas II's reign but there is no evidence that these were anti-Zionist.

the leadership was taken by Dr. Chaim Weizmann,[1] a member of the " Greater Actions Committee" and the moving spirit in the anti-Ugandist " Democratic Faction." We last saw him in Manchester explaining to Arthur Balfour the reasons why Chamberlain's offer had been refused. That meeting remained without a sequel until 1914, when Dr. Weizmann met Charles Prestwick Scott, the editor of the *Manchester Guardian*. As the career of Herzl took a new turn when he met William Hechler, so did that of Dr. Weizmann when Jewish Zionism in his person confronted Gentile Zionism once more in the person of this famous journalist.

Scott was not a Zionist at the time. He was to be converted. He came of a Unitarian family and would have entered the ministry of that sect as a young man if he had not been appalled by what he described as the weight of " external authority" opposed to its doctrine. As a result of these doubts of Unitarian validity, his piety in after life, though ardent, was somewhat vague. It was typical of his times with its Liberal, Modernist, and faintly mystical character. He reverenced Christ as a " moral ideal," hesitating to define the matter further. "Taking the sum of things," he wrote, " is there not something in Matthew Arnold's definition of God (based on the prophets) as ' the power not ourselves that makes for righteousness.' " The passionate religion of Zionism with its ancient continuity and visible sacraments of race and soil was much better suited to the mind of this Bible-reading, energetic and able man than the diluted Christianity and perplexed idealism of the Age of Diffusion.

Unconsciously following Hechler, Scott made the Jewish leader known to people in authority, with the difference that these introductions were to men who were all worth knowing. Through Scott Dr. Weizmann met Lloyd George, and was

[1]This leadership was not taken by Dr. Weizmann without considerable difficulty, but the reader is not invited to explore the elaborate party-strife within Zionism except when necessary. Nahun Sokolov, as appears later, had a strong legal claim to Zionist leadership which he generously allowed to go by default. Dr. Gaster was the most indefatigable challenger of Weizmann's position.

reintroduced to Balfour.[1] The outward purpose in the resulting interviews was to discuss Dr. Weizmann's chemical discoveries and find some means of putting them to a war usage, but the more perennial interests of Zionism and the fate of the Jews were present from the very beginning. "When Dr. Weizmann was talking of Palestine," Lloyd George confided to a Jewish friend, "he kept bringing up place names which were more familiar to me than those on the Western Front." "You know," said Arthur Balfour at the end of his first meeting with him in 1914, "I was thinking of that conversation of ours and I believe that when the guns stop firing you may get your Jerusalem."

At the same time a yet more wonderful prospect opened for Zion, in another quarter. In November of 1914 Mr. Asquith asserted in the House of Commons "It is the Ottoman Government and not we who have rung the death-knell of Ottoman Dominion, not only in Europe but in Asia," and in these words the sick man of Europe was officially declared to have forfeited the sympathy of his doctors and to be fair game for their pillage. One member of the Government immediately took action.

The President of the Local Government Board was Mr. Herbert Samuel,[2] the first practising Jew to be a member of a British Government. On the day of Asquith's statement he called on Sir Edward Grey to obtain his sympathy for "the restoration of a Jewish state" following the collapse of Turkish Imperial rule. Grey replied that the idea "had a strong sentimental attraction for him," and added that if France put forward plans for Syria it would be "important to safeguard" this proposition. Grey was true to these ideas for the rest of his career. For the second time in history a British Foreign Secretary gave full and open support to Jewish nationalism; for the second time the aspirations of Zionism were abandoned at what looked like the hour of fulfilment.

[1] Some doubt exists as to the order and circumstances of these meetings. It appears that Dr. Weizmann's own record contains some slips of memory. (See *Fifty Years of Zionism*, a historical analysis of Dr. Weizmann's *Trial and Error* by Oscar K. Rabinovicz, Robert Anscombe & Co., 1950.)

[2] Now Viscount Samuel.

The prose of Mr. Asquith was the rock on which these new hopes were overturned. On January 28th of 1915 he wrote in his diary: " I have just received from Herbert Samuel a memorandum headed ' The Future of Palestine '! He goes on to argue, at considerable length and with some vehemence, in favour of the British annexation of Palestine. . . . He thinks we might plant in this not very promising territory about three or four million European Jews, and that this would have a good effect upon those who are left behind. . . . I confess I am not attracted by this proposed addition to our responsibilities, but it is a curious illustration of Dizzy's favourite maxim that ' race is everything ' to find this almost lyrical outburst proceeding from the well-ordered and methodical brain of Herbert Samuel."

Two months later Mr. Samuel distributed a revised version of his memorandum. Certain rhetorical passages had been removed, and his practical suggestions for a protectorate had been considerably expanded. For the governance of a Jewish Palestine of the future, he proposed several regimes from which the Allies might choose; he suggested a French or international Protectorate, or even the immediate formation of an autonomous Palestinian state. His own preference on political, sentimental and strategical grounds was for a British protectorate within the Empire. Several eminent conversions to Zionism resulted from this document, notably those of Lord Haldane and Lord Bryce. But nothing could move the Prime Minister. On March 13th he returned to the matter in his private journal:

" I think I have already referred to Herbert Samuel's dithyrambic memorandum, urging that in the carving up of the Turks' Asiatic dominions we should take Palestine, into which the scattered Jews would in time swarm back from all the quarters of the globe, and in due course obtain Home Rule. Curiously enough, the only other partisan of this proposal is Lloyd George,[1] who I need not say, does not care a damn for

[1]It is difficult to understand how Asquith could have been unaware of Grey's interest which persisted in active form till his resignation. Among papers published by the Soviet Government in 1924 is a despatch from Grey to Sir George Buchanan of March 13th, 1916, instructing him to obtain from the Russian Government serious consideration of this question.

the Jews or their past or their future, but thinks it will be an outrage to let the Holy places pass into the possession or under the protection of ' agnostic, atheistic France.' " He was never to change his mind. At the end of his life Jewish irredentism still seemed to him " fantastic " and outside all practical policy.

Confronted by the indifference of the Prime Minister, and surrounded by the disaster of the whole Western world, the hopes of Israel began to diminish to their accustomed size, but not before this latest false dawn had been noticed by a man who was to play a decisive part in the ultimate success of the Zionist movement. That success was probably inevitable, but in fact it came about through the further action of Gentile Zionism, and to understand the next turn of events we should consider the character of the man who set these into movement once more. His name was Sir Mark Sykes.

He came of a Yorkshire family. He was born to apparent good fortune, but the happiness of his circumstances was largely an illusion. We should look at these to understand why he acted as he did. Nothing in this man's early life had been propitious. He was the neglected child of parents who had been married against their wills. His father, Sir Tatton Sykes, was a man of harsh and sorrowful disposition which made him loveless even towards his only son. His mother was a woman of passionate will and talent[1] which had been turned inward with destructive effect. From his wretchedly divided home Mark Sykes found no relief in the adventures of upbringing, and was to remember his schooling with lifelong horror. His young manhood was burdened with disappointment in the form of inherited debts and the destruction of his family home through fire. He had been cheated of early happiness; he seemed doomed to be cheated of all the good things of this world, given to him in such profusion, plucked away so often and so inexorably.

His life proves one fact abundantly: that the science of psychology as popularly understood is great nonsense. If ever

---

[1]The curious reader may consult her violent, ill-conceived, but not unamusing novels, notably *The Macdonalds*.

a man had cause for embitterment here he was. But Mark Sykes grew up to be the most joyous of happy beings. The faults of his temperament were not in the direction of melancholia but rather of an exaggerated exuberance, of a wild relish of adventure and of the arresting or droll contrasts to be experienced in a world of marvellous variety. The miseries of his childhood and youth left no rancour in his mind towards his parents, but they did leave some tendency to escapism.

The surface of comedy which he showed the world deceived many people as to his true nature. Remembering him at a distance of a few years, T. E. Lawrence described him in these words: " Laughs were his triumphs. His instincts lay in parody: by choice he was a caricaturist rather than an artist, even in statesmanship. He saw the odd in everything, and missed the even. He would sketch out in a few dashes a new world, all out of scale, but vivid as a vision of some sides of the thing we hoped."

In reality there was a deep strain of gravity constantly forming his mind and actions. His distracted early home had been weakly held together by a great common preoccupation. The family had Protestant traditions which had once been vigorous and were now weakening; they also had the faint but august memory of a Catholic martyr. Sir Tatton Sykes was a major figure in the later stages of the Gothic Revival, and somewhat in the spirit of Pugin his passion for the architecture formed by Catholic liturgy (he built nearly twenty Gothic churches) drew him towards the old faith itself. He presented to his home parish a succession of clergymen of extreme Anglo-Catholic views and practice, whereafter candles, censers, vestments and the like pomps of Rome became the enforced but not welcome spiritual food of the Puritan-minded countryfolk of his part of East Yorkshire. On his wife these innovations had a decisive effect. Jessica Sykes treated one of the extremist clergymen as her confessor, and in the course of their relationship he made a remarkable confession to her. He was convinced, he said, that the Christian establishment and tradition was to be found only in Roman

Catholicism. He urged her to go where he dared not. She was received into the Catholic Church on the 25th of November of 1882. She insisted that she must bring her son with her into the fold. Sir Tatton Sykes hesitated, then agreed. By such extraordinary means Mark Sykes became a Catholic between the ages of three and four, and from his early childhood his religion was his chief preoccupation. He grew up to be an unconventional Catholic, inclined towards modernism, an enthusiast for reunion of the Churches on lines of compromise, but this state of feeling did not mean any indifferentism. He was a man of ardent character and he took no decision either of a public or private kind without considering his duty as a member of his Church. This is the first point to recognise for an understanding of the part he played in the history of the Jewish people. There is a second one of nearly equal importance.

From his mother he inherited the enthusiasm in his character, from his father certain less obvious but profound essentials of temperament. Sir Tatton Sykes, for all his withered heart, was a man of romantic disposition who sought relief from the world in distant things. He loved the vanished Middle Ages. He sought them not only in Gothic building but in frequent travels in Oriental countries. On one expedition to the Near East his son Mark was taken with the impedimenta of the baggage train, and memories of this adventure were among the first of the child's life. They made a lasting impression on him. He inherited his father's Gothic predilections to the full,[1] and from his earliest days he remained fascinated by the archaic splendours and the primitive peasant simplicity of the Islamic world. An event served to deepen these feelings. His education had been of the most haphazard order, obtained, as best he might, from a large variety of schools at none of which he stayed long; but the process ended at Cambridge. In 1897 he entered Jesus College. The Master was Arthur Morgan, who understood the young man thoroughly. Seeing that the outlandish up-

[1] At the end of his life he attempted a Saxon Revival. He designed a War Memorial, later erected at Sledmere, in the Saxon style, and attempted, but without success, to write a Saxon chronicle.

bringing of his charge could not be given a conventional finish he granted him leave of absence for two terms on condition that he spent the time travelling in the Ottoman Empire and producing a record. Since his first childhood adventure Sykes had made other youthful journeys to the East, but the direction of his talents was not settled until this moment. He kept his side of the bargain,[1] and from now on it was his aim to establish himself among the great Orientalists of the English tradition. It is doubtful whether, in the short space of his life, he succeeded in this ambition, during a period which manifested unparalleled excellence in this field, but within the fifteen years which elapsed between his journey from Cambridge and the opening of the war he drew on himself the approval of scholars and the attention of certain leading men, notably Lord Curzon and Lord Kitchener. When he became a Member of Parliament in 1911 this led to political promotion. The rebirth of Jewish nationalism owes an unacknowledged debt to the Gothic Revival and to a generous action by the Master of a Cambridge College.

It is not known, to revert to the main current of our story, how Mark Sykes became a Zionist, but there is no doubt as to who first taught him Zionist principles. This was Dr. Moses Gaster, the Haham, or Chief Rabbi of the Sephardic Community in London. He was a Roumanian Jew who had settled in England after having been expelled from Bucharest as a dangerous agitator for Jewish rights, and he was one of the most versatile scholars of his day, making remarkable contributions to Hebraic, Roumanian and Slavonic studies. How he met Mark Sykes is not known. It is probable that they came to know each other before 1914 as members of learned Orientalist societies to which they both belonged. According to a statement in one of Mark Sykes's speeches,[2] the Rabbi began to open his friend's eyes to the meaning of Zionism in the last days of 1915.

---

[1] The interested reader should consult *Through Five Turkish Provinces* by Mark Sykes. The late Sir Dennison Ross regarded this as containing the best record of Levantine English.

[2] Address to the London Opera House meeting of December, 1917.

SIR MARK SYKES
From a portrait by the Zionist artist Leopold Pilichowski

In the autumn of that year Sykes had been appointed one of the two " Assistant Secretaries to the War Cabinet," the other one being Mr. Leopold Amery.[1] The post was a little more than it sounded. The two Assistants enjoyed the rank of Under-Secretaries of State; their official duty was to prepare " Intelligence Summaries " at regular intervals for the information of Ministers, Mr. Amery dealing with European and Far Eastern affairs, Mark Sykes with the problems of Islam, but beyond these assignments they were allowed what must seem to a later generation extraordinarily wide powers in the making of policy. Sykes had been chosen on Lord Kitchener's recommendation because it was believed that his knowledge of the Turkish Empire together with his partly French education fitted him to conduct negotiations which had been made necessary by the possibility of British success in Syria. At that time the whole structure of the Entente was in danger from French jealousy because of the presence of British armies in a part of the world which many Frenchmen believed they had inherited from the crusaders, and those who approved the Samuel memorandum, notably Sir Edward Grey and Arthur Balfour, felt uneasy at the same time that its proposals might flurry these sensibilities afresh. It is as certain as such things can be that when Mark Sykes read the Samuel Memorandum among the papers entrusted to his official care, his first move was to consult Dr. Gaster.

How weary the Zionists must have grown of planting seeds in fertile soil! We have seen how, since the days of Lord Palmerston, they were never without influential friends who might have turned their dreams into reality, men who listened to them with interest, even emotion, and seemed on the brink of action, and who then drew back, chilled by second thoughts. Mark Sykes seemed no exception. When he learned what Zionism meant from his friend the Haham, he was fascinated by its poetry, but he did not see it as a possible feature of practical policy and for several months he did nothing which might have

[1] Mr. Amery has supplied much of the information for what follows, elucidating the curious official position held by himself and Mark Sykes. In the accounts of the Balfour Declaration written by those who took part in its origins this is rarely described correctly.

served to establish any Jewish rights in the promised land. The British decision to conduct secret negotiations with France for a Syrian understanding was finally taken at a meeting of the War Committee held at 10 Downing Street on December 16th of 1915 in the course of which British policy in the Islamic East was examined.[1] Sir Mark Sykes was summoned to express his views and in so doing he made no mention of Zionism although he spoke at some length on the future of the Levant. Immediately after this he was instructed to begin official talks with Monsieur Georges Picot, a former French Consul-General in Beyrut, who at this time was the Counsellor of the French Embassy in London.

From the diary of Dr. Gaster, a cryptic document, often illegible, in which appointments, private thoughts, and narrative are not easily disentangled, a fragmentary record of Sykes's first steps in Zionism is just discernible. In March of 1916[2] Sykes and Picot went to St. Petersburg, and in a conversation with Sazanov Sykes discussed the possibility that Zionism might solve the Jewish problem of Russia. Then, after his return to England, he showed in one small incident that his Zionist sympathies had by this time grown strong. The most eminent English Jewish scholar of those days was Lucien Wolf. He was also an extreme opponent of Zionism and he presented an aide-memoire to the Foreign Office some time in the early part of 1916, pointing out the dangers of Jewish nationalism. When the document came to Sykes he prevented its communication to the French Government, thereby incurring an official rebuke. In May Sykes saw for the first time a way of using Zionism effectively.

Pro-German feelings in America were supposed to be harming the Allied cause throughout the world, and the idea came to Sykes (evidently from Dr. Gaster) that if American Jewry could be attached to the Allies all might be changed. His first endeavour was to get Picot to share his point of view. Helped by Dr. Gaster, he succeeded to some extent, for after much persuasion Picot accepted the principle, which Sykes most likely borrowed

[1]From a memorandum in the Sledmere Papers.
[2]At this time the Sykes-Picot negotiations were enlarged to include appeasement of Russian Eastern ambitions.

from the Samuel memorandum, that the Sanjak of Jerusalem should be under an international regime sympathetic to the growth of some form of Zionist establishment. With this to offer, so it was believed, the German-minded Jews of America could be won. On Picot's recommendation (we may suppose) the initiative was taken by the French Government, who despatched Professor Guillaume Basch of the Sorbonne on a mission of propaganda to the United States.

The mission was a failure. American Jewish opinion had been moved by the contrast between Russian barbarism and German orderliness. Every Russian retreat left horrible evidence of atrocity towards Jews. Every German advance into Poland was accompanied by exemplary regulations regarding the treatment of Jews in occupied territory. These facts made a profounder impression than the vague propaganda of Basch.[1]

Sykes was an extremely impetuous man, easily led into enthusiasm, liable to sudden revulsions, and the failure of the Basch mission seems to have thrown him into a state of doubt and irritation concerning his new interest. For more than four months there is no mention of Zionism to be found in his papers and his correspondence with Dr. Gaster during the same period is confined to one letter written by the Haham to him in July. The letter is of some significance as it was sent with a copy of a recently published book called *Zionism and the Jewish future*, a collection of essays by Jewish leaders. This book had originated in a proposal of Dr. Weizmann, and from it most British politicians of the time obtained their ideas of Jewish nationalism. On Mark Sykes, however, it made no immediate impression

[1] In the Gaster-Sykes-Picot episode the writer is guided by the Diaries of Dr. Gaster, especially the entries of 2nd and 15th May, 1916, Dr. Gaster's correspondence with Sykes, the memorandum of a conference held on the 7th of February, 1917, at Dr. Gaster's house, the Sledmere Papers, and J. V. Malcolm's *The Origins of the Balfour Declaration*. Dr. Gaster seems to have exaggerated the Zionist part played by Sykes in the first two years of the war, believing that he was responsible for some of the details of the Samuel Memorandum. This was certainly not the case. There is a very puzzling entry on the 16th of April of 1916 where Dr. Gaster speaks of " H. S.'s meeting " at which the Zionists were " offered " (underlined in the original) a Constitution and a Charter under an Anglo-French regime in Palestine. Lord Samuel can give the writer no help in elucidating this passage. It is possible that " H.S." does not stand for " Herbert Samuel " and that the entry refers to internal party matters.

and his revulsion continued. This man who was to play a decisive part in the return of Israel was roused to do so, not by Jewish propaganda, but by a further action of Gentile Zionism applied this time to himself.

The office of the Assistant Secretaries was in Whitehall Gardens. One day in October of 1916 a certain Mr. James Malcolm came to visit Mark Sykes there. This naturalised Englishman, by origin of the celebrated Perso-Armenian family of Malkom,[1] and a financier by profession, was at this time one of the five delegates appointed by the Armenian Catholikos to look after the interests of those of his countrymen who dwelt under Allied Governments. His special charges were the Armenian volunteers, eleven thousand of whom had elected to serve under British command in the Eastern campaigns. He had met Mark Sykes before the war and knew him on familiar terms. He had noted his appointment and used to consult him both officially and unofficially about his multitudinous vicissitudes as the representative of Allies who were technically enemies, a predicament which was more singular in those times than now.

On this day in 1916 Mr. Malcolm was struck by an unaccustomed look of melancholy in Mark Sykes's expression. He asked him what was wrong. Sykes replied that he could see no end to the war. In France there was a military deadlock. At sea the power of the submarines was growing; on land that of the Russian armies failing. In the East the revolt of the Arabs was producing nothing. (This was before the Lawrence phase had begun.) A decisive victory, or indeed a victory of any kind seemed impossible without American participation on an enormous scale, and of that he said he saw little likelihood. He knew nothing of America at first hand, but he saw the reports which reached the Cabinet. They were discouraging. Mr. Malcolm asked if any progress was being made in the winning

---

[1]This family is best known to Europeans by the fame of Malkom Khan, for many years a prominent figure in Persian diplomacy. Wilfred Blunt asserted that one conversation with Malkom Khan was enough to persuade anyone (if persuasion were necessary) that the Eastern mind was superior to the Western.

of American opinion. Sykes shook his head. " Precious little,"
he answered. He then told Mr. Malcolm about the Basch
Mission, saying nothing about its Zionist character, but insisting
that it had revealed the extent of pro-German feeling among
influential American Jews. Mr. Malcolm asked Sykes what
arguments had been used. " Oh," sighed the other, " we told
them we'd win the war and that it was to their interest to be on
the winning side. The usual argument."

At this Mr. Malcolm took occasion to harangue his friend
on the principles which should govern British foreign policy
regarding the Jewish world, and Mark Sykes listened with
interest and good humour, saying nothing. This gave Mr.
Malcolm the impression that he knew nothing about the Jewish
world at all and he proceeded to tell him about Zionism, speaking
as though to an entirely ignorant person. He told him how he
himself came to understand this great movement: how, belonging to a minority with direful and recent memories of persecution,
he had developed an unusually close insight into Jewish feeling.
In South Persia he had seen Jewish families taking refuge in his
father's house during the officially inspired disorders of Nasr ud
Din Shah's reign. When as a young man he migrated from
Shiraz to Balliol College, he was taken under the fatherly care of
a business associate of his father, namely Sir Albert Abdullah
Sassoon. In his later career he continued to enjoy many Jewish
friendships and connections. He knew Colonel Albert Goldsmid,
that romantic nationalist who had grown up in ignorance of
his Jewish birth, had discovered it when serving as a British
officer, and had immediately rejoined the faith of his ancestors,
thereafter becoming a leading spirit among the " Hoveve Zion "
of England. Through the influence of remarkable Jewish personalities such as these, Mr. Malcolm became disposed towards
the idea of Zionism, but in the event he was converted by a
Gentile, the then famous journalist Edward Fitzgerald, who had
known Herzl in Vienna.

As he listened to this recital, Sykes began at last to yield to the process which Dr. Gaster had begun. He broke off the meeting and asked Mr. Malcolm to come back soon.

Conversion was not accomplished quickly. Sykes's first reaction to this second introduction to Zionism was one of renewed excitement, of being moved by the immense antique power of Jewish belief, but this sudden enthusiasm was followed by a second mood of caution. There was no man at that moment, five months after the conclusion of the secret Sykes-Picot Agreement, who knew more than he did about the negotiations which had gone forward and were continuing between Western and Eastern powers. Sykes was the founder of the " Arab Bureau "[1] in Cairo whose bulletins were first edited by T. E. Lawrence, and as Assistant Secretary he was fully informed of the correspondence exchanged the year before between the British High Commissioner in Egypt, Sir Henry MacMahon, and the Sherif Hussein of Mecca, representing the Arab nations. After reflection the opinion of Sykes was that the prospect of Zionism, to which everything in his character assented, had come too late. He told Mr. Malcolm so at their next meeting a few days later. He said that arrangements had already been concluded which made it impossible for the British Government to take on any new policy in the East, and he added that this was not merely his personal opinion: he had consulted Lord Milner, he explained, and Lord Milner, like himself, found the idea of Zionism genial, but too radical for adoption at this late stage. As people often do when obliged to give up what they would like to have, Sykes sought for as many objections as he could. He said: " Whatever you may say, the Jews *cannot* be with us. The memory of the Russian persecutions is far too close to their minds. At best they may be apathetic."

" Why do you say that? " asked Mr. Malcolm.

" I know many Jews," answered Sykes.

Mr. Malcolm, because he believed Sykes to have no knowledge of Zionists, replied that the well-to-do English Jews he

[1]This may be concluded from a letter written by Sykes in October, 1915, to Lord Robert Cecil (now Viscount Cecil of Chelwood), and another of December, 1915, written by General Gilbert Clayton to Sykes. (The Sledmere Papers.)

met were not the real leaders of the Jewish people. "You have not met the other kind of Jews," he said, adding that they were "remarkable types," and were to be counted in hundreds of thousands. He then told Sykes of a very curious and powerful influence which Zionists could exert. One of President Wilson's closest advisers and friends was Justice Louis D. Brandeis, a Jew with the passionate Zionist faith of a recent convert. It was believed, with what if any degree of truth it would be hard to say, that Wilson was attached to Brandeis by ties of peculiar hardiness, because, so the story ran, in his earlier days the future President had been saved by this man from appearing in a damaging law-suit. It was said that Brandeis was regarded by Wilson as the man to whom he owed his career. These allegations may have been nothing but exaggerations of a known situation, but this situation unadorned was important enough: there could be no doubt that Brandeis was Wilson's intimate adviser, and Brandeis was a Zionist. It followed that despite the Basch failure, a Zionist policy was in truth the way to capture American sympathy. When Sykes heard this he was again moved to confer with Lord Milner, and the latter told the Cabinet of Malcolm's proposals and ideas. The Cabinet showed cautious interest. Their reply was that no harm could be done if Malcolm were to open talks with representative Zionists, but that no promise must be made. But Malcolm was not willing to undertake such a mission.

"I cannot go empty-handed," he said to Sykes, "I must be able to tell these people that if the Zionists help the Allied cause, then they will receive the support of the British Government in their claim to rights in Palestine." Mark Sykes explained the chief objection as he saw this at the moment, namely that such a line of action, especially if supported by a British Government, would be profoundly repugnant to French feelings, since these were much influenced by "The Syrian Party" headed by Etienne Flandin, the party which kept alive belief in a historic mission of France to rule the Levant and to protect the diverse Christian communities who had survived more than a thousand years of un-Christian rule. He could not tell Mr. Malcolm that this objection counted for much because by the secret Anglo-French agreement which he had negotiated the British Government, for the sake of the Entente, had recognised many of the pretensions of the Syrian party, thereby adding a considerable complication to our undertakings towards the Arabic-speaking world. He warned him only that the Government could not commit themselves far at the moment.

To these explanations Malcolm replied: "The question is, do you want the help of the Jews in the United States? The only way you can get that help is by offering Palestine to the Zionists."

By this time Sykes's conversion had been completed. In consequence he did not now do the logical thing. He did not reply that in that case American sympathy must be sought in some other way. Instead he discussed the matter afresh with Lord Milner and George Barnes, both of whom shared his inner predilection. The two Ministers put the matter to the Cabinet again. The latter again authorised official conversations though only on the same terms. This time Malcolm agreed to act the part of go-between.

During these days of 1916 there had been other meetings between Zionists and British politicians in London, notably between Dr. Weizmann and Arthur Balfour, between Dr. Gaster and Mr. Herbert Samuel, and perhaps most importantly those which Herbert Sidebotham, a member of C. P. Scott's Manchester staff, and a Zionist of the Oliphant-Gawler "strategic" school, enjoyed with Sir Edward Grey. The glow of the sacred flame was constantly enlarged. Lord Cromer came to take a respectful view and wrote an article on *Zionism and the Jewish Future* for *The Spectator*. But the main line of action from which the historical process of Zionism moved forward appears to have lain in these conversations in Whitehall Gardens during which an Armenian delegate converted a Yorkshire country gentleman to belief in the new "Spes Israelis," and the most curious thing about these first scenes of the last act is how little part the Jews themselves played.

As the go-between Mr. Malcolm now arranged to meet the Zionist leaders through his friend Leopold Greenberg, whom we last noted at the Sixth Zionist Congress in Basle reading Sir Clement Hill's letter on Uganda. Greenberg did as he was asked. He took his friend to No. 67 Addison Road, West Kensington, the house of Dr. Weizmann. Mr. Malcolm noted " his tall figure, his pale face and keen eyes and natural geniality." A small company of Dr. Weizmann's fellow-Zionists, mostly members of the movement's political committee in England, were assembled to see and hear the negotiator. Among them was a member of the Zionist Executive who had come to England in 1914, Nahun Sokolov, who was destined to play a chief role in these events.

The meeting was not immediately dramatic.

When Mr. Malcolm had told everything which had passed between him and Sir Mark Sykes; when he had explained how Sykes had consulted Milner and George Barnes and that the Cabinet had given him a two-fold authorisation to open conversations, he was not received with much acclaim. It may be that these Zionist leaders had often been visited by unfruitful people who believed themselves to possess keys to power, such as grow common in time of war. Having been cheered by false dawns in the past, they watched this new opening in a spirit of incredulity. At the end of Malcolm's recital Dr. Weizmann recalled his own discussions with Mr. Scott and with Balfour and how he had had breakfast with Lloyd George, to no great purpose. Was Mr. Malcolm perfectly certain that he was really authorised by the British Cabinet? That he had not misunderstood? Malcolm assured him of the reality of his mission. Dr. Weizmann then put the following question to him: " Are you really and *personally* convinced that the British Government *seriously* intend to promise Palestine in return for the help of leading American Jews? " Malcolm said that that was his conviction. Dr. Weizmann asked him another question: " Do you advise us to accept the British Government's offer? " " Yes," said Mr. Malcolm, " I do." Dr. Weizmann rose and shook hands with him, a minute ceremony by which he signified the entry of the Jewish leaders into the negotiation. " When can I meet Sir Mark Sykes? " he asked. Malcolm rang Sykes up then and there and arranged for a meeting at the latter's house in Buckingham Gate on the next day.

On the next day Dr. Weizmann was unable to go because of some appointment at the Admiralty where he held an official post, and so his place as leader of a Zionist delegation was taken by Sokolov. This was to be the usual pattern of events throughout the negotiations. Dr. Weizmann was the directing mind, but taking little active part in day-to-day business, which was handled by this other man.

Nahun Sokolov was a Jew of Warsaw of wide cosmopolitan education, the pre-eminent journalist of Zionism, manifesting the brilliant and superficial Jewish culture of the age of Diffusion and Emancipation side by side with a passionate inner preoccupation with his strict Jewish allegiance. The manner of his life in Warsaw, where he published and edited two Jewish newspapers, and the effect on others of his smooth and apparently imperturbable personality have been described by Dr. Weizmann in much detail.[1] He was not easily understood. He gave an impression of somewhat inhuman detachment, but this was not his real character, indeed he was capable of being quite mastered by his feelings, for when he came to write the history of Zionism his work was not a little marred by intemperate language, both in attack and praise. But as a rule not much was visible of his emotion. Dr. Weizmann was with him in Warsaw when the news of the massacres of Kishinev reached the office of one of his papers, and he relates how he was somewhat shocked at Sokolov's calm. The truth was that Sokolov was one of those people who could learn about such horrors without the least outward perturbation, because his life was so entirely dedicated

---

[1] See Dr. Weizmann's account of Sokolov in *Trial and Error*, and Oskar K. Rabinovicz's corrections in *Fifty Years of Zionism*.

to bringing them to an end. He had the inner peace of a man under the compulsion of a vow. He was a diplomat whose smiling manner indicated no lack of patriotism. He could negotiate with the utmost patience about matters of the closest and even the most painful need, only showing the passionate fervour of his faith when ultimate principles were called into the question.

Being new to England, he had not met any of the men in power before this meeting with Sir Mark Sykes.

When introductions had been made by Mr. Malcolm, a memorandum was presented to Sykes for him to convey to the Cabinet. We may suppose that remarks of a formal nature were then exchanged. On the surface this was one of a hundred non-committal interviews such as happen daily in the course of official life. Before the delegation left, Sokolov made a simple request, namely that the Zionist Committee should have facilities for communication abroad. He pointed out that since they were an international body this was especially needful to them, and he suggested that they should be granted governmental privileges, since they could thus attain their object while subjecting themselves to the needs of secrecy and censorship.

Sykes promised to put this to the authorities. Oddly enough, he had once before requested such facilities for the Zionists in a telegram which he sent from Russia, without success, it seems. On this occasion when he repeated the request, the next morning he got what he asked for: it was agreed that the War Office and the Foreign Office would send Zionist letters and telegrams by way of Embassies, Consulates or Headquarters. As usually happens in official life, the permission was repeatedly forgotten, and in the months ahead Sykes often had to intervene afresh, but the permission was never withdrawn and could not be.[1]

It is unlikely that any of those who were present at this meeting at No. 9 Buckingham Gate recognised the immense importance of what was happening when these facilities were asked for. It

[1] For the communication question the Sledmere Papers, the Gaster Papers, Mr. Malcolm's Record, and some letters from Sokolov to Sykes in the Zionist Archives in Jerusalem are followed.

is not too much to say that once the permission had been given the British Government had no alternative but to grant whatever the Zionists demanded, and that they could only get out of so doing by becoming enemies of the Jewish people. The latter course might have become a logical, and even a defensible part of a political programme, but everything that was finest and most essential in the traditions and history of England was so utterly opposed to it that it must have led any political party which dared it to destruction; and so it was literally unpractical so long as England was ruled by free institutions. For, once the news was given out to Jewish communities all over the world that in return for certain services the British Government would use their then massive power in Eastern affairs to satisfy the Jewish longing for Palestine, then Zionism was really put to the test for the first time; and if Zionism could pass that test and could show that this movement for a return of the chosen people to the promised land was at the heart of Jewry, and really represented the force which had preserved it as a living thing for five thousand years, then there could be no going back on the promise, even a little way, either by those who gave it or by those who received. By this act (unless Zionism was a slight thing) the Jewish leaders themselves became powerless to stem the tide that they had set in motion, as they were to find to their cost, sometimes, in the days to come. History has shown that Zionism passed the test. Great as the obstacles to a Governmental declaration sometimes appeared during the months ahead, the decision had been taken on this October day in 1916, and it was irrevocable. The story really ends here, for the rest of what happened between now and the promulgation of the Balfour Declaration, and indeed until the establishment of an Israelite State in Palestine, was in truth only the accomplishment of what was inevitable, little as it seemed so at the time.

Hitherto the career of Gentile Zionism in England had shown a consistent pattern with which we have grown familiar:

on one side churchmen and enthusiasts agitating for a restoration of Israel, on the other side men in power being occasionally interested. From now on it was otherwise. The impetus came from above. The Gentiles were eager to welcome what Zionism had in store for them. The enthusiasm was encouraged in the highest councils of the state.

When Asquith was manœuvred from power in December, 1916, and Lloyd George appointed in his place, we may say, from our present point of view, that a sceptic was replaced by a passionate believer. Asquith never made a more remarkable misjudgment of Lloyd George than when he described his colleague as one who " does not care a damn for the Jews or their past or their future . . ." The contrary would have been much closer to the truth. Lloyd George cared intensely for the Jews; his devotion to them was one of the consistent things in his bewilderingly various nature.

His Welsh traditions had filled him with the Bible; first impressions had been made on this impressionable man by the music of the Old Testament rumbled forth in the bethels of North Wales, and the fact that he could rejoice in poetic trash must never make us forget that he was a man who had been lastingly touched to the very depths of his soul by master strokes of the human spirit. He was a man of whom we may say that the Bible had made him. It so happened, too, that the enormous egotism in his nature was on specially good terms with the Jewish people. As a stranger in a strange land he felt kinship with them, and he prided himself on being one of the few people in the world who understood their character and predicament. An incident had deepened his sympathy. It is said that he never forgot that when he was a young solicitor one of his earliest court cases was in defence of a Jew, and that when he had won and was rejoicing in the glow of this first success, the father of his client embraced him publicly and said, "You are the greatest benefactor of our people since Moses!"

Twenty years or so after that event Lloyd George met Herzl. He acted as his adviser in the El Arish negotiations, and it was Lloyd George who drew up the draft of a charter for Jewish autonomy at the time of the Uganda proposal. Three years after the Uganda affair, we find him sending a telegram to a Zionist meeting in Wales. We have already noted him as one of the first British statesmen whom Dr. Weizmann met during the Great War. His elusive spirit never became enchained to Zionism, but he knew it far better than any of his colleagues, and he liked it very much. To accuse him, as he accused himself, of a passing and rootless interest in the matter is unjustifiable.

In the new Government Arthur Balfour succeeded Sir Edward Grey at the Foreign Office.

If Lloyd George is a difficult man to understand, at least we know where the difficulty lies: in his fantastic many-sidedness, his contradictoriness, in the play-acting, the sincerity, the candour, the generosity and the self-centred ingratitude which all dwelt in him together. About Balfour there was no such ostentatious incomprehensibility. He sails through our history with every show of being precisely identifiable. He remains perplexing none the less. His nature was more open than that of most men, but less is discoverable about him than is usual with those who live public lives.

It is not difficult to see why Lloyd George was a Zionist. To discover why Balfour became one we need to search beyond appearances. The suggestion has been made that his full life was impoverished by the coldness of his nature, that he lacked intense emotional experiences, and, as it were, made the deficiency good in his last years by an intensely emotional partisanship of the Zionist cause. The idea comes from people who knew him.

Certainly the coldness was there; so also was the compensating emotionalism, hidden away in subjection. Whoever studies Arthur Balfour's life must be surprised by unexpected and rare appearances of a strong vein of passion, singular and persistent. How beautifully strange, for example, was his idolatrous love of Handel's music, that deeply passionate adoration! In the middle of the war the Dean of St. Margaret's, Westminster, proposed to him in the course of a conversation that a series of Handel concerts might fittingly be arranged in his church as a distraction for serious-minded men on leave in London. Balfour seized on the idea energetically, helped personally in the work of selection from the oratorios, and, though a member of the War Cabinet, attended every one of these concerts unless he was abroad, giving up whole Wednesday afternoons for the purpose. Of a man capable of such an action at such a time we can say with confidence that he obtained the emotional refreshment he needed with an extraordinary deliberation, the deliberation, moreover, of an essentially cold heart and mind. But to generalise from such incidents to the conclusion that he supported Zionism as he did for the same reasons as he attended these concerts is to accuse him of a crime, or at the very least of hateful irresponsibility.

A temptation arises to see in the most famous of Balfour's deeds the fine flowering of Gentile Zionism as it had been long harboured in the pure ecclesiastical school. Many details of the great career fit: the lifelong churchmanship; the Sunday night prayers and Bible-reading to the assembled household of Wittengehame, and the impressively simple religious sense which made him assert that if reason and its works deny an origin in God, " by this very act they proclaim their own insufficiency." It is not difficult either to imagine that his wholehearted acceptance of Zionist enthusiasm was prompted by his impatience with the excessively refined religious tastes of the Age of Diffusion. In a notable passage of his 1914 Gifford lectures he said: " It may be observed that though no tragic accompaniments attach to the growth of a purely Absolutist philosophy, this by no means implies that metaphysics is better than religion. It is true that, for the sake of a purely Absolute, no man has been moved to do what a later morality condemns—to placate it, for example, with bloody rites or obscene revels. But this is because, for the sake of such an Absolute, no man has ever yet been moved to do anything at all."

In the years after 1917 Balfour made many statements about Zionism both in writing and in public speeches. He occasionally referred to a religious impetus behind what he had done, but he never stressed this. He preferred prosy explanations. When he spoke of an unmaterial interest in his policy, he usually meant that the movement could solve the psychological problems brought about by anti-Semitism. In an introduction to Sokolov's history he thus addressed his readers in a passage characteristic of many others: " Zionism differs in kind from ordinary philanthropic efforts, it appeals to different motives. If it succeeds it will do a great spiritual and material work for the Jews, but not for them alone. For as I read its meaning it is, among other things, a serious endeavour to mitigate the age-long miseries created for Western civilisation by the presence in its midst of a Body which it too long regarded as alien and even hostile, but which it was equally unable to expel or absorb."

It is probable that Arthur Balfour's Zionism was influenced by a paper submitted to the Foreign Office by Herbert Sidebotham in the spring of 1916 (when Balfour was First Lord), since one of the arguments in this document, that the small gifted Jewish people needed but their ancestral hearth to give the world such treasures as the Ancient Greeks had given from Hellas, was often used by Balfour when discussing Zionism in private.[1] This argument, not easily resisted by a late Victorian, was valid in the sense that it rightly interpreted Zionist belief, for (we should remember) the Jews were among the many people to draw inspiration from the Risorgimento, whose excellence was still little questioned. Higher than this ideal Balfour hesitated to fly in his many reserved self-justifications. Of the motives which this enigmatical man showed the world, the most prominent was not a millennial conviction such as Hechler's, but an earthy, secular, Scotch common sense.

What is most strange is not this common sense devoted to a selfless aim, but the ardent pertinacity with which Balfour pursued its object, quite unlike his usual way. The most consistent charge against his statesmanship is that he was so open-minded

---

[1]Sir Harold Nicolson has supplied this information, with other valuable particulars. He saw a great deal of Balfour at this time.

ARTHUR JAMES BALFOUR
From a photograph taken on his arrival in London from the U.S. in 1917

that he was too often satisfied with the harmfully weak solutions of compromise. On Zionism his mind was shut. No argument against it—he heard many—is ever recorded to have influenced him or diminished his purpose for a moment. The strength of his determination, always concealed while he waited inactive for his opponents to be scattered, may be measured by his untypical conduct when leading the British delegation to America in the June of 1917. He was the most discreet of men, but while on this mission he gave assurances first to Clarence I de Sola, the Secretary-General of the Zionist Federation of Canada, and then to Louis D. Brandeis, which both men took to be pledges of British action. He seems to have purposely compromised himself to strengthen the cause he had at heart.

To the end of his life Arthur Balfour gave little sign of weakening powers, and his mind was never conquered by his feelings. To interpret aright the often made allegation that in his Zionism he administered an emotional compensation to himself we may borrow an idea from a modern historian who has pointed to the negative result of perfect balance, and applying that to the surprising last-minute enthusiasm in Balfour's career, we may boldly but perhaps not too boldly surmise that the exquisite disposal of his thought and feeling was prodigiously interrupted in his last years by an appeal, which he could not resist or criticise, to his high sense of passionate needs—not to his personal sentiment (though this was involved), but to his philosophical apprehension of the place that emotion must occupy in human destiny; and we can say further that this appeal was all the more powerful because it was awaited with the enforced calm of his sternly self-disciplined nature. In that sense we may perhaps accept the common judgment that in this instance the fate of a people was formed by an uprush of emotion.

In the life of Courts, Cabinets, General Headquarters and suchlike it is sometimes of small use to have the favour of great men unless their subordinates are of a like mind. In this respect the Jewish cause was unusually fortunate in the London of 1917, where, so far as Eastern questions were concerned, the principals, having given the signal, took little part until the end, leaving the carrying out and even some of the construction of policy to their juniors. Malcolm's work of conversion was carried on.

A curious little man called Fitzmaurice was to be seen bustling in and out of Ministries and official places in those days. For many years he had been Dragoman or local expert at the British Embassy in Turkey and people used to say that when he gave an opinion about Ottoman affairs he was difficult to follow because he was so profound a master of his subject that no one who was not an Osmanli born and bred, and himself involved in a great quantity of Turkish plotting, could even dimly understand what he was talking about. For all that the advice of " Fitz " was much sought in the Foreign Office and the War Office. He had known and admired Mark Sykes in Constantinople, and he now followed him into Zionism. It was Fitzmaurice who converted Sir Henry Wilson, Sir George Macdonough the Director of Military Intelligence, and some others. Being a man of violently emotional opinion, he was easily inclined to optimism, and so, having succeeded so far with his own countrymen, he entertained the ambition of winning over the French, Italian and Russian Governments. Like Mark Sykes, he was a Roman Catholic, and he believed that he could even win the Papal Government to a Zionist policy. He travelled to Rome for the purpose, and in this part of his enormous enterprise he may have influenced events.

By early 1917 Zionism had reached a position where it could not easily be abandoned again by a British Government. The meeting at 9 Buckingham Gate was followed by others, among which one held at Dr. Gaster's house on the 7th February of 1917[1]—a debate of five Jewish leaders with Mark Sykes—has come to be considered as the event which inaugurated the new era. The main purpose of the Jewish argument was to obtain

[1] A detailed Memorandum of the meeting supplied by Mr. Vivian Gaster is followed here. See also Dr. Weizmann's *Trial and Error*, and Dr. Rabinovicz's correction and his quotation of a letter from Mr. Vivian Gaster.

official agreement that the National Home should be established under British protection. The idea had often been put forward by individuals, but never with the urgency and unity of this occasion. Every Jewish speaker insisted on this point, and from certain of their remarks it is clear that rumours had reached them that an Anglo-French undertaking concerning Palestine had been reached, and that they had guessed the outlines correctly. Yet, so well had the secret of the Sykes-Picot Agreement been kept that they did not treat their guess as seriously as we might expect them to have done. Mr. Herbert Samuel (who was present) was no longer a member of the Government, but he had held high office so it was natural that his guidance should have been sought, and there was a strange moment when Sir Mark Sykes invited him, in some desperation it would seem, to tell what he thought could be divulged of the Sykes-Picot Agreement. Mr. Samuel gave a guarded reply which could be interpreted as expressing ignorance or discretion. From this it came about that for the moment the Jewish leaders (with Mr. Samuel's agreement) accepted the guidance of Sir Mark Sykes. Led by him, Zionism once more entered the field of international politics as it had done before under Herzl, and began to move towards a position of strength from which it could assert itself to the world. Thickets, sloughs, and tangles in plenty still threatened the movement's progress, the first of these being the Sykes-Picot Agreement which, with the help of its English author, the Zionists turned to their advantage.

In an extremely important respect the Agreement was what the Zionists wanted, for it gave a geographical identity to Palestine for the first time in hundreds of years. Nor was this merely a remarkable coincidence. In a sense the Sykes-Picot Agreement was of Zionist origin, the special provision for Palestine being to a large extent the result of the Samuel memorandum, of Dr. Gaster's interrupted conversion of Sykes, and of Sykes's influence on Picot. (Sykes's temporary disillusion was nowhere reflected.) Further, it protected the future of Palestine (in an unscrupulous manner as some thought) from the consequences of the British promises to the Sherif of Mecca for Arab independence in the Arab speaking world.[1] In only one respect did it run counter to Zionist wishes, and that was in the insistence on an international zone.

During the three days following the meeting in Dr. Gaster's house further meetings were held between Zionists and Gentiles. On the 8th of February Mark Sykes introduced Sokolov to Picot; on the 9th Picot received Sokolov alone at the French Embassy; on the following day Sykes held a discussion with Sokolov and Dr. Weizmann.[2] At all these meetings the proposal for a British protectorate was pressed vigorously by the Zionists, and Sokolov did not hesitate to tell Picot that in Jewish eyes British suzerainty in Palestine was preferred to French rule. By his extraordinary skill in argument, by renewing the American proposal (which was already being forgotten), by demonstrating that the assimilation of Jews to Western civilisation was not possible in large numbers outside highly cultivated societies such as those of France and England, Sokolov succeeded in making Picot an ally of Zionism, a process which, as we have seen, had been begun by Dr. Gaster and Sykes. But for all his personal sympathies, it was beyond Picot's ability to agree to what the Zionists most wanted namely British suzerainty. No French politician could ignore "the Syrian Party" in Paris, led by Monsieur Etienne Flandin, and devoted primarily to asserting an historical French mission to the Eastern Mediterranean.

There was no great wish on the English side to take on Palestine responsibilities. Mark Sykes would have accepted the proposal to institute a French protectorate, if it had not been that Jewish hostility to the French colonial system made this impracticable.[3] Neither he nor Picot relished the internationalisa-

[1] See Appendix B for details of these promises.

[2] The Gaster papers, in which detailed memoranda of these meetings are preserved.

[3] British views on this matter varied very much during the war. In 1915 British ambitions in Syria were very much to the fore in high places, but not so, strangely enough, in the first part of Lloyd George's premiership despite his suspicion of " agnostic atheistic France." At the meeting of 7th February Dr. Gaster suggested a French protected Zionism and Sykes said that the Foreign Office were not likely to raise difficulties to such a proposal. Sykes's views at this time are to be found in a minute of a discussion

tion of Palestine, but they could see no better solution. Then in late February a conversation with Sokolov made up Sykes's mind that the international proposal was worthless. "He asked me to consider," wrote Sykes to Picot, "the aversion of the Zionists for an ... international regime, as being likely to promote dissension and intrigue, and to increase rather than alleviate the religious and political differences of the situation." He then put forward a new suggestion, namely that the Protectorate of Palestine should be offered to the United States, thus giving the country an undivided Government in a form which disposed of Anglo-French jealousy.[1] But again, in spite of his own moderate views, Picot was not able to support this proposal, out of deference to the powerful group in Paris which used a vague tradition as an instrument of Imperial policy, and which was opposed by its very nature to any but the most trivial development of Zionism in Syria.

From this predicament there seemed no escape by ordinary means, so Sykes and Sokolov resolved to seize the initiative, and the manœuvre by which they brought about the acquiescence of the French Government in a British Zionist policy in spite of the formidable anti-Zionist interest in France fills one of the most remarkable and neglected chapters of the story.

This is what happened.

Sykes was due to leave for Egypt in April as Cabinet representative, and on the 3rd he attended a meeting at 10 Downing Street where he received his instructions from the Prime Minister and Lord Curzon. Lloyd George (who had spoken to Dr.

between him, Weizmann, and Sokolov which took place on February 10th, 1917, at 9 Buckingham Gate. " Sir Mark Sykes said he could see no objection to a purely pro-Zionist propaganda but it was necessary to keep the idea of a British suzerainty in the background for the time being as it was likely to intensify the French opposition. In this connection he repeated his anxiety with regard to the weekly journal *Palestine* (the organ of the British Palestine Committee), which he considered much too emphatic in its exposition of the British interest in Palestine. He was afraid that this emphasis was likely to make their object more difficult of achievement." (The Gaster Papers.)

[1]Letter from Sykes to Georges Picot of 28th February, 1917. (The Sledmere Papers.) In his remarkable book, *The Arab Awakening*, the late George Antonius made no mention of this letter although, with the exception of Sir Shane Leslie he was the only historian to have examined the Sledmere Papers. They were in disorder and he evidently missed this one. Had he read it he must have altered the view he put forward in his book as to the purpose of the Declaration.

Weizmann in the same sense on the same day) told Sykes that he was anxious that no Eastern agreement should be made which could disrupt the Entente, adding nevertheless that it was of the utmost importance that Zionism should be assured of free growth under British auspices. He was more conscious than his colleagues that the Government were making conflicting pledges. He raised the question as to whether a choice should not be made between an Arab and a Jewish policy, and he insisted that Palestine should be excluded from all agreements with the Arabian princes. This was the only personal intervention of Lloyd George in the negotiations leading to the Balfour Declaration and it served to assure Mark Sykes that the Prime Minister's enthusiasm had not weakened.[1]

A few days later Sykes went to Paris taking Sokolov and Malcolm with him. There he arranged for Sokolov to meet under-secretaries in the French Foreign Ministry, and he advised him to go alone to these meetings so as to avoid giving the impression that the Zionism he represented was an English fad. This was a bolder move than appears now. The Zionists of London, notably Mr. James de Rothschild, had urged that their representatives should never negotiate independently with the French, as this might encourage the Syrian party to assemble a team of Rabbis who would implore the protection of France in the Holy Land.[2] But Sykes and Sokolov considered that the importance of Zionism showing its strength was worth the risk, and the event proved them right.

The interviews went forward smoothly. In the meantime Sykes busied himself to discover what he could about the Syrian Party. He had a friend in Paris called Hussey Walsh, an Englishman married to a French duchess, who, at Sykes's entreaty, consented to use his advantageous position to charm the truth out of the Party leader. " Flandin rose like a trout on a dull day . . ." reported Sykes of Walsh's interview: "(he said) Picot was a fool who had betrayed France—France required the whole of

[1] From a memorandum in the Sledmere Papers.
[2] Memorandum of the Meeting of 7th February, 1917. (The Gaster Papers.)

the Mediterranean Littoral down to Arish, and the Hejaz railway
as far south as Ma'an. A small international conclave of Jaffa,
Jerusalem and Bethlehem might be arranged in which France
should predominate . . . but for the rest, the country should be
absolute French territory as far East as the Euphrates. . . . What is
important is that this gang will work without let or hindrance
in Picot's absence, and further, Picot will always have the knowledge of their views and aims at the back of his mind . . . The
backing behind this is Political-Financial-Religious, a most
sinister combination. The Cailloux-Bouillon[1] lot are trying to
run a sort of Christian Socialist party; the nationalists, like
Flandin, are out and out anti-Britishers with concessions in
view. Lastly, a patriotic French priesthood are always easy
victims to the wiles of such combinations of politicians."[2]

Sykes stayed only a few days in Paris. As soon as he had
Hussey Walsh's information he left for Rome in order to discuss
British Eastern policy with members of the Italian Government,
whose interest in Zionism was negligible, and with the Vatican
authorities. On the Church's interest, which was great and
supposedly hostile, a great deal depended.

The idea of Vatican hostility was out of date. It seems that
after Pius X's interview with Herzl, the Pope, or his advisers,
came to regret the brusque manner with which the Zionist
leader had been received. A few weeks after that audience
Cardinal Merry del Val took occasion to soften the impression
by saying to a friend of Herzl: "If the Jews believe that they
might greatly ease their lot by being admitted to the land of
their ancestors, then we would regard that as a humanitarian
question." And he added: "We shall never forget that without
Judaism we would have been nothing."[3] Two years later the
Dreyfus conspiracy was exposed, and this prompted a reaction
against the anti-Semitic wing of the New Ultramontanes. There
were other circumstances reconciling the Papacy to Zionism
which become clear in the course of the story.

[1]Franklin Bouillon was Vice-President of the Syrian Party.
[2]First letter to Sir Ronald Graham of 15th April, 1917. (The Sledmere Papers.)
[3]Interview with Heinrich York-Steiner, reported by Dr. Josef Fraenkel.

Two Studies in Virtue

As soon as he had arrived in Rome Sykes sought an interview with a Vatican official who was of the same rank and influence as himself, someone not a cardinal who had the Pope's ear. He found his man in Monsignor Pacelli,[1] Assistant Under-Secretary for Foreign Affairs. "I spoke to the Monsignor," recorded Sykes,[2] "of the immense difficulties which surrounded the question of Jerusalem, the Arab Nationalist movement, the Moslem Holy Places, Zionism, and the conflicting interests of the Latins and Greeks, beside the aspirations of the various powers.... Although he did not say as much, the Monsignor, by certain turns of speech, let it be easy to see that the idea of British patronage of the Holy Places was not distasteful to Vatican policy. The French I could see did not strike him as ideal in any way. I also prepared the way for Zionism by explaining what the purpose and ideals of the Zionists were, and suggested that he should see M. Sokolov when the latter came to Rome. Of course one could not expect the Vatican to be enthusiastic about this movement, but he was most interested and expressed a wish to see Sokolov when he should come to Rome."

Sykes then obtained a brief private audience of the Pope. This was of a formal kind and nothing was said of Zionism. The next day Sykes left for Egypt.

Sokolov arrived in Rome about three weeks later, and on the 10th May, after conferring with Monsignor Pacelli, he was received by Benedict XV. It was as though Herzl's audience was being annulled. "Have I correctly understood Zionism?" asked the Pope when the opening formalities were over. "What a reversal of history! Nineteen centuries ago Rome destroyed Jerusalem, and now, desiring to rebuild it, you take the path to Rome!"

In his reply Sokolov recalled the fate of the Empire and compared it to that of the Jewish nation: one had vanished, the other was reclaiming its land.

[1]Subsequently Pope Pius XII.
[2]Second letter to Sir Ronald Graham, 15th April, 1917. (The Sledmere Papers.)

" Yes, yes," agreed Benedict with enthusiasm, " this was providential. God willed it."

The Pope then asked Sokolov to explain the Zionist project in detail. Sokolov answered as follows: " Our programme is twofold. It aims first to create in Palestine a spiritual and cultural centre for Jewry, and secondly to establish a national home for oppressed Jews. Our desire is to build up in that country a great centre where Jews will be able to develop their culture freely, to educate their children in the spirit of their ideals, and to devote all their energies to making their National Home a model of Jewish civilisation and morality."

The Pope was deeply impressed. " That is a wonderful idea," he said. Then he wanted to know whether this plan had been contrived with a view to preventing persecutions. Sokolov answered in the rhetorical terms which came naturally to him. He referred to the right of the Jews " to a place in the sun—in our land." "We look forward," he said, " to the rebirth of historical Judaism, to the spiritual and material revival of the homeland that personifies our national genius and our Biblical tradition in its purest sense. We claim the right of Freedom which cannot be denied to any people."

" But is there enough space," asked the Pope, " in Palestine, to carry out your plan? "

To this question which was to be asked so often not only then but in the course of the next thirty years, and on which so much depended, Sokolov returned a skilfully evasive reply. " There is the possibility of reaching our goal," he said, " but first we must prepare the ground." The conversation turned to the small number of Jewish colonists in Palestine at that time, only twelve thousand; and to the different days ahead when British influence would introduce civilised rule in place of Turkish domination. " Great Britain," the Pope interjected, " is the greatest and most experienced colonising power in the world." Then they discussed Zionist intentions regarding the Holy Places, before the Pope returned to the original question, which he posed afresh: " Are many Jews likely to settle in Palestine? "

Sokolov again replied with a skilful and grandiloquent evasion. " The best—and those who have suffered most," he said, and then led the conversation away from that subject to the great agricultural work of the pioneers, and from there to a discussion of the Jews in Eastern Europe.

The last words of Benedict at this audience were spoken in answer to Sokolov's request for moral support, and were to be long remembered by Zionists. He said: " Si, si, io credo che noi saremo buoni vicini "—" Yes, I believe that we shall be good neighbours."[1]

Shortly after this Sokolov returned to Paris.

The importance of this encounter with Benedict XV was very considerable, since by his friendly reception of a Zionist leader, and his openly expressed approval of a Palestinian regime run by Great Britain, the Pope loosened one of the foundation stones of Monsieur Flandin's party. The latter, by the use of skilful propaganda, had for long appeared to enjoy the full support of the Church. Such support was unwelcome to the anti-clerical Government of France, but more than this it was wholly against the interests of the Vatican, who looked with distaste at its consequence: Jerusalem controlled by an anti-clerical and renegade-Catholic power. The logical result of this situation, both for the French Government and the Papacy, was to work for the exclusion of French rule from the Sanjak of Jerusalem, as ultimately came about at Versailles. The first step in that direction can be seen in the diplomacy by which Sokolov and Mark Sykes outmanœuvred Monsieur Flandin, and it was followed immediately by the second step, when the French Government gave strong official support to the Jewish cause. We will relate presently the curious part played by Baron Edmond de Rothschild. For the moment we should notice that

[1]This account of Sokolov's meeting with the Pope is taken from a record made by Sokolov's son, Mr. Florian Sokolov, from his father's papers. See " Zion," Jan.-Feb., 1950.

when Sokolov returned to Paris, he obtained a formal document signed by Jules Cambon, Secretary-General to the Foreign Ministry. It was dated the 4th of June, 1917, and read as follows:

" You were good enough to present the project to which you are devoting your efforts, which has for its object the development of Jewish colonisation in Palestine. You consider that, circumstances permitting, and the independence of the Holy Places being safeguarded at the same time, it would be a deed of Justice and reparation if the Allied Powers, by lending their protection, were to assist the renaissance of Jewish nationality in that land from which the people of Israel were exiled many centuries ago. The French Government which entered the present war to defend a people wrongfully attacked, and which continues the struggle to assure the victory of right over might, cannot but feel sympathy for your cause, the triumph of which is bound up with that of the Allies. I am happy to give you herewith such assurance."

This victory in France was not followed by a similar one in England. The British Government began to hesitate because, strangely enough, at this time they feared the effect on the Entente of a British protectorate more than the French did.

We have noted that the proposal for an American protectorate began with Mark Sykes.[1] During his visit to Paris he discarded it because, as he explained in April in a letter to Arthur Balfour, all Frenchmen interested in Syria (not only those of Flandin's party) were fearful of so powerful a competitor entering the field. They " naturally tremble," he wrote, " at the prospect of ' Dollars ' and ' Go ' being brought into line against their ' Sentiment ' and ' Chicane.' " Henceforth he worked steadily and slowly for a British protectorate. But his advice was not taken at the Foreign Office for some time. Balfour urged Dr. Weizmann to interest the American Government in the idea of

---

[1] It may well have originated elsewhere as well, but if so, this was a case of several independent origins. Mark Sykes's letter to Picot is written in a spirit of initiative.

an Anglo-American Protectorate.[1] Lloyd George[2] had already warned him of the danger of Zionism becoming odious to France by the establishment of a purely British regime.

Then the hands of the Zionists were unexpectedly strengthened by one of their Gentile supporters. C. P. Scott had for some time regarded with distrust the negotiations of the Zionists with Mark Sykes. In February he had warned Dr. Weizmann that as a Catholic Sykes would tend to give in to French claims in the East,[3] supposing, it would seem, that no Catholic could help being attracted to the party of Etienne Flandin. In April Scott went to Paris, and while he was there someone told him of the Sykes-Picot Agreement. His immediate action, and one which showed the extremity of his belief, was to betray the secret to the Zionists. He told all he knew to Dr. Weizmann on the 16th April of 1917, and thus armed him with a certain moral superiority of the utmost value in negotiations of this kind, full of mixed motives of which the higher motive was the essential one. Nine days after the 16th of April, in an interview with the Assistant Secretary of State, Lord Robert Cecil, Dr. Weizmann made it clear in guarded language that he knew the terms and the origin of the British predilection for an international zone. He repeated the objections of his party. Lord Robert renewed the suggestion that the National Home should try to make terms with France by accepting French patronage. Dr. Weizmann would have none of this. Zionist policy was by now unalterable on this point. British patronage was wanted in Palestine because only under the British form of Imperialism was there a constant tendency to independent growth. After long discussion Lord Robert agreed to support the Zionists in this matter.[4] It was not likely that Balfour would maintain a different view against Lord Robert, and Lloyd George had already asserted in private

[1] Dr. Weizmann, *Trial and Error.*

[2] At their meeting on April 3rd, 1917, see page 197 ante. In *Trial and Error* Dr. Weizmann refers to this meeting "with the Prime Minister, Mr. Asquith." There can be little doubt that the meeting was with Lloyd George, whose remarks to Sykes on the same day were similar to those made to Dr. Weizmann.

[3] Dr. Gaster's Diary. (The Gaster Papers.)

[4] Dr. Weizmann, *Trial and Error.*

his own wish for a British regime in Palestine.[1] Unless a French army were to appear in the East, a British Palestinian Protectorate of some kind now seemed certain. Weakened by its own authors as much as by opponents from outside, the Sykes-Picot agreement began to be transformed by Zionist pressure.

The first obstacle had hardly been cleared when another rose up, one which is now almost forgotten but which appeared enormous for a short time. This was the Turkophil party in England which is of interest to this story mainly because it showed a changing temper in Zionism.

The Turkish party contained remarkable men but they never seem to have worked as a single body and so never became powerful. Their leader at this time was a former ambassador, Sir Louis Mallet, and their most active members throughout the war were the author Marmaduke Pickthall,[2] and Aubrey Herbert,[3] Member of Parliament for Yeovil. They represented the Disraeli school of Tory foreign policy and their central belief was that " the disappearance of the Ottoman Empire must be the first step towards the disappearance of our own."[4] Unless Great Britain had the goodwill of the Caliph in Constantinople, they argued, her place in Asiatic affairs would be fatally weakened. They esteemed the Turkish character and abhorred Russia. As happens in party politics, they and their opponents held exaggerated views. Herbert and Pickthall over-estimated the staying power of the Ottoman regime and despised the Arabs and Armenians in a somewhat fantastically extreme way, while

[1]Notes of a conference held at 10 Downing Street, April 3rd, 1917. (The Sledmere Papers.)

[2]Marmaduke Pickthall (1875-1936), Oriental traveller and author, notably of *Said the Fisherman, The House of Islam,* and *The House of War.* This account of the Turkish party is based on several memoranda in the Sledmere Papers and the delightful but somewhat absurdly one-sided biography of Pickthall by Ann Fremantle.

[3]The Hon. Aubrey Herbert (1880-1923), younger son of the 4th Earl of Carnarvon and half-brother of the famous Egyptologist. He was one of the officers charged with the abortive negotiations with Khalil Pasha at Kut-el-Amara in 1916. (See the letters of T. E. Lawrence, edited by David Garnett.) He represented Yeovil from 1911 till the end of his life, and he used his position to make representations in favour of Albania which led the Peace Conference of Versailles to recognise the independence of that country. Throughout his life he was a close friend of Mark Sykes.

[4]Mark Sykes, in the House of Commons, 1914. Before the outbreak of war he was a member of this party.

on the other side Sykes and Fitzmaurice, former lovers of Turkey, sometimes forgot what had once moved them to admiration, the virtues of the simple people of Turkey which were to redeem their country under the then unknown Mustafa Kemal. Both parties inclined to interpret a complex picture into terms of wartime black and white.

The position of the Turkish party in England is not readily understood to-day. The clutch of " security " was not so wide or strong as in our time and it seemed natural to life as it was then lived that throughout the war Marmaduke Pickthall should write polemical articles in *The New Age*, and that he and Aubrey Herbert should address public meetings in favour of an immediate peace with Turkey, calling, in the very strongest terms, for the repudiation of every act and policy of the Government which stood in the way. It was at one of their meetings held in the Caxton Hall on the 9th of June of 1917 that Malcolm obtained information which made the Zionists see danger. He learned that a proposal was afoot, the latest of many, to approach certain Turkish politicians in Switzerland, with a view to a separate peace. He was shocked to hear Party supporters boasting about their coming success, and when Pickthall addressed the audience Malcolm felt obliged to leave in protest because the speaker was using such violently pro-Turkish language.[1] (Marmaduke Pickthall, we should remember, was the extremist of the party and had apostatised to Islam in 1914.)

It so happened that a little while before this Dr. Weizmann had received a mysterious message from Brandeis telling him, without further explanation, that an American commission was travelling to the East. Malcolm and Weizmann compared notes. They made more discoveries: that French emissaries of a French peace party had already gone to Switzerland, to meet members of the " Ottoman League of Peace and Liberation," and that the American Commission was headed by Henry Morgenthau, the former American Ambassador to Turkey. It

---

[1]The whole of this incident is recorded in the Sledmere Papers. The same incident is briefly referred to in *Trial and Error*, chapter xvii.

seemed plain that large-scale political action was being taken. On the next day, Sunday the 10th June, Malcolm and Weizmann went to the Foreign Office together in high rage.

Mark Sykes was still away in Egypt and his place in Whitehall Gardens was being taken by Mr. William Ormsby-Gore.[1] To him Malcolm and Dr. Weizmann delivered a vigorous protest. They told him what they knew and warned him of the folly of forfeiting the goodwill and loyalty of Jews and Armenians by these overtures. Dr. Weizmann went on to give Mr. Ormsby-Gore some remarkable information. The Germans like the English had their Herberts and Pickthalls, their rebels against orthodox policy, and like the English they could use them deftly. The Zionist leaders in Berlin had recently been approached by the then famous philanthropist Johannes Lepsius, a man who had devoted his life to the Armenians, and he had conveyed suggestions from the Imperial Government that Germany might protect Zionism in Palestine, forcing her Turkish allies to give the Jews what they wanted. Dr. Weizmann insisted that if regard for Turkish Imperial integrity (in which Zionism could have little future) were to become a part of British foreign policy, Jews might be tempted by Dr. Lepsius's offer to transfer their loyalty. At the moment this loyalty was closely attached to the Allies and to England in particular. Dr. Weizmann asserted his own loyalty to England, but, he warned, he could not answer for the pertistence of such loyalty among his people under the stress of disillusion and disappointment. Malcolm supported him. They were both in a state of passionate indignation, and before leaving they said that they would oppose Aubrey Herbert in every way they could, and that they considered themselves free to use their information as they chose.

When he came to write his memoirs Dr. Weizmann aptly described the sequel to this remarkable interview as an " Opera Bouffe intermezzo." It is not possible to say whether Mr. Ormsby-Gore's two visitors awoke the Foreign Office to a sense of crisis, or whether they were extremely fortunate in their

[1]Now Viscount Harlech.

timing. On Saturday the 9th of June, Arthur Balfour had returned from America. The protest was met in full. Any intention there may have been to send Aubrey Herbert or Marmaduke Pickthall on a peace-mission was abandoned, and Arthur Balfour personally arranged for Dr. Weizmann to travel to Gibraltar in order to meet Morgenthau. It appears that the latter had but vague instructions from Secretary Lansing and President Wilson, and vague plans of his own to obtain peace somehow by means of his Turkish experience. It is likely that when confronted at Gibraltar by Dr. Weizmann's logical and keener mind he began to lose confidence. Six weeks later, after acquainting himself with political opinion in Europe, he reported against a continuance of his mission. The whole of this pro-Turkish move which appeared so powerful at the beginning of June had almost entirely lost its strength a month later. Nothing remained but Sir Louis Mallet's recommendations for a separate peace, and of this the Zionists appear to have been unaware, probably because his part of the manœuvre was conducted within the Foreign Office by means of memoranda to the Secretary of State. It made some progress, until Mark Sykes returned in the middle of July and set himself to defeat it. " A few right and lefts," he recorded of his contest with Mallet's party, " a breakfast with the P.M., and a successful speech in the House laid them low."[1]

When we consider that Lloyd George and his Foreign Secretary were Zionists there is nothing surprising in this victory over an anti-Zionist party. What is more remarkable is the evidence we find here of the extent to which Zionism's strength had grown in a few months. When they heard the news that three great powers were treating with a fourth one to conclude an arrangement harmful to their interests, they did not appeal to compassion or seek to lodge themselves deeper in their patrons' favour: instead, they came into the arena as a fifth power whom it was dangerous to antagonise. This turn in the career of Zionism is not so surprising to us if we remember how C. P. Scott's

[1]Letter to General Clayton, July 22nd, 1917. (The Sledmere Papers.)

revelations had put Zionists on their mettle against being ignored in favour of larger interests. At this point we should remember, too, that since Sokolov's first meeting with Mark Sykes and the establishment of communications, the Jews of almost the whole diaspora had heard the news and had their eyes on England.[1] We should also remember the unhappy adventures of the Portuguese Government in the Angola business, and the words of the Psalm: " Let them not say We have swallowed him up."

After the defeat of the Turkish party it seemed again that some formal act of state would inevitably be made by the British Government on behalf of the Zionists. Dr. Weizmann accompanied by Lord Rothschild had had an interview with Balfour at the end of June.[2] They had insisted that the time had come for a final decision and Balfour had asked them to draft a declaration for him to discuss with the Cabinet. But these signs were deceptive. There was a last obstacle to be overcome and this the greatest of all. A considerable opposition to Zionism had formed itself in England and France under the leadership of Jews.

It has become the fashion among writers on Zionist matters to dip the pen in vinegar at this point, and to portray these anti-Zionist Jews as monsters of unfeeling. They have been the subject of attacks similar to those conducted by anti-Semites against all Jews. The fact that many of them were rich has been treated as sufficient proof in itself that they were enemies of mankind, and it has become a commonplace assumption that they acted exclusively out of motives of cowardice and treachery. The truth is very different from this electioneering stuff. These men were worthy of the highest respect and what they did was as much a needful consequence of history as the passionate irredentism of the Zionist movement. They represented the continuing tradition of Moses Mendelssohn and the Reformists; they represented the

---

[1]Malcolm records that the news reached the Jadidis, among others, a group of crypto-Jews settled in Meshed in East Persia. As a result of Moslem pressure they had decided to abandon their faith for Islam, but when they heard that the British Government intended to support the Jewish claim to Palestine they changed their minds.

[2]*Arthur James Balfour* by E. C. Dugdale.

amazing success of the emancipated Jews of the nineteenth and twentieth centuries. It would have been a monstrosity of human nature if no Jew had voiced the claims which belonged to these things.

The struggle between the two schools was the last open conflict before the Declaration between the Eastern and Western traditions. This conflict had already appeared in the same form as now during Sokolov's visit to Paris in April. The largest Jewish organisation in France, the *Alliance Israélite Universelle*, was against modern Zionism. The members feared for the French allegiance of Jews if the ordinary patriotism of their people was to be complicated by the attractions of Jewish nationalism, and in this state of anxiety they looked with distrust at the arrival of two Zionist emissaries under the guidance of a romantically minded English Orientalist. They made repeated enquiries at Sokolov's hotel; they began to approach the officials of the Foreign Ministry, when their manœuvres were suddenly brought to an end in a most remarkable way.

Baron Edmond de Rothschild was one of the most arresting characters of his time. He occupied a position in society which was unique in Parisian history. He was the richest man in France, one of the greatest art-collectors of modern times, and in the world of international finance almost as powerful as the legends pretended. This great millionaire, surrounded by the mystery of fashion from his splendid possessions and mode of life, was an extraordinary mixture of egotism and magnanimity. Dr. Weizmann has related that he was conscious of his power and arrogant in the grasp of it, but at the same time afraid of its enormity. In a spirit of the purest philanthropy, with every prospect of loss, he had established his Palestine colonies, and yet for many years his reaction to organised Jewish irredentism was hostile. To a deputation headed by Max Nordau he explained his reasons with fierce candour: he had his own foundations in Palestine, he said, and added: "These are *my* colonies, and I shall do what I like with them." In Palestine itself the Jewish settlers whom he had rescued from persecution groaned at the autocracy of their benefactor. Among Zionists it was usual to regard him as a man too self-preoccupied to help this movement which had begun without him. But in the course of his old age, through the influence of his son Mr. James de Rothschild and of Dr. Weizmann, in whom he recognised a personality as vigorous as his own, Baron Edmond changed his views, and when he saw the approach of the conflict between the *Alliance* and the Zionists he intervened.

On the eve of the Passover he invited two leaders of the *Alliance* to his house, where he argued with them for four hours. " One day you will have to render an account," he said, " if you assume the role of Satan, blocking the road." One of the leaders urged that Zionism would cause hatred between Frenchmen and Jews. " They hate us anyhow," replied the Baron, " regardless of whether we do our duty for Eretz Israel or not. So let us do our duty." His final argument was as follows: that from a strictly French political point of view, the opposition of the Alliance to Zionism might have much to recommend it, but in view of the small size of the French Jewish community, and their happy circumstances compared with the devouring need of the Jewish millions in Russia, it would be a lasting infamy if French Jews should place their interests above those of their more numerous and less fortunate brethren. " Right is with them," he said, " and not with you. Therefore it devolves on you to declare to the French Government that what is asked of it [by the Zionists] is right and fair. To-morrow you will do it."

The leaders were convinced by the argument, and when they conveyed what the Baron had said to their colleagues they convinced the Alliance. The latter not only withdrew their opposition, leaving the road clear for Sokolov, but gave the Foreign Ministry a formal declaration of their support.[1]

Baron Edmond's action was not followed in England, where the Assimilationist party fought till the very end. As with the Turkish party, these enemies of Zionism were not organised

[1]This account of the activities of Baron Edmond de Rothschild is taken from Sokolov's record edited by Mr. Florian Sokolov.

into a coherent group and so they never realised their strength.

Their leader, or rather their most prominent man, was Edwin Samuel Montagu, one of the most gifted English Jews ever to appear in the House of Commons. He was the second practising Jew to be a senior member of a British Government when from June to December of 1916 he was Minister of Munitions. He resigned with Asquith, but after six months of political idleness he accepted a historic Secretaryship of State for India, a move which Asquith foolishly never quite forgave him. He remained a member of Lloyd George's government till 1922.

He portrayed himself vividly in his diaries:[1] a hard short-tempered man easily consumed by a great idea, marvellously far-sighted, but so much the victim of passionate moods that often he could only see prejudice; generous in his conclusions about his fellow-men but harshly, sometimes petulantly critical of them in the course of acquaintance. He made enemies everywhere, and yet he often expressed his need of friendship with a surprising lack of reserve. He could criticise himself unsparingly. He aimed at himself a few of the bitter jibes with which he too often mocked others, and yet for all this self-discipline and self-honesty, he was liable to the egotism of genius in extreme forms. Duality ran right through his forthright and morbid character with its astonishing mixture of idealism and cynicism. When he was not right he was as often wrong beyond all expectation, and nowhere did the double aspect of his nature appear more forcibly than in his response to Zionism. It engaged his feelings with a violence that forced him to look deeply into its consequences, but which brought all his prejudice down to blind him to some of its essential attributes. He wrote thus on August 3rd of 1916 to Sir Eric Drummond:[2]

[1] The interested reader may consult *An Indian Diary*, edited by Edwin Montagu's widow, the late Venetia Montagu, and published in 1930. It was written and dictated by him in the course of his official journey to India from October, 1917, to May, 1918, and though severely specialised in subject is a document of rare general interest. By the kindness of the late Mrs. Montagu and her daughter, Miss Judith Montagu, the writer has been allowed access to the original typescript and other of Montagu's papers.

[2] The late Earl of Perth.

" I return herewith the correspondence between you, Grey, and Buchanan.[1] I am not concerned with the American point of view, but I am concerned with the attitude which is taken up as regards the Jewish question as a whole. It seems to me that Jews have got to consider whether they regard themselves as members of a religion or of a race world-wide in its habitat and striving to maintain in spite of geographical distribution an entity for political as well as religious consideration.

" For myself I have long made the choice. I view with horror the aspiration for national entity. Did I accept it, as a patriotic Englishman, I should resign my position on the Cabinet and declare myself neutral, or at any rate, not primarily concerned in the present war. Nobody is entitled to occupy the position that I do unless he is free and determined to consider, and consider only, the interests of the British Empire.

" I regard with perfect equanimity whatever treatment the Jews receive in Russia. I am convinced that the treatment meted out to Jews in Russia will be no worse or no better than the Russian degree of general civilisation. In that respect Russia is an advancing country. They are behind England, as every country is, in their ideas of religious and civil freedom. But they are developing. Their future is in front of them. They have not reached their zenith, and as they approach it, I am confident that, just as England is, they will become a more habitable country and perhaps, but this is another story, a less efficient military organisation. For the moment the correspondences seem to me to show clearly two things; first that the Russian Jews have not, in Buchanan's opinion, played a very distinguished part in the war (I hope they have played a more distinguished part in England, but be it said in passing, could anything be more disastrous than for Jewish Englishmen and Jewish Americans to be bracketed with the Jewish Russians, sharing the same verdict for their part in the war?), secondly, that Jewish nationalism (which is to my mind horrible and unpatriotic) has already damaged, or con-

[1]See footnote page 172 ante.

tributed to the damage of the Allied cause by helping in the disappearance of Sazonoff.

" I implore the Foreign Office to be content with that achievement and to discountenance this pro-German anti-civilisation tendency."

Views resembling these were widely shared by Western Jews.

In England the Jewish community was centred round a venerable body, the Board of Deputies of British Jews, and the President of this Board, moved by the same anxieties about patriotism which had distressed the *Alliance Israélite*, took action in partnership with his colleague of the Anglo-Jewish Association on the 28th of May. A long letter appeared in *The Times* over the signatures of the two Presidents, David Alexander and Claude Montefiore,[1] in which, " in view of the statements and discussions lately published in the newspapers relative to a projected Jewish settlement in Palestine," they defined their opinion.

Their first objection was to the national basis of the new Jewry. They claimed to share with Zionists the Jewish veneration of the Promised Land and to look for a time when Jerusalem would be a centre to which all Jewish eyes would be turned, and they recalled that they had declared their readiness to co-operate with the Zionists " on the basis of the so-called cultural policy which had been adopted at the last two Zionist Congresses in 1911 and 1913," but as regards establishing the hallowed centre as a national state with frontiers, they protested that it would have the effect of making all Jews of the diaspora strangers in strange lands. They objected vigorously that to deny the possibility of Jewish assimilation was a slander. These were familiar arguments of anti-Zionism, but the two Presidents went on to deduce a novel one:

" The Jewish religion," they said, " being the only certain test of a Jew, a Jewish nationality must be founded on, and limited by, the religion. It cannot be supposed for a moment that any section of Jews would aim at a commonwealth governed

[1]See Appendix A for the text of this letter.

by religious tests, and limited in the matter of freedom of conscience, but can a religious nationality express itself politically in any other way? The only alternative would be a secular Jewish nationality, recruited on some loose and obscure principle of race and ethnographic peculiarity; but this would not be Jewish in any spiritual sense, and its establishment in Palestine would be a denial of all the ideals and hopes by which the revival of Jewish life in that country commends itself to the Jewish consciousness and Jewish sympathy." This raised questions which had never been answered, have never been since, and perhaps never will be.

The letter closed with a last objection: that to accord special rights to the Jews of Palestine, " in excess of those enjoyed by the rest of the population," was immoral and impolitic.

A press controversy arose immediately. Within the next few days answering letters from Dr. Gaster, Lord Rothschild, Dr. Weizmann and the Chief Rabbi were printed. They all asserted that Alexander and Montefiore did not represent a majority opinion, and Dr. Weizmann scored a notable victory by exposing the allegation that the Zionists sought privileges in Palestine which would not be enjoyed by the whole population. The more difficult questions were evaded, but the victory was considered to have gone to the Zionists, in signal of which, on the 29th May, *The Times* published a leading article written by Mr. Wickham Steed, in which its batteries of impressive platitude were put to the service of Jewish nationalism. About three weeks later Alexander and all his followers were compelled to resign their positions on the Board of Deputies. Nevertheless, from this time until the end, there existed a possibility that the British Government would at the last moment refuse a Zionist declaration out of deference to Jewish opinion.

The anti-Zionist party was very strong. It contained many of the best known Jewish names in England. After June, 1917, it was represented in the Government, as we have seen, by Edwin Montagu. It had valuable Gentile support. Its ideas were echoed by many people in the India Office and Government, who found a spokesman in Lord Curzon. Nevertheless, for all their great strength and influence, the anti-Zionists were defeated in a very short time. One reason was that though, contrary to what Zionists believed, they probably represented a majority opinion of Jews in England, this opinion was unheroic and unsuited to a time of war, and so not one that people liked to admit as their own. Another was that with the exception of a few people, such as Edwin Montagu, anti-Zionists did not hold their convictions with the same passion as their opponents did, and many of them were uneasily aware that they represented the way of life which for many years, since the time of Moses Mendelssohn, had given the Jews their besetting fear of disappearance. Another reason why they failed was that they conducted their campaign carelessly.

They were very inaccurately informed about their opponents. We have noted how Alexander and Montefiore accused Zionists of wishing to make the Jews of Palestine into a ruling caste, without any justification. Lord Curzon believed this too.[1] Montagu made one fantastic error. The reader may have been puzzled by the concluding sentence of his letter to Sir Eric Drummond when he asked the Foreign Office " to discountenance this pro-German anti-civilisation tendency." He never looked far enough beyond the Berlin Headquarters of Zionism to detect the movement's Russian ancestry, and he remained convinced to the end of his life that it was Teutonic in character. The idea seems to have obsessed him. In October of 1917 he recorded in his diary:

" Wingate[2] spoke to me about the danger of a Germanised Turkey, which would make our position in Egypt . . . frightfully and fearfully difficult, and that is why I am glad to find in him a strong opponent of Zionism, for this would undoubtedly bolster up German influence in Palestine, most Zionists being of German origin." He put up ideas of that kind, which impressed

---

[1]In the memorandum of 24th October, 1917, mentioned later in this essay. It is quoted in Lord Zetland's life of Lord Curzon, Vol. II.

[2]Sir Reginald Wingate, High Commissioner in Egypt in succession to Sir Henry MacMahon.

his colleagues, until they were knocked down soon after. None of the anti-Zionists made sufficient study for their needs.

One very common misunderstanding of Zionism which led Montagu's party astray was not confined to the anti-Zionists. It was the most important of such errors and concerned a curious party conflict within Zionism at which we should look. We have had a reference to it in the letter of Alexander and Montefiore, when they spoke of " the so-called cultural policy which had been adopted at the last two Zionist Congresses in 1911 and 1913."

There were two main parties within the Zionist movement and they were known as the Politicals and the Practicals. The Politicals believed that it was essential to obtain political guarantees before beginning the work of restoration, the Practicals that it was essential to establish Jewish colonies in Palestine while working for a guarantee. That was the cause of their difference and the shape of Zionism's two-party structure, in which, since 1911, the Practicals had been the ruling party. Now the leaders of the Practicals, among whom were Dr. Weizmann and Nahun Sokolov, were disciples of one of the most influential teachers to rise in Jewry within modern times. This was a man from Kiev called Asher Ginsberg, better known by the Hebrew pseudonym of Ahad Ha'am, meaning " One of the People," under which he published his writings. He was living in London at this time as an agent for the Wissotzki Tea Company. His story was very remarkable.

He had become known in the year 1889 as the author of an article on Hibbath Zion which appeared in a Jewish paper of Odessa. It was a discouraging piece directed against the Jewish migrations from Russia to Palestine and called " This is not the Way." He was preoccupied by the Jewish dread of disappearance, and he insisted that the real solution was to be found, not in seeking amelioration of circumstances but in the preservation and renaissance of the Jewish spirit. For this, he said, it was necessary to begin at the beginning and to establish cultural centres in Palestine first. These are not the kind of messages which are received with irrepressible joy by the hunted and the persecuted during a time of troubles. But Ahad Ha'am was a great man. The Jews not only of Russia but of the world listened to him as to a prophet, and his influence can only be compared to that of Herzl. He had a considerable advantage over the latter. His essays are impressive in translation, but readers of Hebrew declare that Ahad Ha'am is one of the great Jewish writers of all time. Dr. Weizmann asserted that his role in the Jewish revival could only be likened to that of a Gandhi or a Mazzini.

A man of his stature could not fit with precision into any party programme, and it was something of a paradox that the party of the Practicals which was most closely identified with his name and ideas was the one most directly descended from Hibbath Zion, in attacking which Ahad Ha'am first became famous. This complex situation was perfectly consistent, but was the beginning of the misunderstanding.

An idea spread among people that under Ahad Ha'am's influence Zionists had " come to their senses " and had rejected for ever Herzl's wild plans to turn Palestine into a revived Kingdom of Israel. It was said that ever since the Practicals won power in the Zionist Executive in 1911 the purpose of the movement had been directed towards establishing a non-political sacred centre for Jews from which they would draw spiritual sustenance, and that such was the sole aim of the orthodox school.

This was all very well, but it overlooked the main impulse of Ahad Ha'am's propaganda. He was a religious teacher, but this by no means implied that he sought a kingdom not of this world.

He was not a Reformist, and he was bitterly opposed to the Assimilationist school to which Edwin Montagu belonged. He was very much a gradualist, but as regards the aims of Zionism he was as uncompromising as any fanatic. He said: " Life in exile, at its best, will always remain life in exile; that is to say that it will always remain the opposite of that free national life which is the aim of the Zionist movement." He was one of those who went so far in his Zionism as to declare a preference for the wretched life of the Pale with its ardent responses, to the civilised life of Western Jewry. "I may not be emancipated," he once said, "but at least I have not bartered my soul for emancipation. I can proclaim from the housetops that my kith and kin are dear to me wherever they are, without being constrained to find excuses. I at least can remember Jerusalem." It was natural for him to differ from other Zionists over the profane purposes of the Hoveve Zion and of Herzl's school with their emphasis on material requirements alone. "We must all agree," he said, "that Zionism has need not only of subscriptions and shares, but even more of souls. One Jewish soul saved from the pitfall of Assimilationism is worth all the shares in the world." No one who reads the works of Ahad Ha'am can doubt that he wanted more stress on the immaterial not in order to dilute Zionism, but to make it stronger and closer-knit. And yet this was the man whom some anti-Zionists believed to be their ally, and whom the Gentile Zionists and even a few Jewish ones came to consider a moderator of Zionist extremism. The mistake had a great effect on history.

We have already drawn attention to the part religion played in Sykes's life. In his biographical work, Sir Shane Leslie asserted that it was Catholicism that made him a Zionist. The judgment was acute, but it needs qualifying. It was his unconventional Catholicism of which Sykes made use here; modernist nationalist Catholicism with a strong admixture of the Gothic Revival. Though he regarded Jewish nationalism as being separate from theological Judaism; though he did not make the mistake of imagining that the aim of Zionism was the establishment of a Jewish Papacy in the Promised Land, he did see the movement in terms more appropriate to his own religion. He saw it as sacramental, as primarily concerned with an outward sign of inward grace, in this case of the virtues which supposedly attach to the tilling of the soil. The main purpose of the Jewish colonies would be to furnish a proof, he believed, "of the capacity of the Jews to produce a virtuous and simple agrarian population,"[1] and it was his final conviction before the issue of the Declaration that the Zionists were so preoccupied with spiritual values of this kind that they did not wish for any political hold on Jerusalem or the establishment of a republic. The origin of this error by which he saw Zionism as so interested in spiritual treasure that its territorial requirement was only a little less unessential than the Papal States in his own belief, this great misconception lay in that common misconception of Ahad Ha'am which we have noticed, but in this case it was strengthened by the character of Sykes's teacher. Dr. Gaster did not consider himself a follower of Ahad Ha'am, but he resembled him in many of his ideas. He was contemptuous of those who saw in Zionism no more than the adoption to the Jewish world of modern nationalism. In *Zionism and the Jewish Future* he said that "the aim and goal" of the movement was "to create for the Jews a national home not so much for physical as for spiritual life."[2] Sykes believed these to be the views of the majority. He received confirmation in a strange manner.

We must again note the activities of Lucien Wolf. Like Edwin Montagu, this remarkable man seems to have become enamoured of a mistaken view of Zionism to which he gave admirable expression. In March of 1917 he delivered a lecture wherein he sought to elucidate the capture of the Zionist Executive by the Practicals, and he asserted categorically that the Practical Party had suppressed the former Herzlian programme in favour of one for "the peaceful penetration of Palestine, the goal of which should be a spiritual centre instead of a state of Jews." No such proposals are to be found among the resolutions of the Zionist Congresses of 1911 or 1913, and the strange thing is that this had been pointed out to Wolf by Sokolov in a letter

---

[1] Letter to Sokolov of April 14th, 1917, telling him of his interview with Monsignor Pacelli, and offering guidance for Sokolov in his forthcoming interview with Benedict XV. (The Sledmere Papers.)

[2] Dr. Gaster asserted in the same book that the idea that the Jewish future could or should follow the career of modern nationalism with little if any reference to the Jewish faith was Assimilationist in character, being born of an exaggerated acquiescence in Western culture. An opposite point of view is to be found expressed with some violence in Sokolov's History.

written five months before.[1] In spite of this warning, he persisted in his belief. He formed a theory on the basis of his belief, and in his March lecture he declared that the modified new Zionism of the Practicals had since the outbreak of war been overthrown by " an emergency political Junta " whose programme was " more aggressive, more sweeping and dogmatic than any that ever came from Herzl himself." A report of Wolf's address was sent to Mark Sykes by Leopold Greenberg. It was easy for the members of the " emergency political Junta " to prove that in fact they were the authentic representatives of the modifying Practicals whom Wolf professed to admire, and that they were in daily contact with Ahad Ha'am. It was as easy as to disprove Montagu's allegation that they were German spies.[2]

To return to the main current of the story, which is now nearing the end.

Although the manœuvres of the anti-Zionists were not well thought out, they did succeed in weakening the confidence of the Cabinet. From August till October Edwin Montagu seized every opportunity to plead with its members, sometimes with tears, against the British Government's Zionist policy, and he distributed a memorandum explaining how in his own personal case such a policy would fatally divide his loyalties. He began to make an impression. It is conceivable that he might have changed the minds of the majority had it not been that the force of circumstances brought his influence in this matter to a sudden end. On the 4th October he addressed the Cabinet on Zionism for the last time. Two weeks later he left England on his famous mission to India. He was away seven months.

Before going he saw that his pleading had had some effect. To resolve once and for all the doubts which he had sown, the

---

[1]The Gaster Papers.

[2]The sources for the preceding passage are, in chronological order: *Zionism and the Jewish Future*, edited by H. Sacher, 1915; correspondence in the Gaster Papers; a copy of Lucien Wolf's address sent to Mark Sykes with a covering note by Leopold Greenberg on the 21st March; the letter from Sykes to Sokolov previously quoted; and " A note on Palestine and Zionism " by Sir Mark Sykes, evidently written for official circulation and dated 21st September, 1917. One copy is annotated by Dr. Weizmann.

Cabinet decided to obtain the opinions of eight representative Jews and be guided by the result. They applied to Leonard Cohen (Chairman of the Jewish Board of Guardians), Claude Montefiore, Sir Stuart Samuel (who had succeeded Alexander as Chairman of the Board of Deputies), Sir Philip Magnus, Lord Rothschild, Nahun Sokolov, Dr. Weizmann, and the Chief Rabbi Dr. Hertz, inviting them to comment on the draft formula. The result of this momentous " election " was kept secret, but it is said on good authority that four replied in a pro-Zionist sense, three in a hostile sense, and that one was neutral. It is generally agreed that the Cabinet were won back to Zionism by the answer of the Chief Rabbi on the 16th October. This remarkable document ran as follows:

" It is with feelings of the profoundest gratification that I learn of the intention of H.M. Government to lend its powerful support to the re-establishment in Palestine of a National Home for the Jewish people. The proposed declaration of H.M. Government that it ' will use its best endeavours to facilitate the achievement of this object ' will mark an epoch in Jewish history. To millions of my brethren throughout the world, it will mean the realisation of Israel's undying hope of a Restoration—a hope that has been the spiritual lodestar of Israel's wanderings for the last 1,800 years.

" The draft declaration is in spirit and in substance everything that could be desired. I welcome the reference to the civil and religious rights of the existing non-Jewish communities in Palestine. It is but a translation of the basic principles of the Mosaic legislation: ' And if a stranger sojourn with thee in your land, ye shall not vex him. But the stranger that dwelleth with you shall be unto you as one born among you, and thou shalt love him as thyself.' (Lev. xix. 33, 34.) "

He went on to say that he was " anxious " that a phrase which had been inserted out of deference to Edwin Montagu on the rights of assimilated Jews should be shortened, presumably so as to give it less prominence, and this was done. The letter

concluded with a formal expression of his gratitude as Chief
Rabbi to the Prime Minister and Foreign Secretary.

Anti-Zionism had not yet been defeated. The departure of
Edwin Montagu did not appear as a disaster for his side. Lord
Curzon remained to fight the last battle, and he, unlike Montagu,
was a member of the War Cabinet. He failed, as all the anti-
Zionists failed, through insufficient knowledge of his opponents.
On the 26th October he addressed a fine bubble-pricking note
to the Foreign Secretary on the final formula. He pointed out
that a National Home must mean a National State and that such
an innovation was dangerous and impractical. Had he said this
and no more he might have made an impression, but he forgot
" the law of parsimony." He went on to argue that the country
could not contain the Jews of the world (a proposal which was
not entertained), and that the Syrians of Palestine would not be
content to live as expropriated " hewers of wood and drawers
of water " to the new ruling caste (a point dealt with by the
Chief Rabbi). He sent the note and did nothing more. It had
no effect.

Then on the 1st November there were last-minute hesitations
among the Ministers. Either through the forgetfulness and confusion that often attend business at the highest levels of the State,
or because following the Nivelle disaster the French Government
had gone through a rapid succession of changes (there were four
changes of Foreign Minister alone between September and
December of 1917), or for some other reason, the Cabinet was
suddenly doubtful as to the view of their French allies. It was
now that the labours of Sykes and Sokolov bore a second harvest
with dramatic suddenness. Mark Sykes went to the French
Embassy for Georges Picot. He said to him: " Can you come
immediately to Downing Street and tell the Ministers what the
French Government thinks of Zionism? Can you do it straight
away without seeking instructions from Paris? There are
situations," he added, " in which one must act instantly without
referring to others." Picot agreed. " I will come with you,"
he said, " and show the Ministers *notre formule*," (meaning

the document given to Sokolov on the 4th of June). Sykes and Picot went to Downing Street. The declaration of Jules Cambon came as a surprise to several Ministers,[1] but it finally made up their minds.

The last obstacle had been removed, and on November 2nd the famous letter was sent to Lord Rothschild. Although it has been printed many hundreds, perhaps thousands, of times since then we should record its terms again here.

" His Majesty's Government view with favour the establishment in Palestine of a National Home for the Jewish people, and will use their best endeavours to facilitate the achievement of this object, it being clearly understood that nothing shall be done which may prejudice the civil and religious rights of the existing non-Jewish communities in Palestine or the rights and political status enjoyed by Jews in any other country."

Such, in the opinion of the present writer, were the main lines of thought, feeling, influence and action which met in the preoccupations of 1917 and produced the Balfour Declaration. Some lines which were important in the beginning vanished a little later, others which were invisible in 1916 became of the first significance in the course of the next year. Without question the first impulse of the British Government's Zionist policy proceeded from a hope that Jewish influences in America would serve the Allied cause, but, except for one later statement by Lloyd George, no convincing evidence has yet been produced to show that this impulse persisted beyond a very short time. It seemed to disappear with surprising suddenness. Nothing is said about it in the papers of Mark Sykes, or in the numerous later pronouncements of Arthur Balfour. A certain air of mystery still hides, and probably always will hide, the origin of this, the most unexpected action of State in our history.

One explanation can be dismissed immediately. There was

---

[1]This curious episode was disclosed by the late Monsieur Georges Picot in an address given in Paris in 1939. It was brought to the writer's notice by Mr. Leonard Stein.

no Jewish plot such as the ingenious Abbé Barruel would have delighted to expose.[1] Although the initiative was with the Jews from the moment they could communicate with each other throughout the world, the Gentiles never wished to resist that initiative and often acted more rashly for Zionism than the Jews. No Jew " forced the pace " as Balfour did by his calculated indiscretions in America; only at Gentile insistence did the Jews show their strength by negotiating alone in Paris, and C. P. Scott's betrayal of State secrets is not paralleled on the Jewish side. Only one piece of evidence in support of a Jewish plot is worth consideration. Max Nordau's statement in 1920 that the term " National Home " was intended to mislead, and the subsequent history of the Jews in Palestine make it possible to suspect that Nahun Sokolov and Dr. Weizmann deceived Mark Sykes as to the intentions of Jewish irredentism. We have noted Sokolov's evasions in his interview with the Pope, and there is no doubt that Sykes's last recommendation to the Cabinet, on which much depended, gave an assurance that the Jews had no wish to establish a republic in Palestine of any kind.[2] But the suspicion lifts if all the available evidence on the origins of the Balfour Declaration is examined, an enormous task, which the present writer, with deference and conscious of numerous slips of memory and of uneven application, can claim to have accomplished.

In this question of Jewish intentions it is first necessary to remember that at the time these things happened the mass movements of the world were with few exceptions on a much smaller scale than they are to-day. This is entirely true of the Jewish world. The pogroms of Alexander and Nicholas accounted for the death of 5,000 Jews at the very most, such a number as Himmler and Kaltenbrunner were wont to handle in one week,

[1]And as Mr. Douglas Reed has often attempted to expose, but not so far with any success. This literary descendant of Wilhelm Marr has suggested that Hitler was a Jew and that his racial persecutions had the sole object of forcing the Palestine issue in favour of Zionism!

[2]See footnote page 221. It is fair to notice that the copy of Sykes's memorandum annotated by Dr. Weizmann has no mention of the subject of a Jewish state. This is found in the second version, which was written subsequently. Nevertheless it seems valid to suppose that Sykes consulted the Zionist leaders on this occasion.

and even one day.[1] The Angola and Uganda schemes proposed total settlements of around 120,000 people each, and among the objections raised to those schemes small numbers were not mentioned. The El Arish scheme was for 100,000 settlers only. In 1914, when the total population of Palestine was about 750,000, there were 80,000 Jews in Palestine, of whom only 12,000 were settled on the land, in pursuance of the Zionist mysticism of the soil. There was no reason to suppose then that these numbers would or could be multiplied by twenty in thirty years. Added to this it must be remembered that Dr. Weizmann himself was in accord not only with Ahad Ha'am's general policy, but to a large extent with his belief in gradualism. In the state question it was the Gentiles who outran the Jews all the time. It was men such as Herbert Sidebotham who thrust it forward far more than the Jewish Zionists. In the May of 1917, Dr. Weizmann made his own position as Zionist leader, and that of the Zionist movement, perfectly clear in a public utterance.

" One hears from our friends," he said, " both Jewish and non-Jewish that it is the endeavour of the Zionist movement to create a Jewish state in Palestine. . . . We cannot consider [such opinions] as safe statesmanship. Strong as the Zionist movement may be . . . it must yet be admitted that conditions are not yet ripe for the setting up of a State ad hoc. States must be built up slowly, gradually, systematically and patiently. We therefore say that, while the creation of a Jewish Commonwealth in Palestine is our final ideal . . . the way to achieve it lies through a series of intermediary stages."

Dr. Weizmann might have gained immense popularity among the Jews on many later occasions if he had abandoned the principles of gradualism which were a condition of British support, but, to his lasting honour, he never did so, until the force of circumstances fairly compelled him to acquiesce in the

---

[1] It is not possible to obtain accurate statistics for anything which happened in Imperial Russia. This rough figure of 5,000 is given after consulting several fragmentary sources and it is to be taken as covering the intentional governmental pogroms only, not the Jewish casualties of the civil war.

foundation of the Israelite State, and accept the Presidency. All this was done in the open.

We may look at another "Barruelist" interpretation of this strange event, little known in the West, but common throughout the world of Islam. Among Moslems of to-day the Balfour Declaration is usually regarded as the outcome not of a Jewish but of a Gentile plot. Lloyd George, it is said, thirsting for Empire and seeing no way to thwart the Syrian ambitions of France, got hold of some Jews and put them up to demanding a British-protected home so that he could then grab the Sanjak of Jerusalem in defiance of his promises both to King Hussein and his European Allies. Even so grave an authority as George Antonius believed this to be the true explanation of what happened.

The theory obtains colour from the strategical arguments of the first Samuel memorandum, the similar arguments of Herbert Sidebotham, and most of all from the insistence of the Zionists on British protection; but anyone who examines the sequence of events with care can recognise the theory as untrue. To arrive at an understanding, we should first clear our minds of the idea that Lloyd George acted in a dishonourable manner in this question. His "Welsh wizardry," his reputation for an atrocious love of scheming, and what Maynard Keynes called "that flavour of final purposelessness," was largely imagined by other people from the incessant play-acting without which, we may suppose, he could hardly pursue his public destiny. We need not say that this man to whom friendship meant almost nothing had a golden heart, but we should recognise that under his display of Machiavellian cunning he had the honesty of abounding common sense. We have already seen that Lloyd George in April of 1917 drew attention to conflicting pledges in Eastern policy and suggested that a choice might have to be made between an Arab or a Jewish alliance. We have seen that he urged caution, and the exclusion of Palestine from all commitments. He was assured by men of experience in this field that his fears were groundless. It was in no way his doing that tangled arrangements were made which looked to later observers like the remains of an enormous conspiracy.

It may, however, be argued that the plot existed nonetheless, being the work, perhaps, of Lloyd George's colleagues rather than himself. If this is believed, then it must be remembered that a perfect opportunity presented itself to the plotters in the decision to obtain Jewish suffrages for the guidance of the Cabinet. Nothing would have been easier than to manage the vote, and nothing is more clear than that the selection of the voters was made and the verdict recorded by scrupulously fair means. But the strongest and finally conclusive proof that there was no Gentile plot lies in the reluctance of the British Government to accept the consequence of its deed. In spite of Lloyd George's and Mark Sykes's personal predilections, and Lord Robert Cecil's acquiescence in the Zionist view that Britain should be appointed the protecting power, the proposal for an American Mandate was not lost until the Peace Conference of Versailles, and then not through English obstruction, or any dissuading of President Wilson, but through American isolationism alone.

If we dismiss the plot theories, as we must do, because they are untenable, then we may be led to seek the cause of the declaration in the general circumstances of the Great War, which have become easier to understand because of their repetition since that time, though it must be confessed that the explanation which results from their study, since it deals with hidden impulses, can never be susceptible of proof.

Unless human nature reacts it must perish. Amid the responsibilities and atrocities of war the consolations of idealism are not only pleasurable but matters of the utmost need. Those who lived in the Age of Diffusion met in Zionism an idealist cult very exactly suited to the feelings and beliefs most typical of that time. Part of the immense power of this cult among the Jews lay in its breadth, its equal appeal to modernists and those who cherished the past, to nationalists, racialists, progressives, reactionaries, as much as to orthodox believers, and so great was this power that it could extend far beyond Jewry, to the world at large. From the deeply emotional enthusiasm of such Gentile Zionists as C. P. Scott, Fitzmaurice, Herbert Sidebotham, and Mark Sykes, and from the consecrated determination of Arthur Balfour it is allowable to suppose that in a world made hideous by the calamities of 1917 Zionism appeared as a vision of construction and piety, as to a succeeding generation in like case the Beveridge Report, by proposing an ideal, suddenly became the preoccupation and delight of a whole people. If we consider the Zionism of Lloyd George's Government from this point of view we may understand too how a small group of Jews were able to impose their will on a powerful world organisation such as the British Empire, and how it came about that though the Gentiles seemed to have the initiative it had in fact passed to the Jews in the early stages of these negotiations and remained with them to the end thirty years later. Zionism could never mean the same to a Gentile as to a Jew. The former had recourse to it for the idealism of which he stood in the most dire need, but the Jew went to Zionism for more than idealism; for religion and life itself. Even so clear-minded a man as Arthur Balfour was perforce vague as to how he contrived to be a Christian and a Zionist at the same time, and this was the case of all the Gentiles. Among the Jews, on the other hand, it required not a little casuistry on the part of such men as Edwin Montagu and Lucien Wolf to explain how they could be Jews and yet refuse to be Zionists. The Jews understood what they wanted and why they wanted it, and for that reason they got it in the end. The Gentiles never quite knew what they wanted or why they did, and though they acted infinitely more from virtue than from self-seeking, there was, if our explanation is true, this most pardonable, even admirable, but nonetheless fatal insincerity in their state of mind. This can account for their frequent misjudgments not of details so much as of principles, for the way they saw only what they wanted to see, and ignored such plain warnings as Dr. Weizmann's assertion that an Israelite state was the ultimate end, and the Chief Rabbi's implication of that when he referred to the

Syrians of Palestine as " the stranger in your land." The same unclear state of mind and feeling may account for the dreadful later history of British rule in Palestine.

It is possible though unlikely that the problems left by the Declaration might have been solved if the same actors had remained on the stage for longer. As it was the continuity of British Zionist policy was thoroughly broken within four years. Mark Sykes was the first to vanish from the scene. He went to the Near East in 1918 on a desperate mission to reconcile French and Arab claims in Syria, and Arab and Zionist claims in Palestine. There his career ended in failure, disillusion, and grief. The Sykes-Picot negotiations are outside this story, but one detail of them needs to be stressed here. In the Zionist episode of 1917 we may get an idea of Sykes as somewhat anti-French. Such is an entirely wrong impression. His fault as a negotiator lay the other way, and it is arguable (though not justly, in the writer's opinion) that he went too far in his efforts to correct anti-French prejudice among his countrymen.[1] Lloyd George appears to have been consistent in his distaste for French claims in the East Mediterranean and when the war was drawing to a close he turned against Sykes, whom he had hitherto cherished and admired, when he found that the policy which was necessary to the Entente in 1917 had become an irritation in the chilly light of victory. With the knowledge of dwindling support at home, Mark Sykes pursued his mission in Syria, and there he first became fully conscious of what all the Zionists, Jew and Gentile, had either minimised, or pretended did not exist; the simple, home-loving, utterly incompetent but inevitable nationalism of the Moslem inhabitants of Palestine.[2]

He tried to calm the storms which he and others had raised.

[1] For a brief account of the anti-French view of Englishmen in the Near East, the interested reader should consult Mr. David Garnett's introduction to the letters of T. E. Lawrence. It should be remembered that the anti-French prejudice of those times was anti-Russian and was based on the idea that French policy was subservient to the Russian Government. The Turkish Party in England were inclined to encourage this theory.

[2] One Zionist alone recognised the force of Arab nationalism in full, and that was Dr. Gaster, see *The Letters of T. E. Lawrence*, editorial note by Mr. David Garnett on page 285.

A professional civil servant or a politician of longer experience would before now have had a line of retreat well prepared, but because he was who he was Mark Sykes had rushed into this affair with a disregard of personal advantage which he took to extreme lengths,[1] and so he received on himself the whole vast avalanche of blame implicit in these impossible negotiations.

He procured his recall in January and left for Paris in the hope that Balfour and Lloyd George might share his anxieties, but at his journey's end he found that the support he had once enjoyed in full measure was now wholly withdrawn. During his Syrian mission his robust health had given way, and when in February of 1919 he was attacked by influenza he died in two days. He was forty years old.

In October of the same year Arthur Balfour resigned the Foreign Secretaryship. He was succeeded by Lord Curzon under whose administration two years later the conduct of affairs in Palestine was transferred from the Foreign Office to the Colonial Office, a logical and perhaps inescapable move which meant that from then on day-to-day Zionist affairs were in the hands of people whose training had fitted them for very different tasks. Arthur Balfour is not known to have made any representation against the new arrangement. He died in the March of 1930 at the age of eighty-two. He received Dr. Weizmann among his last visitors. He was happy in the hour of his death and never regretted for an instant his part in the Jewish revival. In spite of the Palestinian disorders of 1928 and 1929, the alarm which the Declaration had caused was beginning to die down in the Moslem world at large, and it seemed possible that within ten years Zionism might be permanently reconciled to its neighbours. Lord Milner died in the same year.

Almost alone of the principals, Lloyd George lived to witness the modern calamities of the Jews, and his behaviour towards them in the nineteen thirties has been the subject of distress and puzzlement. Many people supposed that this man who had

[1] In a spirit not unlike that of T. E. Lawrence he refused to accept honours because he believed that he was labouring on behalf of other people and could only receive honours when their happiness was attained.

presided over the Cabinet which issued the declaration, and who in many minds had earned a serious title to be considered " the greatest benefactor of the Jews," would stand forth now as a champion, but during the whole period of Jewish persecution in Germany he recorded no memorable protest either in the House of Commons or in public addresses. He seemed to have forgotten the Jews as he had done many other people and causes. There are signs that even so early as 1919 the exaltations with which Zionism had filled him in early war-days had grown less, for his breach with Mark Sykes was not caused by a belief that through the fault of this adviser contradictory policies had been followed towards Jews and Arabs (a substantial charge), but because, in his view, Sykes had given too much to the French.[1] Unlike Balfour, he rarely spoke of Zionism. In the years after his Premiership he made only two important statements on the subject, one in his memoirs, one in his evidence before the Royal Commission of 1937. They are perplexing. In his memoirs he wrote that the Declaration was Dr. Weizmann's reward for his chemical services to the nation; to the Royal Commission he asserted that it was promulgated in exchange for propaganda work, and for no other reason. These discrepant accounts are not necessarily incompatible or untrue, but the very fact that they are widely different suggests that their author was not deeply interested in the question.[2] From such considerations it is natural to suppose that in his passion for Jewish irredentism we see not only the excitability but the shallowness of Lloyd George's character. This is wrong.

For all his variety Lloyd George was not a versatile man. He could fill a large number of Cabinet posts with equal and incomparable skill, but this was not because he could turn rapidly from one interest to another or use at will any of a large number of irons in the fire, but rather because he could concentrate his

---

[1] Lord Riddell's *Intimate Diary of the Peace Conference and After.*

[2] Friends of Lloyd George have suggested another curious explanation: that he had a boyish side which made him deeply ashamed of the sentimentality of some of his impulses and inclined him to self-explanations of a " tough " and disreputable nature which he did not merit.

mind with a power which was excluding. In that part of the History of Zionism which lies within the years of his premiership we see him in an untypical role, approving from afar, rarely descending to close quarters with the subject of his heart, turning towards it only once or twice from other and chief preoccupations. This was not his usual way.

When the war was over he conceived that one need stood above all others in the world: to solve the problem of unemployment. To this he gave his mind with all his old vigour but none of his old success. For nearly twenty years, during what he believed to be his prime, he was refused office and thus denied any opportunity of carrying out the policy he had devised and which he believed, possibly with justice, to be the remedy for this besetting cause of poverty. On reaching power, Hitler instituted a land policy similar to that of Lloyd George, with the same purpose, and with apparent success. For this, the reputable side of Nazism, Lloyd George conceived an intense admiration, and this admiration explains his visit to Berchtesgaden, his smooth encounter with its occupant, and his blindness to the man's evil, a blindness which allowed him to forget the renewal of atrocity which was not only essential to Hitler's regime but to his personal happiness. In his old age Lloyd George continued to live in the present, wrapped up in enthusiasms and temporarily oblivious of what lay outside them. In this disposition of his character is to be found the explanation of his apparent later callousness, but it is a false exaggeration of its consequences to say that he forgot Zionism. He could no more do this than he could forget the Authorised Version of the Bible or the hymns of Wales. In him the traditions of Gentile Zionism found their greatest expression, and the cessation of his Zionist activity after 1919 need not be deplored. After his fall there was probably nothing more in his power that he could do for the people he loved.

The issue of the Balfour Declaration was the last wholly

independent Imperial act of a British Government done without any reference at all to pressure from any other great State or combine of States. It will probably go down to history as the product of miscalculations not often equalled. None of its political hypotheses proved to be correct. The belief of self-interested British enthusiasts that a Zionist Palestine would enhance British prestige was the most pitiful in its exposure. The humiliation and expulsion of a bewildered British garrison and administration were among the main causes of the swift decline of British influence in the East after the Second World War. The hope that the erection of a Jewish Homeland would dispel anti-Semitism was answered not only by the unconcerned spread of anti-Semitic ideas in the West but by the unprecedented growth of anti-Judaism in Moslem countries, from India to the Mediterranean.

There was one supreme miscalculation in this great act from which all its misfortunes flowed culminating in the slaughter of innocents, the destitution of more than half a million of the "non-Jewish communities" of Palestine, and orgies of in-gratitude. That miscalculation lay in the optimism of the Age of Diffusion. Throughout the episode of 1917 the arguments of Zionists and Assimilationists, among the Jews and the Gentiles, had a great thing in common: they all presumed that the Western world would remain devoted to humane standards of conduct. For that reason the strife between the two parties was from one point of view artificial since the Jewish and Gentile Zionists, despite the hard things they said about their opponents, did rely on Assimilation for the realisation of their dream by peaceful means. Though the Jews understood the perils of modern barbarism better than other people, it was difficult for them not to follow the fashionable ideas of the time and to assume, with the great majority of their fellow-men, that the tolerance which made assimilation possible was an established part of an enduring and perhaps eternal civilisation. No one living then could know that the disasters of the First World War were inflicting a wound on that civilisation so deep that it may have been mortal, and that within relatively few years from 1917 a renascent barbarism was to desecrate the Western world with civil carnage and oppression compared to which the horrors of the Russian Pale were nothing. The refusal or incapacity of any British Government to recognise a new age or new duties when that time came, and the persistence of British politicians of all parties in using Palestine, their solemn trust, as a vote-catching device, must cool sympathy with this total failure of the British genius and the democratic principle.

In the days of Cromwell Jewish liberties were pleaded in England on Scriptural grounds. The presence of the Tribe of Reuben having supposedly been attested in America, it was held by many Hebrew divines and their Puritan champions that it only needed the admission of " the holy people " into England for the total scattering to be complete, and the return made possible. No one seems to have noticed that in 1917 this prophecy was literally fulfilled. Thirty-five years after, confronted by a survival of the Jews which is not easily explained in natural terms, it is perhaps allowable, at some risk of sententiousness, to remember that the words of Daniel which inspired Rabbi Manasseh ben Israel were not an exhortation to the delights of nationalism alone, but pointed to a promise of redemption.

APPENDIX A

Text of the Alexander-Montefiore Letter

On the 24th of May, 1917, the following letter appeared in *The Times*:

" Sir,—In view of the statements and discussions lately published in the newspapers relative to a projected Jewish re-settlement in Palestine on a national basis, the Conjoint Foreign Committee of the Board of Deputies of British Jews and the Anglo-Jewish Association deem it necessary to place on record the views they hold on this important question.

The Holy Land has necessarily a profound and undying interest for all Jews, as the cradle of their religion, and the site of its sacred memorials. It is not, however, as a mere shrine or place of pilgrimage that they regard the country. Since the dawn of their political emancipation in Europe, the Jews have made the rehabilitation of the Jewish community in the Holy Land one of their chief cares, and they have always cherished the hope that the result of their labours would be the regeneration on Palestine soil of a Jewish community, worthy of the great memories of their environment, and a source of spiritual inspiration to the whole of Jewry. Accordingly the Conjoint Committee have welcomed with deep satisfaction the prospect of a rich fruition of this work, opened to them by the victorious progress of the British Army in Palestine.

Anxious that on this question all sections and parties in Jewry should be united in a common effort, the Committee intimated to the Zionist organisation as far back as the winter of 1914, their readiness to co-operate with them on the basis of the so-called 'cultural' policy which had been adopted at the last Zionist Congresses in 1911, and 1913. This policy aimed primarily at making Palestine a Jewish spiritual centre by securing for the local Jews, and the colonists who might join them, such conditions of life as would best enable them to develop the Jewish genius on lines of its own. Larger political questions not directly affecting the main purpose, were left to be solved as need and opportunity might render possible. Unfortunately, an agreement on these lines has not proved practicable, and the Conjoint Committee are consequently compelled to pursue their work alone. They are doing so on the basis of a formula adopted by them in March, 1916, in which they propose to recommend to His Majesty's Government the formal recognition of the high historic interest Palestine possesses for the Jewish community, and a public declaration that at the close of the war 'the Jewish population will be secured in the enjoyment of civil and religious liberty, equal political rights with the rest of the population, reasonable facilities for immigration and colonisation, and such municipal privileges in the towns and colonies inhabited by them as may be shown to be necessary.'

That is still the policy of the Conjoint Committee.

Meanwhile, the Committee have learnt from the published statements of the Zionist leaders in this country that they now favour a much larger scheme of an essentially political character. Two points in this scheme appear to the Committee to be open to grave objections on public grounds.

The first is a claim that the Jewish settlements in Palestine shall be recognised as possessing a national character in a political sense. Were this claim of purely local import, it might well be left to settle itself in accordance with the general political exigencies of the reorganisation of the country under a new sovereign power. The Conjoint Committee, indeed, would have no objection to urge against a local Jewish nationality establishing itself under such conditions. But the present claim is not of this limited scope. It is part and parcel of a wider Zionist theory, which regards all the Jewish communities of the world as constituting one homeless nationality, incapable of complete social and political identification with the nations among which they dwell, and it is argued that for this homeless nationality a political centre and an always available homeland in Palestine are necessary. Against this theory the Conjoint Committee strongly and earnestly protest. Emancipated Jews in this country regard themselves primarily as a religious community, and they have always based their claim to political equality with their fellow citizens of other creeds on this assumption, and on its corollary—that they have no separate national aspirations in a political sense. They hold Judaism to be a religious system with which their political status has no concern, and they maintain that, as citizens of the countries in which they live, they are fully and sincerely identified with the national spirit and interests of these countries. It follows that the establishment of a Jewish nationality in Palestine founded on this theory of Jewish homelessness, must have the effect throughout the world of stamping the Jews as strangers in their native lands, and of undermining their hard-won position as citizens and nationals of those lands. Moreover, a Jewish political nationality, carried to its logical conclusion, must, in the present circumstances of the world, be an anachronism. The Jewish religion being the only certain test of a Jew, a Jewish nationality must be founded on, and limited by, the religion. It cannot be supposed for a moment that any section of Jews would aim at a Commonwealth governed by religious tests, and limited in the matter of freedom of conscience; but can a religious nationality express itself politically in any other way? The only alternative would be a secular Jewish nationality, recruited on some loose and obscure principle of Race and ethnographic peculiarity; but this would not be Jewish in any spiritual sense, and its establishment in Palestine would be a denial of all the ideals and hopes by which the revival of Jewish life in that country commends itself to the Jewish consciousness and Jewish sympathy. On these grounds the Conjoint Committee deprecate most earnestly the national proposals of the Zionists.

The second point in the Zionist programme which has aroused the misgivings of the Conjoint Committee is the proposal to invest the Jewish settlers in Palestine with certain special rights in excess of those enjoyed by the rest of the population, these rights to be administered by a Jewish Chartered Company. Whether it is desirable or not to confide any portion of the administration of Palestine to a Chartered Company need not be discussed, but it is certainly very undesirable that Jews should solicit or accept such a concession, on a basis of political privileges and economic preferences. Any such action would prove a veritable calamity for the whole Jewish people. In all the countries in which they live the principle of equal rights for all religious denominations is vital for them. Were they to set an example in Palestine of disregarding this principle they would convict themselves of having appealed to it for purely selfish motives. In the countries in which they are still struggling for equal rights they would find themselves hopelessly compromised, while in other countries, where these rights have been secured, they would have great difficulty in defending them. The proposal is the more inadmissible because the Jews are, and will long remain, a minority of the population of Palestine, and because it might involve them in the bitterest feuds with their neighbours of other races and religions, which would seriously retard their progress, and would find deplorable echoes throughout the Orient. If the Jews prevail in a competition based on perfect equality of rights and opportunity they will establish their eventual preponderance in the land on a far sounder foundation than any that can be secured by privileges and monopolies.

If the Conjoint Committee can be satisfied with regard to

Appendix A

these points they will be prepared to co-operate in securing for
the Zionist organisation the united support of Jewry.

DAVID L. ALEXANDER
President, Board of Deputies of British Jews
CLAUDE G. MONTEFIORE
President, Anglo-Jewish Association "

The influence of Lucien Wolf is probably to be traced in the
fallacious account of the " cultural " policy which occurs in the
third paragraph.

APPENDIX B

The Conflicting Pledges

SINCE THE essay, "The Prosperity of His Servant," deals only with the origins of the Balfour Declaration little is said in the text about the pledges given to Arabian potentates during the First World War. These pledges, which are held by many people to have been incompatible with our promise to the Jews, were three in number.

1. The original pledge was conveyed by Sir Henry Macmahon on October 24th of 1915 in a letter to the Sharif of Mecca, later King Hussein. The relevant passage runs as follows:

"It gives me the greatest pleasure to convey to you, on their (the British Government's) behalf the following declarations which, I have no doubt, you will receive with satisfaction and acceptance.

The districts of Mersin and Alexandretta, and portions of Syria lying to the West of the districts of Damascus, Homs, Hama, and Aleppo, cannot be said to be purely Arab, and must on that account be excepted from the proposed delimitation.

Subject to that modification, and without prejudice to the treaties concluded between His Majesty's Government and certain Arab chiefs we accept that delimitation.

As for the regions lying within the proposed frontiers, in which Great Britain is free to act without detriment to the interests of her ally France, I am authorised to give you the following pledges on behalf of the Government of Great Britain, and to reply as follows to your note:

(1) That, subject to the modifications stated above, Great Britain

is prepared to recognise and uphold the independence of the Arabs in all the regions lying within the frontiers proposed by the Sharif of Mecca;

(2) That Great Britain will guarantee the Holy Places against all external aggression, and will recognise the obligation of preserving them from aggression;

(3) That, when circumstances permit, Great Britain will help the Arabs with her advice and assist them in the establishment of governments to suit those diverse regions;

(4) That it is understood that the Arabs have already decided to seek the counsels and advice of Great Britain exclusively and that such European advisors and officials as may be needed to establish a sound system of administration shall be British;

(5) That, as regards the two vilayets of Baghdad and Basra, the Arabs recognise that the fact of Great Britain's established position and interests there will call for the setting up of special administrative arrangements to protect those regions from foreign aggression, to promote the welfare of their inhabitants, and to safeguard our mutual economic interests.

I am confident that this declaration will convince you, beyond all doubt, of Great Britain's sympathy with the aspirations of her friends the Arabs; and that it will result in a lasting and solid alliance with them, of which one of the immediate consequences will be the expulsion of the Turks from the Arab countries and the liberation of the Arab peoples from the Turkish yoke which has weighed on them all these long years."

2. On June 16th, 1918, a document generally known as " The Declaration to the Seven " was conveyed from the Foreign Office by the Arab Bureau in Cairo to seven Syrian notables in reply to a memorial submitted to the British Government. It should be noted that the memorial had expressed the concern of the notables not at the prospect of Zionism but at a widespread rumour that King Hussein intended to establish his own administration in Syria and Irak. The author of the declaration was Sir Mark Sykes, according to T. E. Lawrence (Letter 113). The text is as follows:

Appendix B

"His Majesty's Government have considered the memorial of the Seven with great care. They fully appreciate the reasons for the desire of its authors to retain their anonymity, but the fact that the memorial is anonymous has in no way detracted from the value which His Majesty's Government assign to that document.

The territories mentioned in the memorial fall into three categories:

(i) Territories which were free and independent before the outbreak of the War;

(ii) Territories liberated from Turkish rule by the Arabs themselves;

(iii) Territories liberated from Turkish rule by the action of the Allied armies:

(iv) Territories still under Turkish rule.

With regard to the first two categories, His Majesty's Government recognise the complete and sovereign independence of the Arabs inhabiting those territories, and support them in their struggle for freedom.

With regard to the territories occupied by the Allied armies, His Majesty's Government invite the attention of the memorialists to the proclamations issued by the commander-in-chief on the occasions of the capture of Baghdad and of the capture of Jerusalem. These proclamations define the policy of His Majesty's Government towards the inhabitants of those regions, which is that the future government of those territories should be based upon the principle of the consent of the governed. This policy will always be that of His Majesty's Government.

With regard to the territories in the fourth category, it is the desire of His Majesty's Government that the oppressed peoples in those territories should obtain their freedom and independence. His Majesty's Government will continue to work for the achievement of that object. They are fully aware of the difficulties and perils which threaten those who are striving for the liberation of the inhabitants of those territories.

(*Note.*—In June, 1918, the foregoing could be applied to Northern Palestine.)

In spite of those obstacles, however, His Majesty's Government believe that the difficulties can be overcome, and they are prepared to give every support to those who are striving to overcome them.

They are ready to consider any scheme of co-operation which does not conflict with the military operations in hand or with the political principles proclaimed by His Majesty's Government and their allies."

3. On November 7th, 1918, an official declaration of policy generally known as "The Anglo-French Declaration" was issued in Syria, Palestine and Irak in the form of a communiqué from General Headquarters, Egyptian Expeditionary Force. In the text, which follows, the term Syria is used to denote modern Syria, Lebanon and Palestine.

"The goal envisaged by France and Great Britain in prosecuting in the East the War set in train by German ambition is the complete and final liberation of the peoples who have for so long been oppressed by the Turks, and the setting up of national governments and administrations that shall derive their authority from the free exercise of the initiative and choice of the indigenous populations.

In pursuit of those intentions France and Great Britain agree to further and assist in setting up indigenous governments and administrations in Syria and Mesopotamia, which have already been liberated by the Allies, as well as in those territories which they are endeavouring to liberate themselves, and to recognise them as soon as they are set up.

Far from wishing to impose this or that system upon the populations of those regions, the only concern of the Allies is to offer such support and efficacious help as will ensure the smooth working of the governments and administrations which those populations will have elected of their own free will to have; to secure impartial and equal justice; to facilitate the economic development of the country by promoting local initiative; to foster the spread of education; to terminate the dissensions which Turkish policy has for so long exploited. Such is the task which the Allies wish to undertake in the liberated territories."

On the Jewish side Balfour's letter to Lord Rothschild was the sole pledge given by a British Government to the Zionist Movement. In 1922 this pledge was renewed and elucidated by

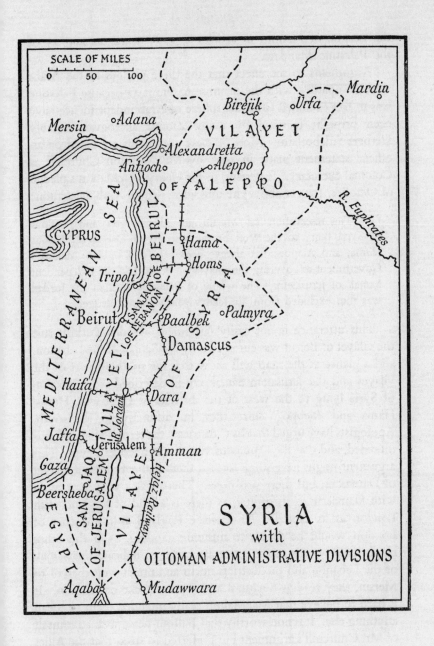

SCALE OF MILES

0   50   100

Mardin

Birejik   Urfa

Mersin   Adana   VILAYET

Alexandretta

Antioch   Aleppo

OF ALEPPO

R. Euphrates

CYPRUS

MEDITERRANEAN SEA

Hama

Homs

Tripoli

Beirut   Baalbek   Palmyra

Damascus

Haifa   Dara

Jaffa

Jerusalem

Gaza   Amman

Beersheba

EGYPT

Aqaba   Mudawwara

OF SYRIA

VILAYET OF BEIRUT

SANJAQ OF LEBANON

VILAYET OF BEIRUT

R. Jordan

SANJAQ OF JERUSALEM

VILAYET OF SYRIA

Hejaz Railway

SYRIA
with
OTTOMAN ADMINISTRATIVE DIVISIONS

the League of Nations in articles 2, 4, 6, 7, 11, 22 and 23 of the Palestine Mandate.

Arguments to the effect that the three pledges to the Arabs were compatible with the promise to the Jews because Palestine was in fact excluded from the sphere of Arab independence have been brought forward by many Zionist apologists, notably Herbert Sidebotham. Most of these arguments are based on an official statement made in 1921 by Mr. Winston Churchill as Colonial Secretary. Referring to Sir Henry MacMahon's pledge of October, 1915 (1 above) he thus addressed an Arab delegation:

" This reservation (i.e. Mersin and Alexandretta, and portions of Syria lying to the West of the districts of Damascus, Homs, Hama, and Aleppo) has always been regarded by His Majesty's Government as covering the vilayet of Beirut and the independent Sanjak of Jerusalem. The whole of Palestine West of the Jordan was thus excluded from Sir Henry MacMahon's pledge."

This utterance is not easily fathomed. Under Turkish rule the vilayet of Beirut was cut in two by the Sanjak of the Lebanon, and a glance at the map will show that the southern part of the vilayet and the Jerusalem Sanjak are ill described as " a portion of Syria lying to the west of the districts of Damascus, Homs, Hama and Aleppo " since they lie distinctly to the south. Apologists have urged that by " district " the term " vilayet " was intended, and that the Damascus vilayet extended to Egypt. This argument might have some force if there had ever been a vilayet of Damascus, but there was none. There was a vilayet of Syria with Damascus as its capital, as there is a land of England with London as its capital. To describe England as the district of London would be to invite misunderstanding. On the other hand, if the words in the letter are taken to indicate the Sanjak of the Lebanon and the districts north and north-west thereof to Mersin, they read as a natural and workmanlike description. It is hard to believe that MacMahon really intended them to mean anything else. It is noteworthy that Balfour never availed himself of Mr. Churchill's argument but preferred to stress that the Allies had obtained Arab independence in a vast area compared to which Palestine was " a notch " which the Arabs should give up.

Incidents such as Mr. Churchill's statement, and a reading of the four pledges may provoke an idea that the Ministers and officials of that time were dishonest men. This is a very harsh judgment which overlooks three vitally important facts. The first of these concerns the nature of nationalism. The men of the early twentieth century thought of nationalism as a European idiosyncrasy which had little force in Asia or Africa. (For this reason when Lord Curzon's statesmanlike treaty with Persia was rejected by the Persian Parliament he could never understand what had happened.) It was generally believed that Syrian nationalism was similar to European nationalism in the Middle Ages, a secondary interest of a few which could be treated lightly without offence. It should be recognised that this idea, though the cause of great calamities through misunderstanding, was not wholly mistaken. The establishment of a Jewish national home in a European country would have been far more difficult than it was in Palestine, where most of the peasantry remained indifferent to Jewish immigration until the last years of the Mandate.

The other two facts that we must remember are two qualifications of the pledges, one of which is described in Lord Samuel's memoirs (*a*), the other being contained in the Weizmann-Feisal agreement (*b*).

(*a*) When Lord Samuel was the first High Commissioner for Palestine he sought to elucidate the confusion of pledges, and he obtained a written statement from General Sir Gilbert Clayton that the exclusion of Palestine from the area of promised independence had been asserted orally to King Hussein, who fully understood that this was a part of British policy. This statement is all the more remarkable in that Clayton was somewhat anti-Zionist in his political ideas. Sir Henry MacMahon endorsed Clayton's statement in two letters to *The Times*, and its truth is borne out by a statement made by Sir Mark Sykes to Lloyd George at the meeting of April 3rd, 1917, and by the fact that at the Conference of Versailles the Arab delegation did not appeal to the MacMahon correspondence. The reason for the suppression of this reservation in the correspondence, and in the Declaration to the Seven, and in the Anglo-French Declaration has never been divulged. Nor has it been explained why Mr. Churchill neglected this important fact which would have saved him the trouble of a tortured argument in 1921, but that the Arab politicians were well aware of such an oral agreement is again suggested by the fact that they did not base an anti-British case on Mr. Churchill's strange utterance.

(*b*) The Weizmann-Feisal Agreement was signed in January of 1919 during the Emir Feisal's visit to London. It was evidently Feisal's mistaken belief that an Arab-Jewish accord would be considered so great a prize by the British Government that for its sake they would stimulate Arab independence throughout Asia. The terms of the agreement are generous to Zionist aspirations, notably in Article XIV, which reads:

> "All necessary measures shall be taken to encourage and stimulate immigration of Jews into Palestine on a large scale, and as quickly as possible to settle Jewish immigrants upon the land. In taking such measures the Arab peasants and tenant farmers shall be protected in their rights, and shall be assisted in forwarding their economic development."

At the end of the document Feisal wrote as follows in his own hand:

> "Provided the Arabs obtain their independence as demanded in my memorandum dated 4th January, 1919 . . . I shall concur in the above articles. But if the slightest modification or departure were to be made (i.e. in meeting the demands) I shall not then be bound by a single word of the present Agreement which shall be deemed void and of no account or validity, and I shall not be answerable in any way whatsoever."

The signatures occur below this codicil.

Since the independence of the Arabs was not attained in

Feisal's lifetime, Arab apologists claim with some force that the Agreement was never valid. However, since Feisal never publicly revoked the Agreement this argument cannot be considered conclusive.

From the foregoing it will be seen that the question of compatibility is extremely difficult to decide, if not impossible. There remains an important point of the " imponderable " kind on the Arab side. As we have noted, the Palestine reservation was never made public to the common people of the country. Although there was no democratic machinery in the Arab countries of that time, it can be maintained that the institution of a measure such as this, which affected the private happiness of several hundred thousand people, without any reference at all to public opinion, was a disregard of the democratic principle too extreme to be practical in any society having any civilisation at all, and from that it can be further argued that impracticability on such a scale has an invalidating power.

On the Jewish side there is an " imponderable " to be noted against the arguments of those who maintain that the pledge to the Zionists was a lesser one than those to the Arabs, and was not sufficient to warrant the establishment of a Jewish Palestine. The Jews are among the most gifted people in the world. The cult of Zion is a force which has inspired them from the time of King David. When this people, encouraged by the most influential Government then in the world, went back to Zion they were confronted by an opposition of the Moslem inhabitants which was ignorant, incompetent and largely venal. To expect the Zionists to take no advantage of that situation, in the interests of justice, was to mistake human nature and to demand of the Jews a feat of altruistic self-restraint of which no people has ever been found capable at any time.

INDEX